Gender
Third Edition

Gender

In World Perspective
Third Edition

Raewyn Connell & Rebecca Pearse

polity

The right of Raewyn Connell & Rebecca Pearse to be identified as Authors of this Work has been asserted in accordance with the UK Copyright, Designs and Patents Act 1988.

First edition first published in 2002 by Polity Press
Second edition first published in 2009 by Polity Press
This third edition first published in 2015 by Polity Press
Reprinted 2015, 2016, 2017, 2018

Polity Press
65 Bridge Street
Cambridge CB2 1UR, UK

Polity Press
350 Main Street
Malden, MA 02148, USA

ISBN-13: 978-0-7456-8071-2
ISBN-13: 978-0-7456-8072-9 (pb)

A catalogue record for this book is available from the British Library.

Typeset in 10 on 12 pt Sabon
by Toppan Best-set Premedia Limited
Printed and bound in the United States of America by RR Donnelley

The publisher has used its best endeavours to ensure that the URLs for external websites referred to in this book are correct and active at the time of going to press. However, the publisher has no responsibility for the websites and can make no guarantee that a site will remain live or that the content is or will remain appropriate.

Every effort has been made to trace all copyright holders, but if any have been inadvertently overlooked the publisher will be pleased to include any necessary credits in any subsequent reprint or edition.

For further information on Polity, visit our website: politybooks.com

In memory of
Pam Benton
1942–1997

She, who had Here so much essentiall joy
As no chance could distract, much lesse destroy;
... she to Heaven is gone,
Who made this world in some proportion
A heaven, and here, became unto us all,
Joy, (as our joyes admit) essentiall.

Contents

Preface

Gender is a key dimension of personal life, social relations and culture. It is an arena in which we face hard practical issues about justice, identity and even survival.

Gender is also a topic on which there is a great deal of prejudice, myth and outright falsehood. Research and theory in the human sciences provide vital tools for understanding the real issues. This book tries to present an accessible, research-based, globally informed and theoretically coherent account of gender.

For people new to the study of gender, we introduce key examples of gender research, describe the main findings on important topics, and provide a map of debates and ideas. For people already familiar with gender issues, we propose an integrated approach that links issues ranging from the body and personality difference to the global economy and world peace. The book draws on a spectrum of the human sciences, from psychology and sociology to political science, cultural studies, education and history.

Modern research on gender was triggered by the women's movement for gender equality. There is a simple reason for this: most gender orders, around the world, privilege men and disadvantage women. Yet the details are not simple. There are different forms of privilege and disadvantage, and the scale of gender inequality varies from place to place. The costs of privilege may be high. Even the definition of who is a man and a woman can be contested.

Gender issues are about men quite as much as they are about women. There is now extensive research about masculinities, fatherhood, men's movements, men's violence, boys' education, men's health and men's involvement in achieving gender equality. We have woven this knowledge into the picture of gender.

We have also emphasized a world perspective. The view from the global North is important, but most people live in other places and have a different social experience. Therefore we give considerable attention to gender research and theory in countries outside the global metropole, places as diverse as Latvia, Chile, Australia, western and southern Africa, Indonesia and Japan.

The world faces urgent issues about gender. Indeed, a whole new realm of gender politics is emerging, with sharp questions about human rights, global economic injustice, environmental change, relations between generations, violence, both military and personal, and the conditions for living well.

If emerging gender orders are to be just, peaceful and humane – which is by no means guaranteed – we need well-founded knowledge and a sophisticated understanding of gender issues. To produce this understanding means sharing knowledge around the globe. Previous editions of this book have been translated into Chinese, Italian, Greek, Japanese, German and Polish. We hope this new edition will be as useful.

This edition includes a wholly new chapter on gender and environment, brings all chapters up to date with current research, includes a new case study, revises the treatment of gender theory, and tries to make the presentation throughout as clear and concise as possible.

A book that attempts to synthesize knowledge across a broad field of study rests on the labour of many people – researchers, theorists, social movement activists, and the many people who participate in research studies.

Most of our intellectual debts are acknowledged in the text. Rebecca owes particular thanks to: James Hitchcock, Bronislava Lee, Stuart Rosewarne and Tim Hitchcock. Raewyn owes particular thanks to: Kylie Benton-Connell, Christabel Draffin, John Fisher, Patricia Selkirk, Carol Hagemann-White, Robert Morrell, Ulla Müller, Taga Futoshi, Teresa Valdés, Toni Schofield, Lin Walker and Kirsten Gomard.

The book is dedicated to the memory of Pam Benton. The epigraph at the start of the book is from Pam's favourite poet, John Donne, and can be found in the poem 'The Second Anniversary'.

Raewyn Connell and Rebecca Pearse
Sydney, December 2013

1

The question of gender

Noticing gender

One night a year, the attention of the TV-watching world is focused on Hollywood's most spectacular event, the Oscar awards ceremony. Famous people are driven up in limousines in front of an enthusiastic crowd, and in a blizzard of camera flashes they walk into the auditorium – the men in tuxedos striding easily, the women going cautiously because they are wearing low-cut gowns and high-heeled shoes. As the evening wears on, awards are given out for film scores, camera work, script writing, direction, best foreign film, and so on. But in the categories that concern the people you see on screen when you go to the movies, there are *two* awards given: best actor *and* best actress; best supporting actor *and* best supporting actress.

The internet is saturated with images of glamorous people, from models in advertisements to all kind of celebrities and public figures. When pop star Mylie Cyrus performed at the MTV Music Video Awards (VMA) in 2013, the images of her sexually provocative dancing travelled at incredible speed across the world. After the event, Cyrus tweeted, 'Smilers! My VMA performance had 306.000 tweets per minute. That's more than the blackout or Superbowl! [*sic*].' Major news and entertainment websites, social media, blogs and YouTube channels sent waves of chatter through cyberspace. Much of it was discussion about whether the public was prepared for the transformation of Cyrus from child star to sex symbol.

Whilst women's bodies are common elements of the visual images we consume on the web, women are much less likely to be producing web content. In a recent member survey, Wikipedia discovered that less than 15 per cent of people who write content for the online encyclopedia are women. Internet access is also uneven. In 2013 the multinational computer technology firm Intel found that nearly 25 per cent fewer women internationally have internet access than men. Whilst in a small number of affluent nations like France and the United States women actually have slightly higher rates of internet access, the gender gap reaches nearly 45 per cent in sub-Saharan Africa.

In politics women continue to be the minority. Every year a 'family photo' is taken at G20 meetings where heads of government and their senior finance and central bank representatives meet to discuss the international financial system. In 2013, four women stood among the twenty national leaders in the photo, representing Germany, Brazil, South Korea and Argentina. The imbalance is commonly more pronounced. There has never been a woman head of government in modern Russia, China, France, Japan, Egypt, Nigeria, South Africa or Mexico. There has only been one each in the history of Brazil, Germany, Britain, India, Indonesia and Australia. Statistics from the Inter-Parliamentary Union showed that in 2013 79.1 per cent of members of the world's parliaments were men.

Among senior ministers the predominance of men is even higher. In 2012, only four countries in the world had women making up half of a national ministry (Norway, Sweden, Finland and Iceland). More typical figures for women in ministerial roles were 21 per cent (Australia, Mexico), 11 per cent (China, Indonesia, Japan), 6 per cent (Malaysia) and 0 per cent (Lebanon, Papua New Guinea). The few women who do get to this level are usually given the job of running welfare or education ministries. Men keep control of taxation, investment, technology, international relations, police and the military. Every Secretary-General of the United Nations and every head of the World Bank has been a man.

Women's representation in politics has changed slowly over time, and with difficulty. French lawyer Christine Lagard was the first woman ever to head the International Monetary Fund in 2011. The world average number of women in parliaments increased from 10 per cent in 1995 to 20 per cent in 2012. Australia's first woman Prime Minister, Julia Gillard, served for three years with a record eight women in ministry and five in cabinet. She was then thrown out of power in a party coup. The new conservative government elected in 2013 had only one woman in cabinet.

What is true of politics is also true of business. Of the top 200 businesses listed on the Australian stock exchange in 2012 (including those that publish the mass-circulation magazines), just seven had a woman as CEO. Of the 500 giant international corporations listed in *Fortune* magazine's 'Global 500' in 2013, just 22 had a woman CEO. Such figures are usually presented by saying that women are now 4.4 per cent of the top business leadership around the world. It's more informative to say that men compose 95.6 per cent of that leadership.

Women are a substantial part of the paid workforce, lower down the hierarchy. They are mostly concentrated in service jobs – clerical work, call centres, cleaning, serving food, and professions connected with caring for the young and the sick, i.e. teaching and nursing. In some parts of the world, women are also valued as industrial workers, for instance in microprocessor plants, because of their supposedly 'nimble fingers'. Though the detailed division between men's and women's work varies in different parts of the world, it is common for men to predominate in heavy industry, mining, transport, indeed in most jobs that involve any machinery except a sewing machine. World wide, men are a large majority of the workforce in management, accountancy, law and technical professions such as engineering and computers.

Behind the paid workforce is another form of work – unpaid domestic and care work. In all contemporary societies for which we have statistics, women do most of the cleaning, cooking and sewing, most of the work of looking after children, and almost all of the work of caring for babies. (If you don't think childcare is work, you haven't done it yet.) This work is often associated with a cultural definition of women as caring, gentle, self-sacrificing and industrious, i.e. as good mothers. Being a good father is rarely associated with cutting school lunches and wiping babies' bottoms – though there are now interesting attempts to promote what in Mexico has been called '*paternidad afectiva*', emotionally engaged fatherhood. Normally, fathers are supposed to be decision-makers and bread-winners, to consume the services provided by women and represent the family in the outside world.

Women as a group are less likely to be out in the public world than men, and, when they are, have fewer resources. In almost all parts of the world, men are more likely to have a paid job. Conventional measures of the economy, based on men's practices, exclude women's unpaid domestic work. By these measures, the world 'economic activity rate' for women has crept up, but is still just over two-thirds of the rate for men. The main exceptions are Scandinavia and parts of West Africa, where women's paid labour force participation rates are unusually high. But in some Arab states women's participation rates are one-quarter the rate for men, and in much of South Asia and Latin America they are about half.

Once women are in the paid workforce, how do their wages compare? Over thirty years after the United Nations adopted the Convention on the Elimination of All Forms of Discrimination against Women (CEDAW, 1979), nowhere in the world are women's earned incomes equal to men's. Women are often engaged in low-wage employment, and still receive 18 per cent less than men's average wages. In some countries, the gender pay gap is much bigger. Zambia has the largest gender pay gap at almost 46 per cent (2005), followed by South Korea with 43 per cent (2007) and Azerbaijan with 37 per cent (2008). Part of any gender gap in income can be explained by the pattern of women being more likely to work fewer hours and more likely to be unemployed. Other reasons relate to discriminatory wage practices and to women's overrepresentation in low-paid jobs.

Therefore most women in the world, especially women with children, are economically dependent on men. Some men believe that women who are dependent on them must be their property. This is a common scenario in domestic violence: when dependent women don't conform to demands from their husbands or boyfriends, they are beaten. This creates a dilemma for the women, which is very familiar to domestic violence services. They can stay, and put themselves and their children at high risk of further violence; or go, and lose their home, economic support, and status in the community. If they go, certain husbands are so infuriated that they pursue and kill the wives and even the children.

Men are not beaten up by their spouses so often, but they are at risk of other forms of violence. Most assaults reported to the police, in countries with good statistics on the matter, are by men on other men. Some men are beaten, indeed some are murdered, simply because they are thought to be homosexual; and some of this violence comes from the police. Most of the prisoners in gaols are men. In the United States, which has the biggest prison system in the world, the prison population in 2011 was 1.59 million, and 93 per cent of them were men. Most deaths in combat are of men, because men make up the vast majority of the troops in armies and militias. Most industrial accidents involve men, because men are most of the workforce in dangerous industries such as construction and mining.

Men are involved disproportionately in violence partly because they have been prepared for it. Though patterns of child rearing differ between cultures, the situation in Australia is not unusual. Australian boys are steered towards competitive sports such as football, where physical dominance is celebrated, from an early age – by their fathers, by schools, and by the mass media. Boys also come under peer pressure to show bravery and toughness, and learn to fear being classified as 'sissies' or 'poofters' (a local term meaning effeminate or homosexual). Being capable of violence becomes a social resource. Working-class boys, who don't have the other resources that will lead to a professional career, become the main recruits into jobs that require the use of force: police, the military, private security, blue-collar crime, and professional sport. It is mainly young women who are recruited into the jobs that repair the consequences of violence: nursing, psychology and social work.

So far, we have listed an assortment of facts, about mass media, about politics and business, about families, and about growing up. Are these random? Modern thought about gender starts with the recognition that they are not. These facts form a pattern; they make sense when seen as parts of the overall gender arrangements, which this book will call the 'gender order', of contemporary societies.

To notice the existence of the gender order is easy; to understand it is not. Conflicting theories of gender now exist, as we shall see in chapter 4, and some problems about gender are genuinely difficult to resolve. Yet we now have a rich resource of knowledge about gender, derived from decades of research, and a fund of practical experience from gender reform. We have a better basis for understanding gender issues than any previous generation had.

Understanding gender

In everyday life we take gender for granted. We instantly recognize a person as a man or woman, girl or boy. We arrange everyday business around the distinction. Conventional marriages require one of each. Mixed-doubles tennis requires two of each, but most sports require one kind at a time.

Most years, the most popular television broadcast in the United States is the American Super Bowl, which, like the Oscars, is a strikingly gendered event: large armoured men crash into each other while chasing a pointed leather bladder, and thin women in short skirts dance and smile in the pauses. Most of us cannot crash or dance nearly so well, but we do our best in other ways. As women or men we slip our feet into differently shaped shoes, button our shirts on opposite sides, get our heads clipped by different hairdressers, buy our pants in separate shops, and take them off in separate toilets.

These arrangements are so familiar that they can seem part of the order of nature. Belief that gender distinction is 'natural' makes it scandalous when people don't follow the pattern: for instance, when people of the same gender fall in love with each other. So homosexuality is frequently declared 'unnatural' and bad.

But if having sex with a fellow-woman or a fellow-man is unnatural, why have a law against it? We don't provide penalties for violating the third law of thermodynamics. Anti-gay ordinances in US cities, police harassment of gay men in Senegal, the criminalization of women's adultery in Islamic Sharia law, the imprisonment of transsexual women for violating public order – such things only make sense because these matters are *not* fixed by nature.

These events are part of an enormous social effort to channel people's behaviour. Ideas about gender-appropriate behaviour are constantly being circulated, not only by legislators but also by priests, parents, teachers, advertisers, retail mall owners, talk-show hosts and disc jockeys. Events like Oscar Night and the Super Bowl are not just consequences of our ideas about gender difference. They also help to *create* gender difference, by displays of exemplary masculinities and femininities.

Being a man or a woman, then, is not a pre-determined state. It is a *becoming*, a condition actively under construction. The pioneering French feminist Simone de Beauvoir put this in a famous phrase: 'One is not born, but rather becomes, a woman.' Though the positions of women and men are not simply parallel, the principle is also true for men: one is not born masculine, but has to become a man.

This process is often discussed as the development of 'gender identity'. There are some questions to raise about this concept (see chapter 6), but it will serve for the moment as a name for the sense of belonging to a gender category. Identity includes our ideas of what that belonging means, what kind of person we are, in consequence of being a woman or a man. These ideas are not presented to the baby as a package at the beginning of life. They develop (there is some controversy about exactly when), and are filled out in detail over a long period of years, as we grow up.

As de Beauvoir further recognized, this business of becoming a gendered person follows many different paths, involves many tensions and ambiguities, and sometimes produces unstable results. Part of the mystery of gender is how a pattern that on the surface appears so stark and rigid, on close examination turns out so complex and uncertain.

So we cannot think of womanhood or manhood as fixed by nature. But neither should we think of them as simply imposed from outside, by social norms or pressure from authorities. People construct *themselves* as masculine or feminine. We claim a place in the gender order – or respond to the place we have been given – by the way we conduct ourselves in everyday life.

Most people do this willingly, and often enjoy the gender polarity. Yet gender ambiguities are not rare. There are masculine women and feminine men. There are women in love with other women, and men in love with other men. There are women who are heads of households, and men who bring up children. There are women who are soldiers and men who are nurses. Sometimes the development of 'gender identity' results in intermediate, blended or sharply contradictory patterns, for which we use terms like effeminate, camp, queer and transgender.

Psychological research suggests that the great majority of us combine masculine and feminine characteristics, in varying blends, rather than being all one or all the other. Gender ambiguity can be an object of fascination and desire, as well as disgust. Gender impersonations are familiar in both popular and high culture, from the cross-dressed actors of Shakespeare's stage to movies starring transsexual women and drag queens like *Hedwig and the Angry Inch* (2001), *Priscilla, Queen of the Desert* (2004) and *Hairspray* (2007).

There is certainly enough gender blending to provoke heated opposition from movements dedicated to re-establishing 'the traditional family', 'true femininity' or 'real masculinity'. By 1988 Pope John Paul II had become so concerned that he issued an encyclical, *On the Dignity and Vocation of Women*, reminding everyone that women were created for motherhood and their functions should not get mixed up with those of men. In a Christmas address in 2012, Pope Benedict XVI criticized gender theory directly. He argued: 'People dispute the idea that they have a nature, given by their bodily identity that serves as a defining element of the human being. They deny their nature and decide that it is not something previously given to them, but that they make it for themselves.' This is a good summary of a central insight from gender theory. Of course the Pope was arguing against it, saying that an essential, biological nature should determine our personal and public lives. These efforts to maintain essentialist ideas about fixed womanhood and manhood are themselves strong evidence that the boundaries are none too stable.

But these are not just boundaries; they are also inequalities. Most churches and mosques are run exclusively by men, and this is part of a larger pattern. Most corporate wealth is in the hands of men, most big institutions are run by men, and most science and technology is controlled by men. In many countries, including some with very large populations, women are less likely than men to have been taught to read. For instance, recent adult literacy rates in India stood at 75 per cent for men and 51 per cent for women; in Nigeria, 72 per cent for men and 50 per cent for women. On a world scale, two-thirds of illiterate people are women. In countries like the United States, Australia, Italy and Turkey, middle-class women have gained full access to higher education and have made inroads into middle management and professions. But even in those countries many informal barriers operate to keep the very top levels of power and wealth mostly a world of men.

There is also unequal respect. In many situations, including the cheerleaders at the football game, women are treated as marginal to the main action, or as the objects of men's desire. Whole genres of humour – bimbo jokes, woman-driver jokes, mother-in-law jokes – are based on contempt for women's triviality and stupidity. A whole industry, ranging from heavy pornography and prostitution to soft-core advertising, markets women's bodies as objects of consumption by men. Equal-opportunity reforms in the workplace often run into a refusal by men to be under the authority of a woman. Not only do most religions prevent women from holding major religious office, they often treat women symbolically as a source of defilement for men.

Though men in general benefit from the inequalities of the gender order, they do not benefit equally. Indeed, many pay a considerable price. Boys and men who depart from dominant definitions of masculinity because they are gay, effeminate, or considered wimpish are often subject to verbal abuse and discrimination, and are sometimes the targets of violence. Differences between classes and races also affect the benefits that different groups of men gain. Men who conform to dominant defini-tions of masculinity may also pay a price. Research on men's health shows that men as a group have a higher rate of industrial accidents than women, have a higher rate of death by violence, tend to eat a worse diet and drink more alcohol, and (not surprisingly) have more sporting inju-ries. In 2012 the life expectancy for men in the United States was calcu-lated at 76 years, compared with 81 years for women. In Russia, after the restoration of capitalism, life expectancy for men is 63 years com-pared with 75 years for women.

Gender arrangements are thus, at the same time, sources of pleasure, recognition and identity, and sources of injustice and harm. This means that gender is inherently political – but it also means the politics can be complicated and difficult.

Inequality and oppression in the gender order have repeatedly led to demands for reform. Movements for change include campaigns for women's right to vote, and for women's presence in anti-colonial move-ments and representation in independent governments. There are cam-paigns for equal pay, for women's right to own property, for homosexual law reform, for women's trade unionism, for equal employment opportu-nity, for reproductive rights, for the human rights of transsexual men and women and transgender people; and campaigns against discrimination in education, against sexist media, against rape and domestic violence.

Political campaigns resisting some of these changes, or seeking coun-ter-changes, have also arisen. The scene of gender politics currently includes anti-gay campaigns, anti-abortion ('pro-life') campaigns, a spec-trum of men's movements, and a complex international debate about links between Western feminism and Western cultural dominance in the world. One of the most striking waves of change underway now is the legalization of gay marriage. Same-sex couples are now able to marry in 13 US states and Washington DC. This is a fast-growing reform movement mostly in the global North, but also in Latin America. Of the 16 countries that permit gay men and lesbians to marry, 9 have made this reform since 2010.

In all this history, the feminist and gay movements of the 1960s–1970s were pivotal. They did not reach all their political goals, but they had a profound cultural impact. They called attention to a whole realm of human reality that was poorly understood, and thus created a demand for understanding as well as action. This was the historical take-off point of contemporary gender research. Political practice launched a deep change – which increasingly seems like a revolution – in human knowledge.

This book is an attempt to map this revolution. It describes the terrain revealed by gender politics and gender research, introduces the debates about how to understand it and change it, and offers solutions to some of the problems raised.

Defining gender

As a new awareness of issues developed, a new terminology was needed. Over the last 30 years the term 'gender' has become common in English-language discussions to describe the whole field. The term was borrowed from grammar. Ultimately it comes from an ancient word-root meaning 'to produce' (cf. 'generate'), which gave rise to words in many languages meaning 'kind' or 'class' (e.g. 'genus'). In grammar, 'gender' came to refer to the specific distinction between classes of nouns 'corresponding more or less' – as the nineteenth-century *Oxford English Dictionary* primly noted – 'to distinctions of sex (and absence of sex) in the objects denoted'.

Grammar suggests how such distinctions permeate cultures. In Indo-European and Semitic languages, nouns, adjectives and pronouns may be distinguishable as feminine, masculine, neuter or common gender. Not only the words for species that reproduce sexually may be gendered, but also many other words for objects, concepts and states of mind. English is a relatively un-gendered language, but English speakers still call a ship 'she', even an oil well ('she's going to blow!'), and often masculinize an abstraction ('the rights of man').

Language is important, but does not provide a consistent framework for understanding gender. German, for instance, has 'die Frau' (the woman) feminine, but 'das Mädchen' (the girl) neuter, because all words with such diminutives are neuter. Terror is feminine in French ('la terreur'), but masculine in German ('der Terror'). Other languages, including Chinese, Japanese and Yoruba, do not make gender distinctions through word forms at all. A great deal also depends on how a language is used. A relatively non-gendered language can still be used to name gender positions and express opinions on gender issues. On the other hand there are many communities where certain words or tones of voice are specifically thought to belong to men or women, or to express the speaker's masculinity or femininity.

Most discussions of gender in society emphasize a dichotomy. Starting from a biological division between male and female, they define gender as the social or psychological difference that corresponds to that divide, builds on it, or is caused by it.

In its most common usage, then, the term 'gender' means the cultural difference of women from men, based on the biological division between male and female. Dichotomy and difference are the substance of the idea. Men are from Mars, women are from Venus.

There are decisive objections to such a definition:

- Human life does not simply divide into two realms, nor does human character divide into two types. Our images of gender are often dichotomous, but the reality is not. Abundant evidence will be seen throughout this book.
- A definition in terms of difference means that where we cannot see difference, we cannot see gender. With such a definition we could not recognize the gendered character of lesbian or homosexual desire (based on gender similarity). We would be thrown into confusion by research which found only small psychological differences between women and men, which would seem to imply that gender had evaporated (see chapter 3).
- A definition based on dichotomy excludes the differences among women, and among men, from the concept of gender. But differences within groups may be highly relevant to the pattern of relations between women and men: for instance, the difference between violent and non-violent masculinities (see chapter 6).
- Any definition in terms of personal characteristics excludes processes which lie beyond the individual person. Large-scale social processes are based on the *shared* capacities of women and men more than on their differences. The creation of goods and services in a modern economy is based on shared capacities and cooperative labour – yet the products are often strongly gendered (e.g. what's on sale in a toyshop), and the wealth generated is distributed in highly gendered ways. Environmental problems are connected to patterns of intensifying global production and consumption, which in turn have gendered dimensions.

Social science provides a solution to these difficulties. The key is to move from a focus on difference to a focus on *relations*. Gender is, above all, a matter of the social relations within which individuals and groups act.

Enduring or widespread patterns among social relations are what social theory calls 'structures'. In this sense, gender must be understood as a social structure. It is not an expression of biology, nor a fixed dichotomy in human life or character. It is a pattern in our social arrangements, and the everyday activities shaped by those arrangements.

Gender is a social structure of a particular kind – it involves a specific relationship with bodies. This is recognized in the commonsense definition of gender as an expression of natural difference between male and female. We are one of the species that reproduce sexually rather than vegetatively like bacteria (though cloning may change that soon!). Some aspects of our anatomy are specialized for this purpose, and many biological processes in our bodies are affected by it (see chapter 3). What is wrong with the commonsense definition is not the attention to bodies, nor the concern with sexual reproduction, but the squeezing of biological complexity and adaptability into a stark dichotomy, and the idea that cultural patterns simply 'express' bodily difference.

Sometimes cultural patterns do express bodily difference, for instance when they celebrate first menstruation as a distinction between girl and woman. But often they do more than that, or less than that. Social practices sometimes exaggerate the distinction of female from male (e.g. maternity clothes), sometimes deny the distinction (many employment practices), sometimes mythologize it (computer games), and sometimes complicate it ('third gender' customs). So we cannot say that social arrangements routinely 'express' biological difference.

But we can say that, in all of these cases, society *addresses* bodies and *deals with* reproductive processes and differences among bodies. There is no fixed 'biological base' for the social process of gender. Rather, there is an arena in which bodies are brought into social processes, in which our social conduct *does something* with reproductive difference. The book will call this the 'reproductive arena', discussed further in chapter 3.

We can now define gender in a way that solves the paradoxes of 'difference'. Gender is the structure of social relations that centres on the reproductive arena, and the set of practices that bring reproductive distinctions between bodies into social processes.

To put it informally, gender concerns the way human societies deal with human bodies and their continuity, and the many consequences of that 'dealing' in our personal lives and our collective fate. The terms used in this definition are explained more fully in chapters 4 and 5.

This definition has important consequences. Among them: gender, like other social structures, is multidimensional. It is not just about identity, or just about work, or just about power, or just about sexuality, but about all of these things at once. Gender patterns may differ strikingly from one cultural context to another, and there are certainly very different ways of thinking about them, but it is still possible to think (and act) between cultures about gender. The power of structures to shape individual action often makes gender appear unchanging. Yet gender arrangements are in fact always changing, as human practice creates new situations and as structures develop crisis tendencies. Finally, gender had a beginning and may have an end. Each of these points will be explored later in the book.

In chapter 2 we discuss five notable examples of gender research, to show how the broad issues just discussed take shape in specific investigations. Chapter 3 considers the issue of 'difference', the extent of sex differences, and the way bodies and society interact. Chapter 4 discusses theories of gender, worldwide, and the intellectuals who produce them. An account of gender as a social structure is presented in chapter 5, exploring the different dimensions of gender and the process of historical change. Chapter 6 discusses gender in personal life, and the politics of identity and intimate relationships. Chapter 7 discusses gender and environmental change, introducing debates between feminists about how to understand the relationship between gender and nonhuman nature. Finally, chapter 8 looks at gender relations in institutions and world society, and discusses what is at stake in movements for change.

Note on sources

Most of the statistics mentioned in this chapter, such as income, economic activity rates and literacy, can be found in the United Nations Development Programme's *Human Development Report* (UNDP 2013; see list of references at back of book), or online tables regularly published by the United Nations Statistics Division. Figures on parliamentary representation and numbers of ministers are from Inter-Parliamentary Union (2013), and on managers, from the Workplace Gender Equality Agency, *Fortune* and CNN. Sources of information on men's health can be found in Schofield et al. (2000). Gender wage gap figures are taken from the International Trade Union Confederation report *Frozen in Time: Gender Pay Gap Unchanged for 10 Years* (ITUC 2012). The quotation on 'woman' is from Simone de Beauvoir's *The Second Sex* (1949: 295). Definitions and etymology of the word 'gender' are in *The Oxford English Dictionary*, vol. 4 (Oxford, Clarendon Press, 1933: 100).

2

Gender research:
five examples

Often a complex problem is best approached through specifics, and the results of research are best understood by looking at the actual research projects. In this chapter we discuss five notable studies of gender issues published in recent decades. They come from five continents. Three focus on everyday life in local settings – a school, a workplace, a community, a personal life. One deals with gender change in a great historical transition, and another with gender issues in the environment. Though they deal with very different questions, they reveal some of the main concerns of gender research in general.

Case 1: The play of gender in school life

One of the most difficult tasks in social research is to take a situation that everyone thinks they understand, and illuminate it in new ways. This is what the US ethnographer Barrie Thorne achieves in her subtly observed and highly readable book about school life, *Gender Play* (1993).

At the time Thorne started her work, children were not much discussed in gender research. When they were mentioned, the usual assumption was that they were being 'socialized' into gender roles, in a top-down transmission from the adult world. It was assumed that there are two sex roles, a male one and a female one, with boys and girls getting separately inducted into the norms and expectations of the appropriate role. This idea was based on a certain amount of research using paper-and-pencil questionnaires, but not on much actual observation of children's lives.

Thorne did that observation. Her book is based on fieldwork in two elementary (primary) schools in different parts of the United States. She spent eight months in one, three months in another, hanging about in classrooms, hallways and playgrounds, talking to everyone and watching the way the children interacted with each other and with their teachers in work and play.

Ethnography as a method sounds easy, but in practice is hard to do well. Part of the problem is the mass of information an observer can get from just a single day 'in the field'. You need to know what you are looking for. But you also need to be open to new experiences and new information, able to see things that you did not expect to see.

As an observer, Thorne was certainly interested in transmission from older people, in the ways children pick up the details of how to do gender. Her funniest (and perhaps also saddest) chapter is called 'Lip Gloss and "Goin' With"', about how pre-adolescent children learn the techniques of teenage flirting and dating. She was also interested in the differences between the girls' and the boys' informal interactions – the games they played, spaces they used, words they spoke, and so on.

But Thorne was able to see beyond the patterns described in conventional gender models. She became aware of how much these models predisposed an observer to look for difference. She began to pay attention not only to the moments in school life when the boys and girls separated, but also to the moments when they came together. She began to think of gender difference as *situational*, as created in some situations and ignored or overridden in others. Even in recess-time games, where the girls and boys were usually clustered in separate parts of the playground, they sometimes moved into mixed activities without any emphasis on difference. There were many 'relaxed cross-sex interactions' in the school's daily routine. Clearly, the boys and girls were not permanently in separate spheres, nor permanently enacting opposite 'sex roles'.

Recognizing this fact opened up a number of other issues. What were the situations where gender was emphasized or de-emphasized? Thorne noticed that, though teachers sometimes emphasized gender – for instance, arranging a classroom learning game with the girls competing against the boys – most teacher-controlled activities de-emphasized gender. This is true, for instance, of the commonest teaching technique in schools, the 'talk-and-chalk' method where the teacher at the front of the room demands the attention of all the pupils to an exposition of some lesson that they all have to learn. In this situation the basic division is between teacher and taught, not between groups of pupils; so girls and boys are in the same boat.

Next, how did the children establish gender difference when they did emphasize it? Thorne began to identify a kind of activity she called 'borderwork':

When gender boundaries are activated, the loose aggregation 'boys and girls' consolidates into 'the boys' and 'the girls' as separate and reified groups. In the process, categories of identity that on other occasions have minimal relevance for interaction become the basis of separate collectivities. (1993: 65)

There are different kinds of borderwork in a primary school. One of the most interesting is chasing, a kind of game that is sometimes very fluid and sometimes not. In the schools Thorne studied, boys and girls could play together, and often chased each other, playing 'girls-chase-the-boys' and 'boys-chase-the-girls'. Indeed one game would often merge into the other, as the chased turned around and became the chasers. Thorne notes that often boys chased boys, or girls chased girls, but these patterns attracted little attention or discussion. However girls-chasing-boys/boys-chasing-girls often resulted in lively discussion and excitement. It was a situation in which

[g]ender terms blatantly override individual identities, especially in references to the other team ('Help, a girl's chasin' me'; 'C'mon Sarah, let's get that boy'; 'Tony, help save me from the girls'). Individuals may call for help from, or offer help to, others of their gender. And in acts of treason, they may grab someone from their team and turn them over to the other side. For example, in an elaborate chasing scene among a group of Ashton third-graders, Ryan grabbed Billy from behind, wrestling him to the ground. 'Hey girls, get 'im,' Ryan called. (1993: 69)

Thorne's observation of children alerts us to parallel processes among adults. Borderwork is constantly being done to mark gender boundaries, if not by chasing, then by jokes, dress, forms of speech, and so on. Gender difference is not something that simply exists. It is something that happens, and must be made to happen; something, also, that can be unmade, altered, made less important.

The games in which the children make gender happen do something more. When the girls chase the boys and the boys chase the girls, they seem to be acting equally, and in some respects they are – but not in all respects. A rough-and-tumble version of the chasing game is more common among the boys. Boys normally control more of the playground space than the girls do, more often invade girls' groups and disrupt the girls' activities than the girls disrupt theirs. That is to say, the boys more often make an aggressive move and a claim to power, in the limited sense that children can do this.

In the symbolic realm, too, the boys claim power. They treat girls as a source of contamination or pollution, for instance calling low-status boys 'girls' or pushing them next to the space occupied by girls. The girls do not treat the boys that way. Girls are more often defined as giving the imaginary disease called 'cooties', and low-status girls may get called 'cootie queens'. A version of cooties played in one of the schools is called 'girl stain'. All these may seem small matters. But as Thorne remarks, 'recoiling from physical proximity with another person and their belongings because they are perceived as contaminating is a powerful statement of social distance and claimed superiority' (1993: 75).

So there is an asymmetry in the situations of boys and girls, which is reflected in differences among the boys and among the girls. Some boys often interrupt the girls' games; other boys do not. Some boys have higher status; others have lower. Some of the girls move earlier than others into 'romance'. By fourth grade, homophobic insults – such as calling another boy a 'fag' – are becoming common among the boys, most of whom learn that this word is a way of expressing hostility before they know what its sexual meaning is. At the same time, however, physical contact among the boys is becoming less common – they are learning to fear, or be suspicious of, displays of affection. In short, the children are beginning to show something of the differentiation of gender patterns, and the gender and sexual hierarchies, that are familiar among adults.

There is much more in Thorne's fascinating book, including a humorous and insightful discussion of what it is like for an adult to do research among children. Perhaps the most important lesson her book teaches is about these American children's *agency* in learning gender. They are not passively 'socialized' into a gender role. They are, of course, learning things from the adult world around them: lessons about available identities, lessons about performance, and – regrettably – lessons about hatred. But they do this actively, and on their own terms. They find gender interesting and sometimes exciting. They move into and out of gender-based groupings. They sometimes shore up, and sometimes move across, gender boundaries. They even play with and against the gender dichotomy itself. Gender is important in their world, but it is important as a human issue that they deal with, not as a fixed framework that reduces them to puppets.

Case 2: Manhood and the mines

In the late nineteenth century the fabulous wealth of the largest gold deposit in the world began to be exploited by the Dutch and British colonists in South Africa. The Witwatersrand gold deposits were immense. But the ore was low grade, so huge volumes had to be processed. And the main deposits lay far below the high plateau of the Transvaal, so the mines had to go deep. The first wild gold-rushes soon turned into an organized industry dominated by large companies, with a total workforce of hundreds of thousands.

Because the price of gold on the world market was fixed, the companies' profitability depended on keeping labour costs down. Thus the industry needed a large but low-paid workforce for demanding and dangerous conditions underground. To colonial entrepreneurs, the answer was obvious: indigenous men. So black African men, recruited from many parts of South Africa and even beyond, became the main labour force of the gold industry – and have remained so ever since.

Over a 20-year period T. Dunbar Moodie worked with a series of partners to document the experience of men who made up this labour force, a key group in South Africa's history. Their story is told in his book *Going for Gold* (1994). Moodie studied the company archives and government records, directed participant-observation studies, and interviewed miners, mine executives and women in the 'townships' where black workers lived. A key moment came when one of his colleagues, Vivienne Ndatshe, interviewed 40 *retired* miners in their home country, Pondoland (near the south-eastern coast). Her interviews revealed aspects of the miners' experience which changed the picture of migrant labour profoundly.

Because the mines were large-scale industrial enterprises owned by European capital, it had been easy to think of the mineworkers as 'proletarians' on the model of European urban industrial workers. But the reality was different. The racial structure of the South African workforce – whites as managers, blacks providing the labour – might have kept labour costs down, but it also created a barrier behind which the mineworkers could sustain cultures of their own, and exercise some informal control over their work. Most lived in all-male compounds near the mines, where they had to create their own social lives.

When the men signed on with recruiting agents – generally on contracts lasting four months to two years – and travelled hundreds of kilometres to the mines, they did not take families with them and did not intend to become city dwellers. This was not just because the wages were too low to support families in the cash economy of the cities. More importantly, the mineworkers mostly came from areas with a smallholder agricultural economy, such as Pondoland. They kept their links to that economy, and intended to return to it.

For most of them, the purpose of earning wages at the mine was to subsidize rural households run by their families, or to accumulate resources that would allow them to establish new rural households on their return – buying cattle, financing marriages, and so on. Being the wise and respected head of a self-sufficient homestead was the ideal of 'manhood' to which Mpondo migrant workers (alongside others) subscribed. The mine work was a means to this end.

This situation led to gender practices very different from those of the conventional European breadwinner/housewife couple. First, the men working at the mines and living in the compounds had to provide their own domestic labour, and, if sexually active, find new sexual partners. Some went to women working in nearby towns. Others created sexual and domestic partnerships, known as 'mine marriages', between older and younger men in the compounds. In such an arrangement the young man did housework and provided sexual services in exchange for gifts, guidance, protection and money from the senior man. This was a well-established if discreet custom, which lasted for decades. For the individual partners it was likely to be temporary. In due course the younger man would move on; he might in turn acquire a 'mine wife' if he became a senior man in a compound. These relationships were not taken back to the homeland.

Back in the homeland, the rural homesteads had to keep functioning while many of their men were away at the mines. This too led to a significant adjustment, because the person left to run the homestead might well be a woman, such as the mineworker's wife. Now the older Mpondo men did not define manhood, *ubudoda*, in terms of warrior virtues, but in a very different way. As one ex-miner, Msana, put it:

> 'Ubudoda is to help people. If somebody's children don't have books or school fees or so, then you are going to help those children while the father cannot manage. Or if there is somebody who died, you go there and talk to people there. Or, if someone is poor – has no oxen – then you can take your own oxen and plow his fields. That is ubudoda, one who helps other people.' [The interviewer writes:] I ... asked whether there was not also a sort of manhood displayed by strength in fighting. Msana replied at once: 'No, that is not manhood. Such a person is called a killer.' (1994: 38)

Manhood, in this cultural setting, principally meant competent and benevolent management of a rural homestead, and participation in its community. Since a woman could perform these tasks, almost all the older Mpondo men logically held the view that a woman could have *ubudoda*. They were not denying that in a patriarchal society men ultimately have control. But they emphasized a conception of partnership between women and men in the building of homesteads, in which women could and often did perform masculine functions and thus participated in manhood.

But these gender arrangements, brought into existence by specific historical circumstances, were open to change. As the twentieth century wore on, the homestead agricultural economy declined. The apartheid government's policies of resettlement disrupted communities and created huge pools of displaced labour. The gold mining industry also changed. The workers became increasingly unionized, and the mine managements abandoned old forms of paternalism and sought new ways of negotiating with workers (though they continued to foment 'tribal' jealousies). In the 1970s the old wage rates were abandoned and miners' incomes began to rise. This made it possible to support an urban household, or a non-agricultural household in the countryside, and broke the economic reciprocity between homestead and mine.

In these changed circumstances the old migrant cultures were eroded, including their distinctive gender patterns. Younger Mpondo men no longer define 'manhood' in terms of presiding over a rural homestead. They simply equate it with the biological fact of maleness – which women cannot share. 'Thus,' remarks Moodie, 'for the present generation of Mpondo, maleness and femaleness have been dichotomized again' (1994: 41). The women with manhood have disappeared from the scene.

Proletarianization has arrived at last, and with it a gender ideology closer to the European pattern. Among the younger mineworkers – more unionized, more militant and much better paid than their fathers – masculinity is increasingly associated with toughness, physical dominance and aggressiveness. This pattern of masculinity requires no reciprocity with women, who are, increasingly, left in the position of housewives dependent on a male wage earner.

There is much more in Moodie's complex and gripping work than can be summarized here, including the labour process in the mines, life in the compounds, and episodes of violence and resistance. As with Thorne's *Gender Play*, the research provides strong evidence of people's active creation of gender patterns. But the story of the mines gives a stronger impression of the constraints under which this creation is done, the impact of economic and political forces. There is a clearer view of the consequences of different gender strategies – prosperity and poverty, dominance and dependence. Above all, Moodie gives us a sense of the complex but powerful processes of historical change that transform gender arrangements over time.

Case 3: Bending gender

In the early 1980s a new and devastating disease was identified, eventually named 'AIDS' (acquired immune deficiency syndrome). It was soon shown to be connected with a virus (human immunodeficiency virus, HIV) that killed people indirectly, by destroying their immune systems' capacity to resist other diseases.

The global HIV/AIDS epidemic has called out a massive research response, ranging from the biological studies which discovered HIV, to social science studies of the practices in which HIV is transmitted. The commonest form of 'behavioural' research in health studies is survey research using questionnaires. But research of that kind, though it yields useful statistics, gives limited understanding of the meanings that sexual encounters have for the partners, or the place of sexual encounters in the lives of the people involved.

It is precisely that kind of understanding that is crucial for AIDS prevention strategies – which, to be successful, must involve people in protecting themselves. Therefore some researchers have turned to more sensitive and open-ended research strategies. One of the most notable products of this approach is Gary Dowsett's *Practicing Desire* (1996). This Australian study used a traditional sociological method, the oral life-history, to create a vivid and moving portrait of homosexual sex in the era of AIDS.

Dowsett's study is based on interviews with 20 men. This may seem like a small number, but good life-history research is remarkably complex, produces a tremendous volume of evidence and many theoretical leads, and so cannot be hurried. Dowsett's study took nine years from first interviews to final publication. Each of the 20 respondents gave a narrative of his life, talked in intimate detail about relationships and sexual practices, discussed the communities he lived in, his jobs and workplaces, his relations with the wider world, and his connections with the HIV/AIDS epidemic. The evidence is remarkably rich, and raises important questions about gender. It is so rich, indeed, that we will discuss just one of the participants here.

Huey Brown, better known as Harriet, was in his late thirties at the time of the interviews. He is a well-known figure in the homosexual networks of an urban working-class community, 'Nullangardie', which has been proletarian (in Moodie's sense) for generations. His father was a truck driver, his mother a housewife. He left school at 14, and went to work at the checkout of a local supermarket. He has held a succession of unskilled jobs, mostly in cafés or hotels; he currently works as a sandwich maker. He doesn't have much money or education and has no professional certificate in anything. But Harriet is a formidable AIDS educator, not only organizing and fundraising for AIDS-related events, but also being an informal teacher of safe sex and an influential community mentor.

Harriet became involved in homosexual sex in adolescence, not as a result of any identity crisis or alignment with a 'gay community' (which hardly existed in Nullangardie at the time), but simply by engaging in informal and pleasurable erotic encounters with other boys and with men. Dowsett points out that homosexuality does not necessarily exist as a well-defined 'opposite' to heterosexuality. Among the boys and men of Nullangardie there are many sexual encounters and sexual networks which never get named, yet make an important part of sexuality as it really is.

Harriet is an enthusiast for sex, has had a very large number of partners, is skilful in many sexual techniques, adopts different positions in different sexual encounters, and gets diverse (and perverse) responses from different partners. As Dowsett remarks, this kind of evidence – by no means confined to Harriet's case – undermines any doctrine that there is a single, standard pattern of male sexuality.

Like many other people, Harriet wanted stable relationships, and has had three. The first was with a jealous man who beat him severely; the third was with a pre-operative transsexual woman, which was stressful in other ways. The second, with Jim, the love of Harriet's life, lasted nine years. 'It was a husband and wife team sort of thing. I looked after him and he looked after me.' Jim took the penetrative role in sex: 'He was that straight that he just didn't like a cock near his bum.' Jim worked in the building trade, they lived together, they baby-sat Jim's nieces and nephews, and some of Jim's family accepted the relationship quite well.

Still, Harriet was no conventional wife. And as Dowsett remarks, what are we to make of Jim?

> It sounds like an ordinary suburban life, except that his partner is a drag queen with breast implants and a penchant for insertive anal intercourse with casual partners on the odd occasion! ... Whatever Jim was or is, he certainly cannot be called 'gay,' and when Harriet says: 'He [Jim] was that straight!' he means a sexually conventional male, not a heterosexually identified one. (1996: 94)

Yet after nine years Jim left Harriet – for a 16-year-old girl. There are gender practices here, but not gender boxes. The reality keeps escaping from the orthodox categories.

In some ways the most spectacular escape from the box was becoming a drag queen. In his late teens Huey began to hang out in a cross-dressing scene and became Harriet, working as a 'show girl'. In Australia, as in many other countries, there is a local tradition of drag entertainment involving mime, lip-synch singing, stand-up comedy and striptease.

Harriet learned the techniques of being a 'dragon', was good enough to pass as a woman on occasion, and even had operations to get breast implants. He acquired the camp style of humour and self-presentation which was part of the local tradition. Harriet now uses these techniques, and the local celebrity they gave him, for AIDS fundraising. But he notes a generational change. The younger men, more 'gay' identified than 'camp', now like beefy male strippers better than the old-style drag shows.

Hotel work and drag shows do not pay well, and in a de-industrializing economy the economic prospects of unskilled workers are not good. In his late twenties Harriet tried another form of work, prostitution. He worked in drag, and many of his customers presumed he was a woman. Some knew the score, or suspected, and for them his penis became part of the attraction. Harriet did some brothel work, but mostly worked independently on the street.

As Wendy Chapkis (1997) shows in a US/Dutch study, there are tremendous variations in the situations that sex workers face and in their level of control over the work. Harriet was right at one end of the spectrum, remaining firmly in control. He did not use narcotics, he offered only certain services, and he insisted on safe sex. He was skilful in sexual technique, and acquired loyal customers, some of whom stayed with him after he retired from the street – and after he took off the frocks. Even so, there was risk in street work, and a price to pay. Harriet learned to keep constantly aware of where the client's hands were. After several years and two arrests, he gave it up. Even so, his sexual reputation stayed with him, and on this account he was refused a job as an outreach worker with a local AIDS service organization.

Harriet's story (of which this is the barest outline) constantly calls into question the conventional categories of gender. It is not just that Harriet crosses gender boundaries. He certainly did that, with ingenuity and persistence, as a drag artist, surgical patient, wife, prostitute and activist. Yet Harriet is a man, not a transsexual woman, and has mostly lived as a man. (In recognition of that, Dowsett writes 'Harriet ... he', and we follow this example.) The gender perplexity is also a question about Harriet's partners, customers and social milieu. Every element in the story seems to be surging beyond the familiar categories.

Dowsett argues that the ordinary categories of gender analysis are seriously inadequate to understand what is going on here. He mentions critiques of gender theory for being 'heterosexist', preoccupied with heterosexual relations and unable to understand people who are not heterosexual. Even when gender terms are used, in the context of homosexual sex they are transformed. An example is Harriet's comment on 'husband and wife'.

Sexual desire and practice thus seem to act like a powerful acid dissolving familiar categories:

> But Harriet also teaches us that these gender categories are subject to deconstruction in sex itself: some like being penetrated by a fully frocked transsexual; some clients eventually do not need the drag at all; pleasure and sensation, fantasy and fixation, are the currency in a sexual economy where the sexed and gendered bodies rather than determining the sexual engagement *desire* to lend themselves to even further disintegration. (Dowsett 1996: 117)

Dowsett thus ponders the limits of gender analysis, and questions the concept of gender identity. It is clear that gender is *present* in most of the episodes of Harriet's life. But it is also clear that gender does not *fix* Harriet's (or his partners') sexual practices.

In his continuing research around the HIV/AIDS epidemic, Dowsett (2003) has argued forcefully that sexuality cannot be reduced to gender categories and must be understood in its own terms. Nevertheless, Harriet's story shows the constant *interplay* between gender and sexuality. Harriet's work as a prostitute rested on a gendered economy in Nullangardie which put money in the pockets of his clients – all of them men. Equally their practice as clients rested on a masculine culture which regarded men as entitled to sexual gratification.

One of the lessons of this research is that we cannot treat gender relations as a mechanical system. Human action is creative, and we are always moving into historical spaces that no one has occupied before. At the same time we do not create in a vacuum. We act in particular situations created by our own, and other people's, past actions. As shown by Harriet's sexual improvisations on materials provided by the gender order, we work on the past as we move into the future.

Case 4: Women, war and memory

One of the world's great experiments in gender equality was undertaken by the Soviet Union. The Bolshevik government established after the Russian revolutions of 1917, and the bitter civil war that followed, was formally committed to equal rights for women. At a time when, in much of the world, women were not even allowed to vote, a prominent feminist, Alexandra Kollontai, became minister for social welfare in the first Soviet government. The new regime made a major investment in girls' and women's education, women's health services and childcare facilities. Women's participation in industry and other forms of technical employment rose to levels never matched in the capitalist 'West'. The regime claimed to have achieved equality between women and men, and opened access for women to all spheres of social and public life.

At the end of the 1980s the system that held these ideals collapsed with stunning speed. In the countries that emerged from the former Soviet Union, different ideas about gender also emerged. Irina Novikova (2000: 119) notes how the attempt to create a new national identity for the post-Soviet regime in Latvia involved an appeal to surprisingly archaic models of gender:

> This started with a 'return to the past', to the patriarchal traditions embedded in the paternalist and authoritarian model of the state that existed before Soviet annexation in 1939. ... In this process, men were supposed to reorganize the state, while women/mothers were supposed to enshrine the 'umbilical' role of a cultural gatekeeper within the family/home/nation/state.

What happened in Latvia appears to have happened in most post-Soviet regimes. They are openly dominated by men, they marginalize women, they have re-emphasized patriarchal religion, and they weave together their nation-building with a hard, aggressive masculinity – exemplified by Vladimir Putin himself. It is, on the face of it, a stunning historical reversal, from a system of gender equality to a militant patriarchy. Why has this occurred?

Novikova, by profession a literary critic and historian, offers a fascinating answer in her essay 'Soviet and Post-Soviet Masculinities: After Men's Wars in Women's Memories'. This is an impressive example of the cultural analysis of gender, a research genre that raises questions not about individual lives, or particular institutional settings, but about the broad cultural meanings of gender and the way those meanings frame individual experience.

Novikova argues that the reassertion of local patriarchies was fuelled by the desire to reject the Soviet experiment as a whole.

> It is commonly believed that men were emasculated, made effeminate, by the official Soviet model of sex equality. It is popularly believed that men's historic identity was lost, and now has to be restored. Thus the critical response to the failure of the whole Soviet utopian project is reflected in a gender dynamic. In the arguments of post-Soviet nationalist and conservative state rebuilding, the essential falseness of the utopian project is proved by the fact that it attributed feminine features to men and masculine features to women, thus reversing the 'natural' sex roles. (2000: 119)

This reaction is reinforced by the precarious position of the new regimes. The smaller ones are poor and dependent economies in a global capitalism dominated by the West, and even Russia suffered a terrible collapse of pride and strength at the end of the 1980s, from superpower to disaster area in a mere 10 years. The celebration of a strong, competitive masculinity can be seen as a means of adjusting to this new, hostile and potentially overwhelming environment.

So far, the story seems straightforward; but it is more complicated than that. As Novikova also points out, the reassertion of masculine privilege could hardly have happened so quickly if the Soviet system had truly been as egalitarian as it claimed, if women had really been in a position of equal power with men.

Within 10 years of the Bolshevik rising, its radicalism was in retreat and an authoritarian system was consolidating under Joseph Stalin. Stalin's regime was not just a violent dictatorship controlled by a group of ruthless men; it was a dictatorship that specialized in egalitarian lies. Under the progressive façade of 'communism' lived a system of inequality, not as spectacular as the inequalities of capitalism over in the United States, but certainly as deeply entrenched.

Part of this was a structure of gender inequality. Many of the gains women had made at the Revolution were rolled back in subsequent decades, for instance abortion rights. Women won a higher proportion of parliamentary seats in the USSR than in almost any other part of the world, but the Soviet parliaments had no power. In the bodies that held real power (e.g. the central executive of the Communist Party), women were a small minority. Women were present in the paid economy, certainly, but they also did a second shift, unpaid housework and childcare.

Yet, Novikova points out, women had an important symbolic place in Soviet culture, which derived from earlier periods of Russian history. This was a place as *mother*, especially as mother to sons. The regime put a lot of energy into reconciling the needs of women as workers with their role as mothers. But it also drew on powerful cultural themes about maternity. Indeed there was a level at which woman-as-mother was symbolically identified with Russia itself, sending forth sons-as-soldiers to liberate the world. A gendered myth of war was created, which grew to full flower in the Second World War, and still existed when the regime tried to justify its disastrous military intervention in Afghanistan in the 1980s.

But women's actual experiences might be very different from the role in which they were cast by the regime. To explore this issue, Novikova turns to a little-discussed genre, women's war memoirs. She discusses the work of two writers. For lack of space we will skip over Elena Rzhevskaya, author of *Distant Rumble* (1988), a Red Army intelligence officer person-ally involved in the search for Hitler, dead or alive, in Berlin in 1945. Here we will concentrate on the more recent writer, Svetlana Alexievich.

Alexievich is the author of *Zinc Boys* (1992), a controversial book about the 'unknown war' the Soviet Union fought in Afghanistan. The title is an ironic allusion, on the one hand, to the zinc coffins used by the Red Army in this war, on the other to the Soviet imagery of 'steel men', i.e. soldiers and workers in heroic narratives of earlier wars. The regime presented the Afghanistan war too as a crusade for peace and social justice. But it failed, despite superior technology, and heavy casual-ties on both sides. Eventually the Soviet forces retreated from Afghani-stan and the socialist government they supported – which was attempting reforms in women's position – collapsed. The eventual victors were the militant misogynists of the Taliban movement, who were in turn over-thrown by a US-led invasion, leading to the neo-colonial wars still being fought across Afghanistan and the borderlands of Pakistan.

Alexievich interviewed Soviet veterans of the war, including women who had been there as military nurses. It is clear that the trauma created by this war was comparable to the failed American war in Vietnam, with similar levels of brutality, horror and doubt. Though the Soviet regime was more successful in suppressing public opposition, as the American regime was to be in the Iraq invasion, this merely drove the trauma underground. *Zinc Boys* opened the wounds again, to the anger both of veterans and of non-participants who wanted to have the whole ghastly mess forgotten.

Zinc Boys is an attempt at multiple autobiography, in which Alex-ievich as editor/author uses – and challenges – the familiar cultural representation of the mother–son relationship in war. The writer's posi-tion is like that of the mother, but also unlike it, especially confronting the emotional havoc among the Russian participants in this war. Instead of the welcoming and supportive national/maternal body, Alexievich and her readers confront body-memories of a different kind: male bodies, dead, torn apart, tortured, piled up and waiting for the zinc coffins – which happened to be in short supply.

The memories of defeat and mental devastation, and the powerful image of the war cemetery with unmarked graves, shatter the traditional imagery of the heroic male soldier at war. But the symbolic position of women in relation to this war is also untenable. The code of the strong woman, the amazon, the fighter for a larger cause, is destroyed by women's real memories of harassment, humiliation, and being sexu-ally exploited in the war zone by the men of their own side. Women's activism – i.e. participation in the crusade – simply made them vulnerable to exploitation, tearing up romantic dreams of marriage and love.

Returning from the war, women found this experience impossible to reconcile with the cultural expectations for womanhood, with the model of a virtuous worker-wife. The only way to handle the contradiction was to erase the memory. Hence some of the outrage created by Alexievich's text, which contested this erasure.

The men returning from the war turned in another direction. For them, the failed war had been an experience of collective impotency. After the American defeat in Vietnam, as a gripping study by Susan Jeffords (1989) has shown, American films and novels put a lot of energy into the reassertion of men's potency and authority vis-à-vis a more available target: local women, and the fiction of sex equality. Novikova shows the parallel in the late Soviet Union: 'Women are reminded that the masquerade is over, that equality was only a gift, and that female warriors are not to transgress the normal, biologically prescribed confines of their sex' (2000: 128).

Women's memoirs, Novikova argues, unveil the hidden gender dynamics behind the Soviet façade. This helps us understand the post-Soviet shift away from the principle of gender equality. Especially this helps us understand why it is often women themselves who support this shift. Having been through these traumas, they want 'only the right to forget their activism'. Many women become staunch supporters of the new patriarchy and the image of a powerful man.

Thus we can gain an understanding of the paradoxical gender patterns in post-Soviet life by a careful attention to cultural history, to the ways traditional gender images were both changed and preserved in the Soviet era of apparent 'sex equality'.

Case 5: Gender, marginality and forests

In South Kalimantan, the Indonesian part of the island of Borneo, the people of the Meratus Mountains live in rugged and marginal terrain. They are politically marginal to the Indonesian state, and marginal to the global economy, which was beginning to take off at the time Anna Lowenhaupt Tsing was doing her ethnographic work in the 1980s. Tsing's book *In the Realm of the Diamond Queen* (1993) is made up of a series of vignettes from life in the mountains.

The first vignette describes Tsing's relationship with a Kalawan woman named Uma Adang – a colourful and tireless figure in a village community who takes the visitor into her home, adopting her as a 'sister'. Uma Adang and her friends make theatrical formal speeches to Tsing, who reads these statements as a kind of mockery of the Indonesian state bureaucracy and Muslim orthodoxy.

Uma Adang's leadership in the community involves an assertion of authority with interesting gender dimensions. For instance, she instigates gender segregation in seating arrangements for local meetings she convenes. This is counter to the Meratus tradition, where no such formal distinction is made. Uma Adang's practice draws from the practice of the local Muslim Banjar people. The Banjar are also a minority in the national and international political economy. But they are intermediaries in the regional economy. Banjar people often dominate markets and tend to be in district-officer roles, or are police, army and other officials who routinely assert political authority over Meratus 'Dayaks' (a term used to describe the numerous ethnic groups in Kalimantan that fall outside Islam and its political sponsorship).

On the tensions of Uma Adang's leadership, Tsing remarks:

> These are not easy discrepancies to resolve, and they draw Uma Adang into a flurry of contradictions around the gender consequences of her leadership. Her leadership requires continual revision as it argues for and against local expectation about gender, ethnicity, and state power. (1993: 35)

Dynamics like these illustrate the ways in which marginality is lived and contested in geographically and politically remote areas of the globe. Tsing is concerned with gender-differentiated responses to peripheral political status. She argues that the contestations over gender difference can also disrupt ethnic unity and spark divergent attitudes towards the state.

Tsing takes up the concept of marginality in an interesting way. Two key dynamics are visible in her account of life in the Meratus Mountains: constraint and creativity. First, the marginalization of Meratus people, particularly by state authority, is clear. Under Suharto's 'New Order', officials deployed a similar style of authoritarian government to the Dutch administration of Indonesia's late colonial period (1920s and 1930s). For example, the Dutch distinguished between national and customary law. This is overlaid by another political dichotomy between Indonesia's Javanese centre and the island periphery. The Meratus people are 'tribal' minorities peripheralized through processes such as the central government's restricting definition of citizenship; its programme for Javanese transmigration and the 'Management of Isolated Populations'; forest land title reform favouring timber and other extractive industries; and the consistent presence of travelling military personnel.

Crucially, there is a second dimension of marginality Tsing emphasizes. She observes ways that marginality can be deployed as a basis for social agency. Uma Adang's self-titled 'woman's shamanism' is an example. Her spiritual teaching involves the education of her followers about symmetrical dualities (*dua-dua*) of gender (man and woman), nature (man and rice), economic organization (rich and poor) and more (Tsing 1993: 270). It is a kind of separate-but-equal approach to gender. No named duality is present in spiritual practice most often conducted by men.

Tsing argues the practice of Uma Adang illustrates that Northern social scientists should pay attention to the creative agency of subaltern people. Importantly, she also attends to the limits of this agency for a woman in Uma Adang's position. For instance, Uma Adang has trouble rousing other women spiritual leaders, and at times has difficulty cultivating her own audience outside the 'central proceedings' of men in community discussion.

The Meratus experience of state authority is likewise gendered. Tsing's description of family planning fertility control is an encounter with the bureaucratic imperatives of the modem Indonesian state. In the 1970s and 1980s, a government-sponsored family planning programme was expanded rapidly across the country. When the programme reached South Kalimantan, resistance came from the Banjar Muslim leadership. In the smaller villages, the administration of the programme was put into the hands of local office-bearers.

In one village where at the time there was no village head, a state official reportedly told one young Meratus man, Pa'an Tini, that village elections would be held on the condition 40 women were recruited to the family planning programme. The prospect of conducting these elections attracted a group of men eager to discuss the process. Tsing argues that their enthusiasm stemmed from the wish to align with the prestige of state authority through the village elections, not from support for the cause of birth control. She observed that there was opposition when the matter of contraception was aired, but just as often misunderstanding about contraception was visible amongst these men and broader village networks.

In the end, neither the village election, nor the delivery of the contraception for the state occurred. Instead, Pa'an Tini opted to perform the bureaucratic task in the most convenient way. He compiled a list of 40 married women to meet the nominal requirements from the central government, but did not pursue the use of contraception with those listed. He took this approach to other aspects of reporting to the state about household arrangements, for instance where family planning statistics required reporting on the 'heads' (*kepala keluarga*) of discrete families in the population. The reality of the households reported on is much more complex. For instance, a household can be formed by a brother and sister, or some other combination of non-conjugal couples, and dependants in a household are highly varied. The effect of this approach to complying with state authority, Tsing notes, is that Pa'an Tini 'protected only the community envisioned in his leadership. His leadership effectively barred women from access to state-provided contraception' (1993: 111).

The political ecology of the mountainous forests of South Kalimantan is an important feature of the dynamics of marginality captured in Tsing's work. The Meratus Dayaks, like many other Dayak communities in Kalimantan, have collected forest products for world markets since before European control. Trade was regulated by court centres from the fourteenth century and in the sixteenth century by the growing Banjar Kingdom in alliance with the Muslim Javanese state of Demak. Dutch colonial rule in the eighteenth and nineteenth centuries was accompanied by new export production programmes for rubber.

In the 1970s the Suharto regime pursued more direct military and economic control over these resource-rich islands. The 1975 Forestry Law made all forests property of the state. Lots of areas without trees, even towns and villages, were included in the first maps (Tsing 2005 194). The first timber concessions drawn up at the time divided the forests up as sites of production, focused on particular species of tree. The forest land of Kalimantan is valuable because it contains dipterocarps – giant trees that are exploited as huge sources of plywood for export markets. The legal construction of forest concessions assumed that commercial value flowed from these specific trees, rather than from the diversity of species of plants and animals that the Meratus use in their shifting cultivation practices.

At the time Anna Tsing was writing *In the Realm of the Diamond Queen*, large-scale timber extraction in Kalimantan was still relatively new. The new timber industry was operating at the greatest scale in the east of the island, but rapidly shifting south and up the Meratus Mountains. When Tsing returned to the Meratus Mountains in the late 1990s, she found that gold mining had produced devastating mercury poisoning in river ecosystems, and huge tracts of land had been assigned to logging and mining companies and firms producing pulp-and-paper and palm oil. Suharto's New Order was overthrown in the wake of the Asian financial crisis in 1997. However, the developmentalist model and increasing imposition of extractive industries in Kalimantan continued apace under President Habibie and his successors.

Tsing's book *Friction: An Ethnography of Global Connection* (2005) captures the dynamics of Kalimantan as a frontier of capitalism. Tsing's argument in the second book is that capitalism, science and politics strive for global connection and aspire to universal knowledge. But neither the processes of capital expansion, nor the universal claims on which they are based make everyplace and everything the same. South Kalimantan is the 'frontier' Tsing uses to illustrate this point.

Uma Adang features again, in the second book, and her anger at the chaos of capitalist development is clear. She tells Tsing that all the trees are coming down, and remarks more than once: 'better you had brought me a bomb, so I could blow this place up' (Tsing 2005: 25). Upon Uma Adang's request, the two embark on a process of recording a comprehensive list of plant and animal species of the local region in anticipation of further destruction. In reflecting on this process, Tsing recalls the debates within the global North on the relation between local knowledge in the periphery and Northern conservationism. She cites the critical reflection of US ecofeminist Noël Sturgeon that ecofeminist attention to indigenous knowledge reconstitutes white privilege. This can occur through reproducing racial essentialist views of 'Third World' women and 'local' knowledge (Tsing 2005: 160). Rather than divest her interest in the importance of indigenous knowledge, Tsing describes and reflects on the process of collaboration as a negotiation of overlapping motivations and pleasure derived from list-making that she, Uma Adang and other Meratus Dayaks share.

The question of gender is not central to Tsing's second book focused on the Meratus Mountains, but a few sections raise questions about gender and environmental change. One example is the impact of stories of ecofeminism which spread through Indonesian environmental activist networks. Tsing travelled with friends in the Indonesian environmental movement that bloomed in the late 1990s and particularly since the fall of Suharto's regime. Stories of women engaged in environmental activism, such as the Chipko movement in India, where women were involved in non-violent resistance to protect forests, and the story of ecofeminism more generally, sparked local attention (Tsing 2005: 236).

Tsing argues that the story of the Chipko movement established a cosmopolitan view of indigenous knowledge, and it was one of a series of international stories which contributed to a new kind of environmental politics in South Kalimantan where Muslim and non-Muslim Meratus Dayaks began to collaborate. She also describes the way in which young Indonesian women engaged in 'nature loving' activities were excited about gender as a new term, and wanted to know more about it. They wanted to walk forest trails without fear, and carry their own packs. The translation of these ideas illustrates that activists borrow travelling feminisms and environmentalisms for their own uses.

Tsing demonstrates that the global periphery is not a static location that stands in contrast to the dynamic core of elite-led globalization. Further, the politics of marginality are gendered in important ways. Tsing illustrates the possibilities for agency in the political ambitions of figures like Uma Adang. Finally, the process of knowing and acting on environmental change poses profound challenges to society, and the gender order. These themes will be further discussed in chapter 7.

Other notable studies might have been included in this chapter, and more will be mentioned through the book. Hopefully these five are enough to show the diversity of gender dynamics, their complexity, and their power. Gender dynamics are at work in many issues that are not conventionally labelled gender issues, such as the environment or war. In talking about gender, we are not talking about simple differences or fixed categories. We are talking about relationships, boundaries, practices, identities and images that are actively created in social processes. They come into existence in particular historical circumstances, shape the lives of people in profound and often contradictory ways, and are subject to historical struggle and change.

3

Sex differences and gendered bodies

At the centre of commonsense thinking about gender is the idea of natural difference between women and men. A whole industry of pop psychology tells us that women and men are naturally opposites in their thinking, emotions and capacities. The most popular book in this genre, which assures us that men and women are like beings from different planets, has sold *50 million* copies and is translated into 50 languages. Other books in this genre, and endless articles in popular magazines, tell us that men and women communicate in different ways, that boys and girls learn differently, that hormones make men into warriors, or that 'brain sex' rules our lives.

Most of the claims in these books are, in scientific terms, complete nonsense – refuted by a mass of research evidence. The US psychologist Janet Hyde (2005), the leading authority on gender difference research, points out that the pop-psychology doctrine of natural difference is harmful to children's education, to women's employment rights, and to all adults' emotional relationships. Clearly we need better ways of thinking about differences and bodies. The development of gender studies now provides some of the necessary tools.

Reproductive difference

Why is there any difference at all between women's and men's bodies? Humans share with many other species, plants as well as animals, the system of sexual reproduction – a method of reproducing which allows genetic information from two individuals to be combined, rather than just one to be copied. Sexual reproduction is itself a product of evolution, perhaps 400 million years old. Life forms existed earlier that reproduced by cell division from one individual; many species still do this, including bacteria and rotifers. Other species, including orchids, ferns and grasses, reproduce both sexually and asexually. Gardeners exploit the reproductive capacities of plants when they take cuttings from a neighbour's garden. Biologists debate why sex evolved, for this odd scheme has some evolutionary disadvantages, such as energy use or unfavourable genetic recombination. One speculation is that sex may have evolved because sexual reproduction allows faster change; another is that it prevents the accumulation of harmful mutations.

Sexual reproduction does not require bodies to be specialized by sex. Among earthworms, for instance, each individual is hermaphrodite, producing both sperm and ova (eggs), and thus every worm is able to perform both male and female functions. In other species, individuals produce either sperm or ova but not both. Their bodies are to some extent 'dimorphic', i.e. in a given species there exist two forms. Humans are among these species.

Genetic information is encoded in DNA and carried on chromosomes, microscopic structures within the nucleus of each cell in a plant or animal. In sexual reproduction, the genetic information that is combined at fertilization comes half from a female, in the egg nucleus, and half from a male, in the sperm nucleus. Human cells have 46 chromosomes, which come in pairs. One pair, the so-called 'sex chromosomes', influences the development of the body's male and female sexual characteristics. Females have two X chromosomes in this pair, males have one X and one Y chromosome. Under the influence of the genetic information here, and given the usual environmental conditions, male and female bodies develop specialized organs – wombs, testes, breasts – and certain differences in physiology, such as the balance of hormones circulating in the blood, and the menstrual cycle in women.

Among mammals, females not only produce ova but also carry foetuses in a protective womb (except for monotremes such as the platypus, which lay eggs). They feed infants with milk from specialized organs – in humans, women's breasts. Among some mammal species, but not all, males have extra bulk, or extra equipment: the antlers of male deer, for instance. Humans are mammals with well-differentiated reproductive systems, but modest physical differences between sexes in other respects. Human males do not have antlers.

In several ways, human bodies are not fully dimorphic. First, there are a considerable number of intersex categories, such as females lacking a second X chromosome, males with an extra X chromosome, anomalous or contradictory hormonal patterns, and a surprising variety of un-standard forms taken by the internal and external genitals. The biologist Anne Fausto-Sterling (2000: 51) estimates that the different intersex groups, taken together, may account for 1.7 per cent of all births; others think the proportion is lower (Sax 2002). There is continuing debate on how broad the category should be, what terminology applies, and how intersex people should be recognized in law (Holmes 2012). A major debate concerns a new term proposed in 2006 by European and US endocrinologists called 'Disorder of Sexual Development'; intersex advocates are worried about the way medical terms such as 'disorder' influence forms of treatment.

Katrina Karkazis's *Fixing Sex: Intersex, Medical Authority, and Lived Experience* (2008) traces the history of medical treatments of people diagnosed intersex. Drawing on interviews in the United States with clinicians, adults with intersex conditions and their parents, she shows that over five decades the health movement has changed medical diagnoses of intersex, but most clinicians still hold heteronormative and homophobic ideas about genital appearance. These views often mean doctors encourage parents to choose surgical procedures for their children. Interviews with patients in Karkazis's book and a collection of life stories published in Catherine Harper's *Intersex* (2007) offer a strong critique of the rush to 'correct' these variations by surgery on small children.

Second, physical differences between male and female change over the lifespan. In the early stages of development, male and female bodies are relatively undifferentiated; there are only small differences between a 2-year old girl and a 2-year-old boy. Even the external reproductive organs – penis, clitoris, scrotum and labia – develop embryonically from common starting point. In a number of ways, male and female bodies so become more similar in old age, for instance in their hormonal balance.

Third, even in early adulthood, the physical characteristics of males as a group, and females as a group, overlap extensively. Height is a simple example. Adult males are on average a little taller than adult females, but the diversity of heights within each group is great in relation to the average difference. Therefore a very large number of individual women are taller than many individual men. European cultures tend not to notice this physical fact because of social custom. When a man and a woman form a couple, they usually pick partners who show the 'expected' difference in height.

A more complex example is the brain – the site of a great deal of recent debate on sex differences. There are some differences in brain anatomy and functioning between women and men, for instance in the tendency to use particular areas of the brain in language processing. But the differences are fewer, and less reliably established, than aggressive popular accounts of 'brain sex' suggest. In many areas of brain anatomy and functioning, there are no significant sex differences. Where there are differences, these may be caused by different behaviours rather than causing them. Brain research now places a lot of emphasis on 'brain plasticity', the capacity of the brain to form new neural connections and lose old ones, i.e. to learn and change. As the neuroscientist Lesley Rogers (2000: 34) puts it: 'The brain does not choose neatly to be either a female or a male type. In any aspect of brain function that we can measure there is considerable overlap between females and males.' As we shall see, this is also a key point about human behaviour.

Conflicting accounts of difference

The fact of reproductive difference between male and female humans is hardly controversial, but its significance certainly is. On this question, approaches to gender diverge sharply. Some treat the body as a kind of machine that manufactures gender difference; some treat the body as a kind of canvas on which culture paints images of gender; some try to staple the machine and canvas images together. None of these is a satisfactory way of understanding the problem.

Many writers about gender assume that reproductive difference is directly reflected in a whole range of other differences: bodily strength and speed (men are stronger and faster), physical skills (men have mechanical skills, women are good at fiddly work), sexual desire (men have more powerful urges), recreational interests (men love sport, women gossip), character (men are aggressive, women are nurturant), intellect (men are rational, women have intuition), and so on. It is widely believed that these differences are large, and that they are 'natural'.

The claim that natural difference provides the basis for the social pattern of gender takes many forms. One is that men dominate in society because, with their higher levels of testosterone, they have a hormonal 'aggression advantage' in competition for top jobs. Therefore society needs patriarchy – Steven Goldberg claimed in *Why Men Rule* (1993) – to protect women from failure!

Arguments in 'sociobiology' and 'evolutionary psychology' deduce social gender from reproductive strategies. From this vaguely Darwinian starting point, theorists have deduced human kinship loyalties, mothers' commitment to their children, husbands' sexual infidelity, women's coyness, men's interest in pornography, male bonding and a remarkable range of other gender patterns. In *Male, Female* (1998), David Geary tries to link psychological research on sex differences with Darwin's concept of 'sexual selection' (the choice of mates in sexual reproduction) as a mechanism of evolution. For each topic where a sex difference can be located, Geary offers an account of how it *might* be linked to sexual selection, i.e. how humans choose, win and control mates. In *Sex, Genes and Rock 'n' Roll* (2011), Australian evolutionary biologist Rob Brooks applies the same view to popular culture. He argues that rock 'n' roll music can be understood as a reproductive agenda for men. That is, fame serves the male search for access to sexual partners.

Models of the body as a gender machine are mainly advanced by men, and have often been used to defend the existing gender order and ridicule feminist ideas about gender roles. However, there are also feminist arguments which present bodies as direct sources of gender difference. US feminists in the 1980s often saw male aggression and female peacefulness as natural. The terms 'male violence' and 'male sexuality', which became common at this time, implicitly linked behaviour to the body, and some activists directly identified the penis as the source of male power. This perspective reinforces the view that bodies are a separate aspect of our subjectivity that causes mental and social phenomena.

The idea of natural difference runs into difficulties on several fronts. Sociobiological explanations of human kinship, for instance, foundered when the predictions from genetics failed to match the realities of kinship systems actually documented by anthropologists (Sahlins 1977). The explanation of gender hierarchy by a hormonal 'aggression advantage' fails when it is discovered that higher testosterone levels *follow from* social dominance as much as they precede it (Kemper 1990). The 'evolutionary psychology' arguments are based on an unrealistic individualism, which takes no account of institutionalized gender arrangements. For instance, in discussing the higher levels of violence among men than among women, all that Geary (1998) can see is male vs male competition for reproductive resources. He cannot see armies, governments, insurgencies, mafias or cultural definitions of manhood – let alone football. But the most striking problem is that these arguments, while appealing to science, are actually entirely based on speculation. Not one sex difference in psychological characteristics has actually been *shown* to result from evolutionary mechanisms.

It is clear that bodies are affected by social processes. The way our bodies grow and function is influenced by food distribution, sexual customs, warfare, work, sport, urbanization, education and medicine, to name only the most obvious influences. And *all* these influences are structured by gender. So we cannot think of social gender arrangements as just flowing from the properties of bodies. They also precede bodies, forming the conditions in which bodies develop and live. There is, as Celia Roberts (2000) puts it, a co-construction of the biological and the social.

Starkly opposed to the body as machine is the idea of the body as a canvas on which culture paints images of womanhood and manhood. Second-wave feminism was very much concerned with the way women's bodies were represented and moulded. One of the very first Women's Liberation demonstrations was against the Miss America beauty pageant at Atlantic City in 1968. (Contrary to an almost universal media myth, no bras were burned at this demonstration. Rather, bras and other constricting underclothes were thrown into a 'Freedom Trash Can'.)

Research on gender imagery is abundant. Historical studies such as Lois Banner's *American Beauty* (1983) trace the changing systems of signs through which women's bodies are defined as elegant, beautiful and desirable, or unfashionable and ugly. The imagery of men's bodies has come in for more recent scrutiny. A nice example is Dorinne Kondo's (1999) study which looks at the advertising campaign through which a Japanese manufacturer of expensive suits created an appeal to a supposed Japanese aesthetic, embodied by the elite of salarymen who stalked around in their particular brand.

Recent cultural studies of the body often focus on language or discourse, under the influence of the French historian Michel Foucault. In a number of celebrated studies, most completely in *Discipline and Punish* (1977), Foucault showed how modern systems of knowledge had come to sort people into categories, and how these categories were interwoven with techniques of social discipline that policed their bodies. The categories and the discipline were applied by professions such as medicine, psychology and criminology, in an amalgam that Foucault called power/knowledge (it rhymes in French: *pouvoir-savoir*).

Foucault, notoriously, failed to theorize gender, though most of his stuff is actually about men in masculinized institutions. However, his approach was taken up by many post-structuralist feminists (e.g. Fraser 1989), and is readily turned into a theory of gender by treating gendered bodies as the products of disciplinary practices. Bodies are 'docile' and biology bends to the hurricane of social discipline.

Field research shows how such disciplining is done. The Los Angeles body-building gyms studied by the ethnographer Alan Klein (1993) reveal a whole subculture of men subjected to a fierce regime of exercise, diet and drugs. Over years of subjection to this regime their bodies are sculpted into the ideal masculine forms desired in body-building competitions. This is an extreme case, but more moderate disciplining of bodies is very widespread. It is undertaken by such powerful institutions as sport, education and medicine. Nancy Theberge (1991) shows how the different exercise regimes for men and women, the disciplinary practices that both teach and constitute sports, are designed to produce gendered bodies. Michael Messner (2007), meanwhile, has shown, through a long research programme, how pervasive are gender stereotyping and gender inequality in the US sports world.

And if social discipline cannot produce gendered bodies, the knife can. The silicon breast implant scandal made public the scale on which cosmetic surgery has been done in the United States, where big breasts are thought sexy. This whole industry, one might think, flies in the face of the ideology of natural difference. Research on cosmetic surgeons and their clients by Diana Dull and Candace West (1991) shows a startling solution. Cosmetic surgery has become considered 'natural' for a woman, but not for a man. The exception is penile surgery, where penis enlargement is now a considerable business. However, a growing number of men in the global North are also undertaking procedures like rhinoplasty (nose jobs), breast reduction, eyelid surgery and liposuction.

Body-as-canvas approaches, though they have been wonderfully productive, also run into difficulty. The approach emphasizes the signifier to the point where the signified practically vanishes. With gender, the difficulty is crucial. What makes a symbolic structure a gender structure, rather than some other kind, is the fact that its signs refer directly or indirectly to the way humans reproduce.

Post-structuralist research often exaggerates the docility of bodies. Bodies may participate in disciplinary regimes not because they are docile, but because they are active. They seek pleasure, experience, transformation. Some startling examples of this can be found in sadomasochist sexual subcultures. People submit to corsets, chains, piercing, branding, rope bondage and a whole spectrum of painfully restrictive clothes in rubber and leather – voluntarily, indeed with delight (Steele 1996). The same is surely true, in milder forms, of the whole system of fashion. Nobody compels young women to wear shoes with stiletto heels. They hurt after a few minutes, and they wreak havoc after a few years, but they are also enjoyable.

Some feminist philosophers, such as Elizabeth Grosz, have argued there is no consistent distinction between body and mind, and that our embodiment itself is adequate to explain our subjectivity. In her book *Volatile Bodies: Towards a Corporeal Feminism* (1994), Grosz uses ideas from a range of Western European philosophers, such as Jacques Lacan, Sigmund Freud, Maurice Merleau-Ponty, Friedrich Nietzsche and Luce Irigaray, to critique the mind/body dualism. She argues that bodies and minds are two aspects of the one element making up ourselves and the world, and uses active language to describe gendered embodiment as dynamically shifting over time. On the question of sexual difference, Grosz maintains that there is an irreducible distinction between sexes.

Bodies are also recalcitrant and difficult. They are vulnerable to epidemic disease. The HIV/AIDS pandemic, one of the great challenges of our time, is interwoven with embodied gender relations and gender practices on a global scale, from domestic violence to forms of sexuality (Schneider and Stoller 1995). As Wendy Harcourt shows in her powerful book *Body Politics in Development* (2009), a whole series of issues in global economic development involve troubles about bodies – in childbirth and childcare, violence, sexualization, technology and more.

Studies of men in industries such as construction and steelmaking show another side of embodiment. The masculinity of industrial labour in these settings consists in its heaviness, risk and difficulty, where men put themselves 'in harm's way', as a vivid ethnographic study of the US construction industry puts it (Paap 2006). In such labour, bodies are consumed: worn down, injured, sometimes killed. As Mike Donaldson (1991) remarks, 'The very destruction of the physical site of masculinity, the body, can be a method of attaining, demonstrating and perpetuating the socially masculine.'

So bodies cannot be understood as just the objects of social process, whether symbolic or disciplinary. They are active participants in social process. They participate through their capacities, development and needs, through their recalcitrance, and through the directions set by their pleasures and skills. Bodies share in social agency, in generating and shaping courses of social conduct. Yet all the difficulties of biological determinism, outlined above, remain. Can we solve these problems by holding both a machine and a canvas image of the gendered body at the same time?

In the 1970s a number of feminist theorists did exactly this, proposing a sharp distinction between 'sex' and 'gender'. Sex was the biological fact, the difference between the male and the female human animal. Gender was the social fact, the difference between masculine and feminine roles, or men's and women's personalities.

To many at the time, this two-realms model was a conceptual breakthrough, showing why biology could not be used to justify women's subordination. The constraints of biological difference were confined to the realm of biology itself. A broad realm of social life ('culture', 'roles', etc.) remained, a realm of freedom, where individuals or societies could choose the gender patterns they wanted. Eleanor Maccoby and Carol Jacklin, the authors of a vast and influential survey of *The Psychology of Sex Differences*, concluded:

> We suggest that societies have the option of minimizing, rather than maximizing, sex differences through their socialization practices. A society could, for example, devote its energies more toward moderating male aggression than toward preparing women to submit to male aggression, or toward encouraging rather than discouraging male nurturance activities. (1975: 374)

The concept of 'androgyny' put forward by Sandra Bem (1974) and other psychologists at this time was a popular attempt to define an alternative gender pattern. Androgyny meant a mixture of masculine and feminine characteristics, which an individual or a society could choose.

At the high tide of North American liberal feminism in the 1970s, the two-realms model supported an optimistic view of change. Oppressive gender arrangements, being the products of past choices, could be abolished by fresh choices. Whole reform agendas were constructed around this principle. Among them were media reforms (to change sex role models), educational reforms (to change the expectations transmitted to girls and boys) and new forms of psychotherapy (to help individuals make the change to new roles).

A notable example of educational reform is the pioneering Australian Schools Commission's report *Girls, School and Society* (1975). This described the ways girls were held back by restrictive social stereotypes, and proposed action to break down educational segregation and to widen girls' job choices. From this report flowed many projects in Australian schools encouraging girls to work in areas such as mathematics, science and technology.

However, the two-realms model soon ran into trouble, as Rosemary Pringle (1992) shows in a careful critique. The idea of gender as culturally chosen difference ('sex roles') was unable to explain why one side of that difference, the masculine, was more highly valued than the other. The separation of gender from bodies ran counter to developments in feminism which were placing stronger emphasis on bodies.

If the two realms cannot be held strictly apart, perhaps they can be added together? A commonsense compromise would suggest that gender differences arise from *both* biology and social norms. This additive conception underlies most discussions of gender in social psychology, where the term 'sex role' is still widely used. This very phrase adds together a biological and a dramaturgical term.

But there are difficulties in the additive conception too. The two levels of analysis are not easily comparable. In such discussions, it is almost always assumed that biology's reality is more real than sociology's, its explanations more powerful, and its categories more fixed. The passage from Maccoby and Jacklin quoted above continues, saying: 'A variety of social institutions are viable within the framework set by biology.' Maccoby and Jacklin argue for social choice, and want change, but the priority in their analysis is clear. Biology determines; only within its 'framework' may humans choose their gender arrangements. Sex role theory and sex difference research constantly collapse back into biological dichotomy.

A further difficulty is that the patterns of difference at the two levels need not match. As we have seen already, human bodies are dimorphic only in limited ways. On the other side, human behaviour is hardly dimorphic at all, even in areas closely related to sexual reproduction. For instance, while few men do childcare with infants, it is also true that, at any given time, most women are not doing this work either.

In current social life there is a whole spectrum of gender variations. In *Breaking the Bowls* (2005), the US sociologist Judith Lorber observes that for any individual, gender is composed of: sex category; gender identity; gendered marital and procreative status; gendered sexual orientation; gendered personality; gender processes (in everyday interaction); gender beliefs; and gender display. Since there is variety in most of these elements, the number of available gender positions rises into the hundreds, perhaps into the thousands. So much for 'dimorphism'!

It is impossible to sustain a two-realms model of gender difference, any more than we can sustain the machine or canvas models. It is time to look more closely at the evidence about difference itself.

Facts about difference: 'sex similarity' research

In pop psychology, bodily differences and social effects are linked through the idea of *character dichotomy*. Women are supposed to have one set of traits, men another. Women are supposed to be nurturant, suggestible, talkative, emotional, intuitive and sexually loyal; men are supposed to be aggressive, tough-minded, taciturn, rational, analytic and promiscuous. These ideas have been strong in European-origin cultures since the nineteenth century, when the belief that women had weaker intellects and less capacity for judgement than men was used to justify their exclusion from universities and from the vote.

The belief in character dichotomy was one of the very first issues about gender to be addressed in empirical research. Starting in the 1890s, generations of psychologists have measured various traits with tests or scales, and compared the results for women with those for men. This body of research, long known as 'sex difference' (sometimes 'gender difference') research, is huge; this is one of the most-researched topics in psychology. There is also a large parallel literature in sociology and political science, looking at group differences in attitudes and opinions, voting, violence, and so forth.

The beginning of this research is described in a fascinating historical study by Rosalind Rosenberg, *Beyond Separate Spheres* (1982). The first generation of psychological researchers found, contrary to mainstream nineteenth-century belief, that the mental capacities of men and women were more or less equal. It is an interesting fact that this finding of 'no difference' was rapidly accepted by men as well as women in the mental-testing field. Indeed, as they developed standardized tests of general ability or intelligence (the so-called 'IQ tests') during the first half of the twentieth century, psychologists incorporated the 'no difference' finding as a given. They chose and scored test items in such a way that males and females would have equal average scores. Later attempts to find gender differences in this field have come to nothing (Halpern and LaMay 2000). It is now widely accepted that in general intelligence, there are no significant gender differences.

An even more interesting fact is that this is the usual finding in the gender difference research on other variables too. In table after table of Maccoby and Jacklin's book, the commonest entry in the column for the finding about difference is 'none'. Study after study, on trait after trait, comparing women's results with men's, or girls' with boys', finds no significant difference. In summarizing their findings, the first thing Maccoby and Jacklin (1975: 349) did was list a series of 'unfounded beliefs about sex differences'. On the evidence they compiled, it is not true that girls are more social than boys, that girls are more suggestible than boys, that girls have lower self-esteem, that girls are better at rote learning and boys at higher-level cognitive processing, that boys are more analytic, that girls are more affected by heredity and boys by environment, that girls lack achievement motivation, or that girls are auditory while boys are visual. All these beliefs turn out to be myths.

Maccoby and Jacklin were not alone. Other reviewers too noted that the main research finding is a massive psychological *similarity* between women and men in the populations studied by psychologists. If it were not for the cultural bias of both writers and readers, we might long ago have been talking about this as 'sex *similarity*' research (Connell 1987: 170).

It is therefore intensely interesting to find that this conclusion is widely disbelieved. The acceptance of gender similarity in the field of intelligence testing turns out to have been exceptional. Most people still believe in character dichotomy. Pop psychology is utterly committed to this idea. In the academic world, generations of researchers, in the teeth of the evidence their own disciplines have produced, have gone on relentlessly searching for, and writing about, psychological gender differences.

The gap between the main pattern *actually* found, and the widespread belief about what *should* be found, is so great that Cynthia Epstein entitled her admirable book about dichotomous thinking and gender reality *Deceptive Distinctions* (1988). Two decades later, when she was President of the American Sociological Association, Epstein (2007) was still having to argue against the conventional 'master narrative' that holds 'that men and women are naturally different and have different intelligences, physical abilities, and emotional traits'.

Why the huge reluctance to accept the evidence of similarity? A large part of the explanation lies in the cultural background. Dichotomous gender symbolism is very strong in European culture, so it is not surprising that when researchers look at sex and gender, what they 'see' is difference. Within our usual research design, gender similarity is not a positive state; it is merely the absence of proven difference (literally, the 'null hypothesis'). Epstein gives an example of journal editors not liking to publish null results. So the true evidence for gender similarity may be *even stronger* than the published literature reveals.

But are the facts as solid as they seem? Conventional psychological tests, it is sometimes said, are too superficial to detect the underlying patterns of gender. The real character differences between women and men may be lodged at a deeper level in personality – say, in the unconscious. (Jungian psychology makes a dichotomy of the 'deep masculine' and the 'deep feminine'.) This could be true. Certainly most quantitative tests in psychology measure only the immediately apparent aspects of behaviour, often through self-report. But if the 'deep' differences don't show up at the level of everyday life, and keep on failing to show up across a wide range of behaviours – which is what the quantitative research reveals – then one wonders how important such deep differences really can be.

A second issue is that the finding of 'no difference' is not uniform. Maccoby and Jacklin also pointed to a small number of traits where gender differences *did* exist, according to the bulk of their evidence: verbal ability, visual-spatial ability, mathematical ability and aggressiveness. It was these findings, not the larger 'no difference' finding, which went into the textbooks, and have been emphasized by most subsequent writers.

A third issue concerns research method. Maccoby and Jacklin had a large amount of data, but most of it came from hundreds of small studies with ill-defined samples. It may be that the number of 'no difference' findings reflects the methodological weakness of the individual studies. If a way could be found to strengthen the method by combining the results of many studies, the picture might change.

Exactly this became possible when a new statistical procedure, known as 'meta-analysis', was introduced to gender difference research in the 1980s. The procedure relies on finding a large number of separate studies of the same issue: for instance, many studies attempting to measure gender differences in aggression, or intelligence, or self-esteem. In meta-analysis each study (rather than each person) is taken as one data point, and the task is to make a statistical analysis of the whole set of studies.

Obviously before this can be done the findings have to be expressed on a common scale. Unless all the studies have used exactly the same measurement procedures, which in practice is rarely the case, this is a problem. The ingenious solution is to define a common scale based on the variability of individual scores in the original studies. For each study, the difference between the average scores of women and men (on whatever test is being used) is obtained, and this is rewritten as a fraction of the overall variation in people's scores found in that study on that same test. (Technically, the difference between means is divided by the mean within-group standard deviation.) The standardized gender difference, known as 'd', found for each individual study is the measurement taken forward into the meta-analysis. By an unfortunate convention, a positive d means that men as a group score higher; a negative d means that women as a group score higher.

The first impact of meta-analysis was to revive confidence in the existence and importance of gender differences generally. This can be seen in Alice Eagly's *Sex Differences in Social Behavior* (1987). Even when most studies in a group individually show non-significant differences, meta-analysis may find an effect size significantly different from zero in the group as a whole. A few examples from the many effect sizes reported are: +.21 across 216 studies of self-esteem (Kling et al. 1999), −.28 across 160 studies of 'care orientation' in moral choice (Jaffee and Hyde 2000), +.48 across 83 studies of aggression (Hyde 1984), zero across 22 studies of 'meaning orientation' in learning styles (Severiens and ten Dam 1998), and between .01 and .17 in large surveys of the frequency of sexual intercourse (Petersen and Hyde 2011).

The question then arises, what do these effect sizes mean? An effect may be significantly different from zero, which means it is not a result of pure chance, but may still be so small that it does not tell us much about the world. Here meta-analysis has its limits. By convention, an effect size of .20 is called 'small', .50 is called 'medium', and .80 is called 'large'. But there is debate about how to interpret this convention. Eagly (1987) argued that even small effects may be practically important, but other meta-analysts are much less convinced.

As meta-analyses built up, so did a renewed scepticism about the size and scope of gender differences. Maccoby and Jacklin in the 1970s considered that 'verbal ability' was one of the traits where a difference (favouring women) was definitely established. But Hyde and McKinley (1997), reviewing meta-analyses of research since then, report effect sizes clustering around zero. Mathematics ability, another claimed area of difference (favouring men), proves to have only very small effect sizes, between −.15 and +.22 for 242 studies, supporting the view that males and females perform similarly (Lindberg et al. 2010).

In 2005 Janet Hyde published a grand meta-survey of meta-analyses, combining the findings of this technique across the whole field of psychology. She found 46 published meta-analyses of gender difference, which analysed over 5,000 research studies, which in turn were based on the testing of about 7 million people. The research covered cognitive variables, communication, social and personality variables, psychological well-being, motor behaviours and assorted other topics. The overall finding is simply stated:

> The striking result is that 30% of the effect sizes are in the close-to-zero range, and an additional 48% are in the small range. That is, 78% of gender differences are small or close to zero. (Hyde 2005: 582, 586)

Hyde provocatively titles her paper 'The Gender Similarities Hypothesis'. It is hardly a hypothesis. The idea of a character dichotomy between women and men has been overwhelmingly, decisively, refuted. *The broad psychological similarity of men and women as groups can be regarded, on the volume of evidence supporting it, as one of the best-established generalizations in all the human sciences.*

Hyde also recognizes that there are some traits on which average gender differences do persistently show up. In her review they include physical performances (e.g. in throwing); some aspects of sexuality, but not all; and some aspects of aggression.

What is particularly interesting in the meta-analytic studies is that when clear psychological gender differences do appear, they are likely to be specific and situational rather than generalized. Studies of aggression often show a gender difference – but in physical aggression more than in verbal aggression, and not in all circumstances. Ann Bettencourt and Norman Miller (1996) find an overall *d* of +.22 in experimental studies of aggression, but report that this effect depends on whether or not there are conditions of provocation. Unprovoked, men have a modest tendency to show higher levels of aggressiveness than women (mean effect size +.33); provoked, men's and women's reactions are similar (mean effect size +.17). Hyde cites a meta-analysis of gender differences in making interruptions in conversation. The effect size varied, according to the type of interruption, the size of the group talking together, and whether they were strangers or friends. She comments: 'Here, again, it is clear that gender differences can be created, erased, or reversed, depending on the context' (Hyde 2005: 589).

Meta-analysis reveals that gender differences in masculinity/femininity, as measured by tests like the 'Bem Sex Role Inventory', change over time. Jean Twenge (1997) showed that men and women (in samples of US undergraduates) became more similar in their responses on these scales over a period of 20 years, from the 1970s to the 1990s. This was not, as many people fear, because men are becoming feminized – both groups' scores on the femininity scales changed little. It was rather because the women increased their scores markedly (and men a little) on masculinity scales over this period.

Meta-analysis has not entirely revolutionized the study of gender difference, since the basic data collection methods remain the same. But it has certainly clarified what this body of research is saying. Confirming earlier conclusions, it tells us that across a wide range of the traits and characteristics measured by psychology, sharp gender differences are rare. Broad similarity between women and men is the main pattern. Meta-analysis adds a clearer recognition that specific and situational sex differences often appear. Very specific skills (e.g. in one science rather than another), specific social circumstances (e.g. provocation), specific times and places (e.g. US colleges in the 1990s) and specific ways of measuring traits all affect the extent of gender differences recorded in the research.

We thus get a picture of psychological gender differences and similarities not as fixed, age-old constants of the species, but as the changing products of the active responses people make to a complex and changing social world. With the aid of meta-analysis, psychology has gradually moved towards the way of understanding gender that has also gradually emerged in sociology.

How far can we generalize this picture? It is often observed that the modern science of psychology is mainly based on the behaviour of white middle-class students in Psychology 101 courses in US universities – not exactly a representative sample of humanity.

Given the impressive evidence of cultural and historical variations in gender arrangements (see chapters 2 and 5), we cannot simply assume that the psychological patterns documented for the contemporary US hold true across the world. Yet this very point, that gender differences can vary between different circumstances, has been emerging from meta-analytic research. The gender similarity research now includes increasing numbers of large-scale studies with better samples of the population of countries in the global North, and increasing numbers of studies in other parts of the world. The conclusions outlined above are a solid starting point for understanding the psychology of gender.

Social embodiment and the reproductive arena

Now that gender similarity research has decisively refuted the concept of character dichotomy, we must reject all models of gender that assume social gender differences to be caused by bodily differences producing character differences. How, then, can we understand the relation between body and society in gender?

Bodies have agency *and* bodies are socially constructed. Biological and social analysis cannot be cut apart from each other. But neither can be reduced to the other. Within a 'difference' framework, these conclusions sit as paradoxes. We must move towards another framework.

There are many, many differences among the 7,000 million human bodies in the world. There are old and young, sick and well, plump and starving. There are differences of physical ability and disability. There are skins permanently stained with soil and skins softened with expensive creams; hands cracked from washing and hands spotless and manicured. Each body has its trajectory through time; each changes as it grows older. Some bodies encounter accident, traumatic childbirth, violence, starvation, disease or surgery, and have to reorganize themselves to carry on. Some do not survive these encounters.

Yet the tremendous multiplicity of bodies is in no sense a random assortment. Our bodies are interconnected through social practices, the things people do in daily life. Bodies are both *objects of* social practice and *agents in* social practice. The same bodies, at the same time, are both. The practices in which bodies are involved form social structures and personal trajectories, which in turn provide the conditions of new practices in which bodies are addressed and involved. Bodily processes and social structures are linked *through time*. They add up to the historical process in which society is embodied, and bodies are drawn into history.

In this book, this historical process is called *social embodiment*. From the point of view of the body, it could be called 'body-reflexive practice', i.e. human social conduct in which bodies are both agents and objects.

Bodies have a reality that cannot be reduced; they are drawn into history without ceasing to be bodies. They do not turn into signs or positions in discourse (though discourses constantly refer to them). Their materiality continues to matter. We are born, we are mortal. If you prick us, do we not bleed?

Social embodiment involves an individual's conduct, but also involves groups, institutions and whole complexes of institutions. Consider the body-reflexive practice that goes into making the exemplary masculinity of a sports star – for instance, Steve, a champion in 'iron man' surf competitions, whose life is described in *The Men and the Boys* (Connell 2000). Steve's practice includes the training routines worked out by coaches, drawing on the professional expertise of physical education and sports medicine. It includes the practice of the sport itself, which is organized by multi-million-dollar corporations. It includes participating in publicity and getting fees via other corporations (commercial media, advertisers). A major sports star, like other media figures, practically turns into a one-person corporation, employing lawyers, accountants, marketing agents and public relations flacks. There is an elaborate social process here. Yet all of this specialized work is based on, and refers back to, Steve's bodily performances.

Gender is a specific form of social embodiment. The distinctive feature of gender is that it refers to the bodily structures and processes of human reproduction. Gender involves a cluster of human social practices – including childcare, birthing, sexual interaction – which deploy human bodies' capacities to engender, to give birth, to give milk, to give and receive sexual pleasure. We can only begin to understand gender if we understand how closely the social and the bodily processes mesh. We are born in blood and pain, *and* we are born in a social order.

These bodily capacities, and the practices that realize them, constitute an arena, a bodily site where something social happens. Among the things that happen is the creation of the cultural categories 'women' and 'men' (and any other gender categories that a particular society marks out). This may be called the *reproductive arena* in social life. The beginning of the chapter noted that we are one of the species that reproduce sexually, and this is where that fact becomes central for gender analysis.

The idea of a 'reproductive arena' is not the same as the traditional idea of a 'biological base', a natural mechanism that produces automatic social effects. Sexual reproduction does not *cause* gender practice, or even provide a template for it. There are many fields where strongly gendered behaviour occurs which has not the slightest logical connection with sexual reproduction (football, shoe design, futures markets, lesbian sex, Handel oratorios, the appointment of bishops ...). We may be one of many species that reproduce sexually, but we are the only one of them that has produced complex, historically changing social structures in which that reproductive capacity is deployed and transformed. Gender, in fact, is one of the most striking things that is unique about our species.

Though it is often forgotten in the excitement of gender politics among adults, the reproductive arena very much concerns children. Not all sex results in pregnancy – in fact the great majority of sexual encounters, even heterosexual ones, don't, and aren't intended to. But the fact that children do arrive this way, and have to be nurtured and taught, and will become the next generation of parents, matters immensely for any society that intends to last beyond next Thursday. The way caring for children is organized is a large part of the domain of gender.

The reproductive arena can be reshaped by social processes. Indeed it constantly is being reshaped in social struggle. For instance, the fertility of a woman's body means something different where contraception is effective and small families are planned from what it means where women are designated lifelong breeders and nurturers – barefoot, pregnant and in the kitchen, as the saying goes.

The reproductive arena is always the point of reference in gender processes, but it is far from incorporating everything that gender is about.

We also need a concept of the *gender domain*, meaning the whole terrain of social life that is socially linked to the reproductive arena. In the gender domain, relations among people and groups are structured by this linkage and can therefore be understood as gender relations.

It follows from this definition that the scope and shape of the gender domain vary from one society to another, and from one period of history to another. They can even be changed by deliberate action. This is attempted in the 'de-gendering' reform strategy (Connell 2006; Lorber 2005). The attempt to de-gender early childhood education in rich countries by employing more men as teachers is a current, though so far not very successful, example. (In some poorer countries there are already more men than women in elementary teaching.)

A few short examples of social embodiment in the gender domain may illustrate what is meant. One of the crudest ways of deploying gender is through sexual harassment – an exercise of power, directed to the body of the target. Meredith Newman and her colleagues (2003) report survey evidence from employees of the US government showing 25 per cent of women report having been sexually harassed on the job, compared with 6 per cent of men. There was little variation from one government agency to another. Greetje Timmerman and Cristien Bajema (1999) found that between 17 and 81 per cent of employed women reported experiencing some form of workplace sexual harassment, according to surveys in 11 European countries.

Miriam Glucksmann's (1990) historical study of women in the electrical engineering and food processing industries in inter-war Britain shows that gender segregation was introduced in the new factories on a massive scale. Nothing about the workers' bodies, or about the technology of chocolate biscuit making, required this. But the factory managers sharply segregated women's from men's bodies. The reason was that to have integrated the workplace would have broken down the existing social dependence of women and the gender division of child care and housework in the workers' homes.

The devastating human immunodeficiency virus, which leads to AIDS, has been spread around the world by contacts between human bodies, usually following gendered paths. Purnima Mane and Peter Aggleton (2001), surveying the role of men in this biological process, note that men's practices in different regions are shaped by local gender orders. The risk of transmission is highest where women have least capacity to control sexuality. Men's bodily practices are also shaped by prevailing definitions of manhood, such as the acceptance of risk, and the idea of proving manhood by sexual experimentation. For instance, in sub-Saharan Africa, where there is a mostly heterosexual HIV epidemic, women who experience more marked gender inequality and violence in relationships are at greater risk of HIV. Risks stem from a lack of control over the circumstances of sex. This inequality and violence in relationships is often related to complicity with a power-oriented ideal of hegemonic masculinity (Jewkes and Morrell 2010).

Bodies are transformed in social embodiment. Some broad changes in recent history are familiar: falling numbers of children born, lengthening expectation of life, rising average height and weight (as child nutrition and healthcare improve), and changing patterns of disease (e.g. polio declining, TB declined but now reviving). The transformation of bodies is structured, in part, on gender lines, as the demographic indicators show. In the rich industrial countries, women's average life expectancy is now noticeably longer than men's. The average expectation of life for women in OECD countries is 83 years, for men 77. But in some poorer countries the difference is noticeably less: in Pakistan, the figure for women is 68 years and for men 66; in the Congo, for women 58 and for men 55.

The idea of social embodiment allows us to recognize a paradoxical aspect of gender. Many gender processes involve bodily processes and capacities that are themselves not gender-differentiated, that are in fact common capacities of women and men. For instance, there are almost no gender differences of any consequence in capacities to work in an industrial economy, apart from those created by different training, the treatment of pregnancy as a disability, or the gendered design of equipment. Most production processes involve the co-operation of very large numbers of men and women in an intricate flow of work. Ironically, this shared labour creates the means through which mass media images of gender dichotomy are circulated.

Recognizing social embodiment also allows a new view of the relation between bodies and change in gender. In sociobiology, sex role theory, liberal feminism and popular ideologies of natural difference, bodily difference is understood to be a conservative force. It holds back historical change, limits what social action can accomplish. But we can now see that bodies as agents in social practice are involved in the very construction of the social world, the bringing-into-being of social reality. Bodies' needs, bodily desire and bodily capacities are at work in history. The social world is never simply reproduced; it is always reconstituted by practice.

Gender as a system of relations is created in this historical process, and accordingly can never be fixed, nor exactly reproduced. The strategic question is not 'can gender change?' but 'in what direction is gender changing?' There are different futures towards which contemporary societies might be moved. We will explore this in the later chapters of the book. First, we need to look at the ways gender has been theorized.

4

Gender theorists and gender theory

Introduction: Raden Adjeng Kartini

A little over a hundred years ago in Java, then part of the Dutch East Indies, a young woman in a ruling-class Muslim family decided to be a writer and teacher. To help prepare herself, she advertised for a pen-friend in the Netherlands. The young woman's name was Kartini (Raden Adjeng is a title of respect) and the pen-friend she found was Stella Zeehandelaar, a social democrat who put her in touch with European progressive thought. Kartini and her two sisters were developing an agenda for reforming Javanese society and culture, especially the position of women. Kartini was vigorously opposed to the institution of polygamy, and critical of the seclusion of women and their lack of education. Therefore she proposed to remain unmarried herself, in order to launch a programme of action. She planned to set up a school for the daughters of the elite, on the idea that the aristocracy should provide a model for change; and she began publishing essays.

These activities by a woman, however, were not thought respectable in elite Javanese society. Though her father had provided a private education for Kartini, he would not send her to train as a teacher in the Netherlands. Nor could she get government support for the planned school. Eventually the family, following custom, arranged a good marriage for her, and she bowed to pressure. She died from complications of her first childbirth, aged 24.

Kartini's letters to Stella, in which this story of hope and disappointment is told, were collected after her death, censored and published in 1911. A little later they were translated into English under the sentimental title *Letters of a Javanese Princess*. (For the tougher, uncensored version, see Kartini 2005.) They became a classic of Dutch and colonial literature, and Kartini became a heroine of Indonesian independence and Indonesian women's movements. Her work is never mentioned in the English-language literature on gender, except for regional studies.

Kartini's writing, and the way her thought has been received and ignored, raise profound questions for studies of gender. She was not trying to develop a 'theory of gender' – she had much more practical goals. Yet her writing deals directly with questions that a theory of gender must address: the institution of the family; gender divisions of labour; ideologies of womanhood; and strategies of change in gender relations. She did this in the context of colonial society, opening up questions about colonialism, racism and the relationship between global centre and periphery that are now, a century later, crucial issues in feminist thought.

Discussions of 'gender theory' and 'feminist theory' usually focus only on theorists in the global North. We begin this chapter with Kartini's story to highlight the need for a genuinely global approach to knowledge. This is not just an issue of geography; it is about a more adequate and more democratic knowledge. In this chapter we combine a narrative of gender theory in the global North, a story often told, with narratives from the global South, which we think equally important.

Ideas are created in changing circumstances, by people with different backgrounds and different training. History throws different problems at them. It is not surprising that they formulate their intellectual projects in differing ways. To understand theories of gender, it is necessary to encounter the intellectuals who produced them and consider the situations they faced. We assume, as Kartini and Stella did, that the attempt at communication, even across huge distances, is always worthwhile.

Imperial Europe and its colonies: from Sor Juana to Simone de Beauvoir

The gender theories of the European metropole (a term that means the economic, cultural and political 'centre' on which other regions are directly or indirectly dependent) are products of a secular, rationalist and sceptical culture. This culture took its modern shape, so far as the human sciences are concerned, in the second half of the nineteenth century. The ideas that emerged then, however, had a deeper background, and understanding this history helps us understand the present. The two key stories were the gradual transformation of older religious and moral discourses, and Europe's encounter with the colonized world.

Mediaeval Christianity inherited, from the saints and sages of the ancient Mediterranean world, a tradition of misogyny that to a modern reader is startling in its viciousness. The writings of Christian intellectuals are peppered with dogmas of the inferiority of women in mind and body, and the danger they represent if men succumb to their wiles (Blamires 1992). There was, nevertheless, a counter-tradition defending women. In fifteenth-century France this was brought together in a great allegory, *The Book of the City of Ladies* (1405), by Christine de Pizan. Christine refuted, point by point, the traditional abuse of women, building an allegorical 'city' in her text which would be a safe space for women. The moral defence of womanhood was taken up in the seventeenth-century colony of Mexico by Sor Juana, a celebrated poet and essayist. Like many educated women, Sor Juana could only find a safe space to work as a nun. In polemics and by her own literary fame, she claimed equal respect for the work of women. However, despite government patronage, the nunnery wasn't safe enough, she fell foul of misogynist church authorities and was silenced.

The counter-tradition continued in Europe among Protestant groups like the Quakers who defended women's right to preach, i.e. to exercise religious authority. It was still alive at the time of the French Revolution, and used in Mary Wollstonecraft's *Vindication of the Rights of Women* (1792), produced in immediate response to the declaration of the 'Rights of Man'. The early suffrage movement in the United States was in large part a religious movement. The Seneca Falls convention in 1848, often seen as the moment when modern feminism appeared, borrowed the moralizing language of the Declaration of Independence for its message.

Already, however, religion was being displaced by science as the major frame of intellectual life. Nineteenth-century science was actively concerned with problems about gender. Charles Darwin, the towering figure in evolutionary thought, in *The Origin of Species* (1859), made inheritance and biological selection into first-rank intellectual issues. He is not usually considered as a gender theorist, but his later work specifically addressed the choice of sexual partners and the evolutionary role of sex as a form of reproduction. This occurred at a moment in European culture when the gender division of labour, and symbolic divisions between women and men, were at an extreme. 'Darwinism' – more than Darwin – popularized the idea of a biological basis for all forms of social difference, including gender division in the metropole, and the racial hierarchies then being constructed by the expanding empires.

Gender issues ran through early attempts by male intellectuals to formulate a science of society. The French philosopher Auguste Comte, the founder of positivism and a figure almost as influential as Darwin, gave close attention to the social function of women in the first-ever 'treatise of sociology', his *System of Positive Polity* (1851). Women were, in his view, an important base for the coming utopian society – but only if they remained in their proper sphere as comforters and nurturers of men. His most distinguished follower, the British philosopher John Stuart Mill, took a more radical view in the famous essay 'The Subjection of Women' (1869), arguing the case for equality, and seeing the basic reason for inequality not in men's moral superiority but in physical force. When Lester Ward wrote the first major theoretical statement in American sociology, *Dynamic Sociology or Applied Social Science* (1883), he offered a long analysis of the 'reproductive forces' with a detailed critique of 'sexuo-social inequalities' such as unequal education for girls and boys. In 1879 the German labour leader August Bebel published a book, *Woman under Socialism*, which became a best-seller. Marx's friend Friedrich Engels wrote a long essay about gender issues, *The Origin of the Family, Private Property and the State* (1884), which became even more famous.

Why did these men do this? First, because the woman question had been placed on the agenda by an emerging movement of women, which was strong in exactly those social groups from which the new social scientists came. Second, because of empire.

Women intellectuals in these generations were operating under such difficulties that they were unlikely to produce theoretical treatises themselves. For instance, women were excluded from almost all universities at the time. One hardly finds a 'theory of gender' in the writings of feminist intellectuals like Harriet Martineau in Britain or Susan B. Anthony in the United States – though one finds critiques of prejudice among men, and practical discussions of the suffrage, law reform and education for women.

When more theoretical writing by women developed, it was often concerned with economic issues, and some key texts came from the margins of European capitalism. From South Africa came Olive Schreiner's *Woman and Labour* (1911), which analysed the 'parasitism' of bourgeois women and the refusal of bourgeois society to recognize its exploitation of working women. From Russia came Alexandra Kollontai's *The Social Basis of the Woman Question* (1909), arguing that there was no general 'women's question', and that support by working-class women for socialism was the only path towards true equality. This did not stop Kollontai from arguing for separate organization of women within the labour movement, and opening debates about sexual freedom and the reform of marriage.

The intellectuals of Paris, London and New York were living in the heartlands of the greatest wave of imperial expansion the world has ever known. Explorers, conquerors, missionaries and curious travellers gathered an immense fund of information about gender arrangements in the non-European world, which they often thought were survivals from the primitive days of mankind. Texts such as Engels's *Origin* show the fascination this information had for metropolitan intellectuals. Early social anthropology is full of it. Popular imperialism put many exotic images and fantasies of gender into circulation: polygamy, marriage by conquest, concubinage, amazon women, primitive promiscuity. A serious comparative science of gender was slow to emerge; but in the late nineteenth and early twentieth centuries the news from the empire was already acting alongside feminism to de-stabilize belief in a fixed gender order.

Meanwhile the peoples being colonized were not standing still. Colonialism had a massive, and often highly destructive, impact on the gender orders of colonized societies. Settler populations also had to negotiate major changes in their way of life, and some important statements came from intellectuals of settler society such as Sor Juana and Olive Schreiner. The historical record is weighted towards the colonizers. Nevertheless it is clear that by the time nineteenth-century feminism and social science crystallized in the metropole, intellectuals of colonized societies were also grappling with changing gender relations.

In Bengal, for instance – the home of a rich intellectual culture as well as the administrative centre for the British occupation of India – there was a sustained debate among men about the position of women and the principle of gender equality. The famous novelist Bankimchandra Chatterjee, for example, sharply criticized men's insistence on the seclusion of women, and even argued for men doing an equal share of the housework! In Egypt, which also fell under British control after a period of self-directed modernization, gender issues were raised in a classic Islamic way by Aisha Taymour. Her *Mir'at Al-Ta'mmul fi Al-Umur* (The Mirror of Contemplating Affairs) (1892) examined Qur'anic texts about women as a way of raising questions about modern patriarchy. The radical Chinese writer He-Yin Zhen (1907) published sophisticated analyses of men's power, women's work and the politics of women's emancipation. Kartini's letters to Stella Zeehandelaar were part of this widespread, though still scattered, questioning.

Already these gender debates were dealing with issues that we can recognize in modern gender research: power ('subjection'), sexuality ('phylogenetic forces', 'free love') and the division of labour ('parasitism'). Yet the categories of 'men' and 'women' remained absolute, in both metropolitan and colonial debates. Until they were questioned, a theory of gender could not emerge.

The crucial steps were taken in the early twentieth century in central Europe. When the Viennese nerve specialist Sigmund Freud became convinced that many of his patients' troubles were psychological not physical in origin, he explored their emotional lives for causes, and developed new interpretive methods to do so. His patients' talk, during long courses of therapy, gave him masses of evidence about the troubled emotional interior of the bourgeois family. This was documented in intensive case histories, the most famous being 'Dora' (1905a) and the 'Wolf Man' (1918). They underpinned the famous theoretical texts in which Freud expounded the concepts of unconscious motivation (*The Interpretation of Dreams*, 1900), childhood sexuality, the Oedipus complex and the transformations of desire in the course of growing up (*Three Essays on the Theory of Sexuality*, 1905b), and the connections between depth psychology and culture (*Civilization and Its Discontents*, 1930).

By the 1920s, Freud's ideas had spread far beyond their first medical audience and had become a cultural force. It was clear that he had put his finger on problems that were troubling and important for European societies. Freud was no feminist, but was probably influenced by contemporary feminism in the problems he addressed. His first major follower, Alfred Adler, did explicitly support feminism. Adler (1927) made the critique of power-oriented masculinity a centrepiece of his revision of psychoanalysis.

Psychoanalysts thus showed that the gender divisions of adulthood were not fixed from the start of life. Rather, the adult patterns were constructed in a conflict-ridden process of development over the life-course. This was a decisive shift in ideas about gender. Nineteenth-century thought, even feminism, had taken for granted the fixed characters of men and women.

The next step followed quickly. The landmark was Mathilde Vaerting's *The Dominant Sex* (1921). Vaerting, a reforming educator, was one of the first two women ever appointed to a professorship in a German university. She met with an extremely hostile reaction, was thrown out of her job when Hitler gained control, and never held a university chair again. Understandably, she had a lifelong interest in the sociology of power! *The Dominant Sex* criticized the notion of a fixed masculine and feminine character, on sociological grounds. Vaerting argued that masculinity and femininity basically reflected power relations. In societies where women held power, men showed the very characteristics which European bourgeois society saw as quintessentially feminine.

In developing this argument, Vaerting created the first extended social theory of gender. Her argument linked psychological patterns with social structure. She distinguished law, the division of labour and ideology as spheres of gender domination. She even offered an amazing prediction of Men's Liberation as a sequel of feminism. Her work was rapidly translated into English, and was a focus of controversy in the 1920s. But in the European upheavals that followed, her work faded into obscurity. Like Kartini, Vaerting is hardly mentioned in English-language discussions now.

While these intellectual upheavals happened in central Europe, practical upheavals with intellectual consequences spread around the colonized and semi-colonized world. A powerful independence movement developed in India, with Mohandas Gandhi emerging as its principal guide. Mobilization of women was an important part of the movement. Though the Ottoman Empire collapsed in the Great War, a Turkish government survived, fought off the colonial powers, and established a modernizing state under Mustafa Kemal. The Turkish republic became an important model, especially in the Muslim world, and one of its features was a self-conscious emancipation of women – perhaps the first state feminism in the world.

In Egypt a second generation of feminists moved into politics as well as literary work. Huda Sharawi launched the Egyptian Feminist Union in 1923 (Badran 1988). In China, as a republic struggled to establish itself against warlords and foreign interventions in the ruins of the ancient empire, a cultural revival began, the 'Fourth of May movement'. Women writers were prominent in this, challenging Confucian doctrines and patriarchal conventions, and writing about women's experience (Ng and Wickeri 1996).

At about the same time, a new way of appropriating knowledge from the colonized world emerged – social anthropology. The Polish scholar Bronisław Malinowski (1927) used ethnographic information in a famous critique of psychoanalysis, arguing that the 'Oedipus complex' as described by Freud was not universal. The American Margaret Mead's widely read book *Sex and Temperament in Three Primitive Societies* (1935), based on fieldwork in New Guinea, rejected the idea of a fixed relationship between biological sex and gendered character. Anthropologists gave sympathetic portraits of non-Western societies where gender arrangements functioned perfectly well, though along different lines from bourgeois life in the metropole.

This helped to popularize the concept of 'sex roles' in the 1940s and 1950s. The concept took the idea that people usually conform to cultural norms for the social positions they occupy, and applied it to gender. The most influential formulation was made by the most influential sociological theorist of the era, the Harvard University professor Talcott Parsons (Parsons and Bales 1956). Parsons treated gender as a consequence of a social system's need for integration and stability. His much-quoted characterization of the male role as 'instrumental' and the female role as 'expressive' defined a difference of social function. Other writers about sex roles simply presumed that the role norms reflected a natural difference.

Sex role theory was concerned also with changes in sex roles, which had become controversial during the Second World War. Mirra Komarovsky (who many years later became president of the American Sociological Association, the second woman ever elected to that position) had good reason to theorize 'Cultural Contradictions and Sex Roles', the title of a 1946 paper. Sex role change was also possible for men, as Helen Hacker suggested in 'The New Burdens of Masculinity' (1957). In consumer capitalism and suburban life, Hacker argued, expressive functions were being added to instrumental ones, so that men were now expected to show interpersonal skills as well as being 'sturdy oaks'.

There was a feminist colouring in some sex role discussions, including Hacker's. But the renewal of gender theory in the global North was basically the work of Simone de Beauvoir in France. *The Second Sex* (1949), the most famous of all modern feminist texts, drew on psychoanalysis, literature and the activist philosophy worked out by de Beauvoir's partner Jean-Paul Sartre, to challenge both gender domination and gender categories.

Refusing to take the polarity of masculine and feminine for granted, de Beauvoir explored how women were constituted as 'other' in the consciousness of men. Then in a remarkable series of social portraits, she explored the ways in which women could respond to this situation and constitute themselves – not escaping from gender, for that was impossible, but realizing gender differently in different life projects. This work, too, was stimulated by the upheaval of war, and de Beauvoir's topics overlapped substantially with those of sex role research. But she saw the same topics differently, because her approach stemmed from a political critique of the subordination of women.

By the mid-century this was exceptional in the global metropole. Psychoanalysis had become a socially conservative branch of medicine, much more concerned to help people conform than to criticize the culture. Sex role theory was also, in the main, a conservative approach – especially as it was applied in counselling, social work and schools. De Beauvoir's cutting edge found many admirers, but no immediate popular response.

From national liberation to Women's Liberation

While the influence of *The Second Sex* slowly spread, the greatest wave of decolonization was breaking since the decolonization of Spanish America over a century before, in the time of Simón Bolívar.

The long struggle of the Indian independence movement triumphed in 1947, though, as a parting gift, the British partitioned the subcontinent, storing up war and sectarian bitterness. Just a couple of years later the Chinese communists won a civil war and both Japanese and American influence in China ended. Indonesian nationalists fought off the attempt to re-impose Dutch rule at the end of the Second World War. Vietnamese nationalists and communists fought the re-imposition of French rule in Indochina, and a few years later had to fight the Americans, both struggles extremely violent though ultimately successful. Kenyan nationalists fought the British, Algerian nationalists fought the French, Mozambican and Angolan nationalists fought the Portuguese, and these movements too ejected the old imperial powers after much blood-letting. Other colonies were liberated by political mobilization without war, notably Ghana, which led the African colonies into independence; or through a complicated handover, as in Egypt, that saw new independent regimes manoeuvring between the new superpowers, the United States and the Soviet Union.

These struggles were led by men, though in almost all cases they involved the mobilization of women, in combat as well as civil politics. The post-colonial regimes, also dominated by men, did little directly for women's emancipation but generally aimed at economic development. This gave leverage to feminist demands for the education of girls and women, and a slow but very powerful global movement arose which has transformed literacy levels in the post-colonial world.

National liberation struggles in the 'third world' had a growing impact on the global North, especially on the youth movement of the 1960s. They gave a political model and a rhetoric to the new wave of feminism that erupted at the end of that decade – the Women's Liberation Movement. An extraordinarily rapid mobilization of younger women occurred in the late 1960s and early 1970s, across much of the capitalist world.

The first great theoretical advance of the new feminism came in Brazil. In 1969 Heleieth Saffioti's pioneering work A *mulher na sociedade de classes* (Women in Class Society) was published in São Paulo. The book presents a sophisticated Marxist-feminist theorization of sex as a form of social stratification, and a detailed account, backed with statistics, of the sexual division of labour, the political economy of the family and women's education. It takes a historical approach to women's subordination and emancipation, analyses the conservative influence of the Catholic church, and has a brilliant discussion of the sexual economy of colonial society in Brazil.

Saffioti was committed to socialist politics, not an autonomous women's movement (Brazil was then ruled by a right-wing military dictatorship), so her account of gender stratification highlights capitalist society's need for social control. She was influenced by structuralist Marxism from Paris, very fashionable in the 1960s; but she also used arguments from the South American 'dependency' economists such as Celso Furtado, concerned with global inequality and how autonomous economic development could happen.

Nothing so sophisticated came from early Women's Liberation in the global North, where the usual view of politics was based on a dichotomous picture of power. The term 'patriarchy' was fished up from an anthropological backwater and used to name systems of male power. Patriarchy had to be confronted by an autonomous women's movement, and the liberation of women was the cutting edge of social revolution. This view was expounded in a torrent of pamphlets and books, from Sheila Rowbotham's *Women's Liberation and the New Politics* (1969) to Robin Morgan's famous anthology *Sisterhood is Powerful* (1970) and Shulamith Firestone's *The Dialectic of Sex* (1970). Even men influenced by the new feminism began to speak this language. Calls for 'Male Lib eration', in solidarity with Women's Liberation rather than against it, soon appeared (Sawyer 1970).

The radical movements of the day shared a belief that all systems of oppression could and would be overthrown. This perspective was immediately shared by the first theorists of Gay Liberation, who added sexual oppression to the agenda – in street politics and in texts such as the Australian Dennis Altman's *Homosexual: Oppression and Liberation* (1971) and Guy Hocquenghem's *Homosexual Desire* (1972), from France.

By the later 1970s, however, a gender-specific view had come to prominence in the United States and Britain. This view sharply separated gender struggles from others, or saw the oppression of women as the root of all social inequality. This perspective was dramatically presented by the US theologian Mary Daly in *Gyn/Ecology* (1978). Daly tried to create not just a new style but practically a new language to express women's culture and women's anger against men. The social radicalism of early Women's Liberation was now defined as an impure variant of feminism.

The impulse of Women's Liberation was so powerful, however, that it launched a whole spectrum of theories. A materialist but non-Marxist theory that focused on the division of labour, emphasizing the economic exploitation of women within the family, was proposed by Christine Delphy in France in a famous essay called 'The Main Enemy' (1970). Debate raged through the 1970s on how to theorize women's domestic labour, and whether capitalists or husbands were the main beneficiaries of women's work (Malos 1980).

The familiar 'sex role' concept was also radicalized. This was now treated as an account of the social controls that hampered women. In the United States there was a wave of enthusiasm for the attempt by the psychologist Sandra Bem (1974) to define and measure 'androgyny' as a goal of sex role reform. A debate about the 'male sex role' and how men could break out of it, or at least bend it, began in the United States and spilled into several other countries (Pleck and Sawyer 1974). It was a Moroccan feminist, however, who produced the most interesting early research on the situation of men and the dynamics of masculinity. Fatima Mernissi's *Beyond the Veil* (1975) is not only an ethnography but also a notable statement of a social-relations view of gender and a pioneering feminist study of men, which happens to be set in a Muslim society.

The nature of women's politics was the subject of immense debate. It was the topic of a modern classic of feminism, Julieta Kirkwood's (1986) *Ser Política en Chile* (roughly: being a politically active woman in Chile), written under the Pinochet dictatorship by one of the leaders of the women's resistance, and published after her death. Kirkwood observed that the problems of women had historically been seen as private issues; the problem for a movement was to transform silence into voice. This meant contesting both the Left's idea of gender as a 'secondary contradiction' and the Right's mobilization of women in defence of 'the family'. The problem of identity was the problem of transforming the group into a historical subject capable of contesting the oppression produced by patriarchy.

Other feminists used the techniques of structuralism rather than historical analysis. A young US anthropologist, Gayle Rubin (1975), combined feminism and anthropology in an abstract but very influential model of 'the sex/gender system'. In 1974, in *Psychoanalysis and Feminism*, the British feminist Juliet Mitchell proposed a complex theory of the reproduction of class society and patriarchy. Mitchell's book, along with the work of Nancy Chodorow (1978) in the United States, reversed English-speaking feminists' coolness towards psychoanalysis. In France the rejection of Freud had not been so marked, and adaptations of Jacques Lacan's version of psychoanalysis were undertaken by a number of feminists. A key goal was to find a level of human reality which escaped the phallocentric structure of ordinary language and consciousness. Julia Kristeva's *Revolution in Poetic Language* (1974) and Luce Irigaray's essay *This Sex Which Is Not One* (1977) were perhaps the most influential.

A simpler feminist adaptation of psychoanalysis and developmental psychology, Carol Gilligan's *In a Different Voice* (1982), captured popular attention in the English-speaking world and became a best-seller. This was a return to categorical gender theory with a psychological twist. It was widely read as proving that men and women had different moral senses, and helped the acceptance of a mild version of feminism as a kind of organizational reform in corporations and the state.

Governments around the world soon took note of the new women's movement, and the United Nations declared 1975 to be International Women's Year, launching a series of world conferences on women. This triggered notable debates and investigations, such as the 1975 national report *Towards Equality: Report of the Committee on the Status of Women in India* (Rai and Mazumdar 2007). An Australian government had already appointed a young feminist philosopher, Elizabeth Reid, as the first Women's Advisor to the Prime Minister, launching a new kind of state feminism.

The 'femocrats' of Australia, Scandinavia and Germany attempted to use bureaucratic and legal reforms to move towards gender equality across the whole society (Eisenstein 1996). Government funding was won for childcare centres, rape crisis centres and women's health centres. This created sharp debate, given the Women's Liberation view of the state as part of the patriarchal system. The work of feminist bureaucrats posed new intellectual questions: how to understand the organizations where they found themselves, as well as how to understand the policy problems they were working on.

Accordingly, new branches of feminist theory and research developed. A number of theorists re-thought the state as a gendered institution of great complexity, with possibilities of internal change (see chapter 8). Research institutes and monitoring programmes were set up, such as the Norwegian Likestillingssenteret (Centre for Gender Equality). A whole genre of feminist or feminist-inspired policy studies began to appear. To take just one field, education: notable policy studies range from the pioneering Australian report *Girls, School and Society* (1975), sponsored by the national Schools Commission, to the very sophisticated British study *Closing the Gender Gap* by Madeleine Arnot and her colleagues (1999).

In universities of the North, the 1970s and 1980s saw a huge growth of feminist or feminist-inspired research in almost every discipline of the humanities and social sciences, and to a lesser extent in the natural sciences. In sociology, for instance, sex and gender – formerly a marginal topic of low prestige – became the most active research field in the whole discipline. Feminist history grew to be a large enterprise, fuelled by the need to correct the massive biases of patriarchal history; gender was recognized as an important category of historical knowledge (Scott 1986). Feminist science studies flourished, casting new light on an area that once was thought a perfect proof of male superiority (Harding 1986).

Journals multiplied which published research and debate about sex roles, gender, women, and eventually men. They included *al-Raida* in Lebanon, *Debate Feminista* in Mexico, *Estudos Feministos* in Brazil, and *Manushi* in India. Some became high-prestige academic journals – such as *Signs* and *Gender & Society* in the United States. In the 1990s and 2000s, women's studies in universities expanded to be 'gender studies' embracing lesbian, gay and transgender issues and non-feminist gender research – amid controversy as to whether this would destroy its political edge. There have been setbacks, including attempts by conservative administrators to close down gender courses in universities in Italy and Australia (among others). Yet only a few years ago the Swedish government established a number of new gender studies chairs, and funded an inter-university 'Centre of Gender Excellence' programme to stimulate research.

At one level, all this was a startling success for feminism. The patriarchal monologue in culture and the sciences was interrupted almost at once. New social bases for feminist thought were established in the state and universities. Yet Women's Liberation movement activists looked on the early stages of this triumph with distrust. They feared that bureaucratic and academic feminisms would lose their political urgency, lose touch with grassroots campaigns, and become unintelligible to working-class women.

Queer, post-colonial, Southern and global

Everything that the activists feared has come to pass. A large part of gender theory in the English-speaking metropole has become abstract, contemplative or analytical in style, or focuses entirely on cultural subversion. A whole literature of gender theory makes practically no reference to girls' education, domestic violence, women's health, gender mainstreaming, the state, economic development or any other policy question that feminists had been grappling with. Instead it deals with sexuality, personal identity, representation, language and difference.

The main points of reference for this kind of theorizing were intellectual developments among men in philosophy who worked on problems other than gender, notably Michel Foucault, Jacques Derrida and Gilles Deleuze in France. The feminist application of Foucault's studies of discourse, micro-politics and the regulation of bodies has been widespread. Derrida's influence has been more indirect, though possibly more profound. His argument on the constant deferral of meaning in language, and his technique of philosophical 'deconstruction', have been read as questioning the stability of all concepts and all identities – including the categories on which feminist thought rested.

A book by a young US philosopher on this theme, Judith Butler's *Gender Trouble* (1990), became by far the most influential text in academic feminism in the 1990s. It was read beyond the academic world, and is still the subject of extensive debate (Lloyd 2007). Butler argued that there are no fixed foundations of gender categories and therefore of feminist strategy. Gender is 'performative', bringing identities into existence through repetitive actions, rather than being the expression of some pre-existing reality. In Butler's treatment, gender radicalism consists not of mobilization around an identity such as 'women', but of actions that subvert identity, disrupt gender dichotomy and displace gender norms.

This book's enormous popularity in the metropole was not only due to post-structuralist fashion. It fed into a new kind of politics. By the 1980s, the social movements of the 1960s and 1970s in the global North had fragmented, and Women's Liberation as a coherent movement was gone – split over issues of sexuality, race and relations with the state. Externally, feminism was running into stiffer resistance. There continued to be gains for gender reform, most spectacularly in Scandinavia, where women arrived en masse in party politics. In 1991, for instance, the leaders of all three major parties in Norway were women, including the Prime Minister, Gro Harlem Brundtland. But the Equal Rights Amendment in the United States was lost, and an anti-feminist militancy, often with religious rhetoric, in the 1980s began rolling back women's reproductive rights. Open homophobia re-emerged in mainstream politics in many parts of the world, and was particularly vicious around the HIV/AIDS epidemic. In 2013, Vladimir Putin's regime in Russia criminalized any action that could be interpreted as promoting homosexual lifestyles to youth.

These events provoked re-examinations of feminism and gender theory. One move was led by Black feminists in North America, who argued that White feminists' uncritical use of a unified category 'women' concealed the realities of racism. For some US Black feminists, including bell hooks (1984), that argument led back to the inclusive radicalism of early Women's Liberation, and a renewed concern with integrating class, race and gender struggles. For others it led to identity politics within feminism, and a kind of standpoint theory, illustrated in Patricia Hill Collins' *Black Feminist Thought* (1991). This suggested there could be multiple perspectives representing the outlook of different groups of women, especially those who were marginalized within the society of the metropole: Black feminism, Latina feminism and lesbian feminism. White feminists had mainly seen the family as a site of women's oppression

– much as Kartini had. But in a context of deeply entrenched racism, the family might be a crucial asset for Black women, and for women in recent immigrant communities.

The most widely influential approach was work that re-examined the founding categories of feminism. Feminist sociologists explored the micro-foundations of the gender order, looking at the way gender categories were created and affirmed in everyday interaction. A classic paper called 'Doing Gender' (West and Zimmerman 1987) crystallized this approach and had a great influence in the social sciences. Feminist philosophers reconsidered the relationship of the body to gender categories. Some returned to the idea of an unbridgeable difference between women's and men's bodies, seeing gender as embodied experience in which the supposed gap between 'sex' and 'gender' is reduced to nothing (Grosz 1994).

The most influential approach emphasized the fragility of all identity categories, and saw gender as, in principle, fluid rather than fixed. A new wave in lesbian and gay thought, which became known as queer theory, took up this idea. Its core was a critique of the cultural constraints, summed up in the word 'heteronormativity', that pushed people into fixed identities within gender binaries. Energy came from new forms of political and cultural activism that defied conventional categories, played radical games with gender meanings, and set about 'queering' everything in sight – troubling older forms of lesbian and gay activism as well. (For a wry and perceptive account by a historian, see Reynolds 2002.) Butler's *Gender Trouble* became an icon for this whole cultural movement.

Recently there has been some reaction against the focus on identity and culture. Some Northern feminist philosophers, in a trend that has been labelled 'new materialism', have emphasized that actual bodies and their characteristics are important, not just representations and norms about bodies. There is a worry that feminist theory has too sharply separated culture and society from nature, and needs to pay attention again to biology, and the material world more generally (Hird 2009; for debate see Ahmed 2008). This is hardly a problem about feminism in the global South! Here material issues such as poverty, nutrition, perinatal death, AIDS and patriarchal violence have always been central. But it is a useful corrective in the metropole. Most new materialist writing is theoretical and deals with embodiment and subjectivity (Coole and Frost 2010). Some connects with deepening concerns about climate change, global food production, waste and biotechnology (Gibson-Graham 2011; Hird 2013).

Studies of these issues are now an active area of gender research. Eco-feminism began to crystallize in the 1970s, mostly using essentialist ideas that connected women with nature and saw men as naturally violent. As the environmental movement grew in strength, and feminist social perspectives became more sophisticated, new generations of theory developed that put more emphasis on the gender politics of colonialism and capitalist development (Agarwal 1992; Shiva 1989) and the gendered character of new global authorities for 'green' governance (Litfin 1997; MacGregor 2010). We will discuss these debates in chapter 7.

During the 1980s, partly as a result of the UN Decade for Women (1975–85), Northern feminists' interest in other parts of the world rose sharply. Conferences multiplied, book series appeared, and Robin Morgan, editor of the famous US Women's Liberation anthology *Sisterhood is Powerful*, now edited a sequel, *Sisterhood is Global* (1984).

Soon afterwards, Chandra Talpade Mohanty, an Indian intellectual working in the United States, published a brilliant critique in an essay called 'Under Western Eyes'. This literature, she argued, homogenized 'third world women' into a single category of victimhood:

> This average third world woman leads an essentially truncated life based on her feminine gender (read: sexually constrained) and her being 'third world' (read: ignorant, poor, uneducated, traditionbound, domestic, family-oriented, victimized, etc.) ... in contrast to the (implicit) self-representation of Western women as educated, as modern, as having control over their own bodies and sexualities, and the freedom to make their own decisions. (Mohanty 1991: 56)

Feminists in the North, it seemed, were making the same kind of error that white male ethnographers often made. As Diane Bell shows in *Daughters of the Dreaming* (1983), central desert Aboriginal societies in Australia had been persistently pictured as male-centred, basically because the ethnographers failed to collect information from Aboriginal women. Starting from the indigenous women's perspective yielded a very different picture of women's traditional authority. But women's situation had deteriorated sharply with colonization.

Mohanty's essay became the keynote of a collection published in the United States called *Third World Women and the Politics of Feminism* (Mohanty et al. 1991). This book had a considerable impact, showing the global diversity of women's politics, and arguing for another kind of theory. In a long introduction called 'Cartographies of Struggle', and in later essays collected in *Feminism without Borders* (2003), Mohanty spelled out an approach to gender that started with the historical experience of imperialism. The making and remaking of gender is interwoven with the making of race and the dynamic of global capitalism. Mohanty agrees with deconstructionism that there is no pre-given universal category of 'woman'. But this is for a practical, not a philosophical, reason:

because systems of domination constantly divide people. For instance, capitalism uses local gender ideologies to incorporate 'women's work' into strategies of profit-making. This approach allows Mohanty to move in a different direction from queer theory, to emphasize the practices of solidarity, the possibilities of common struggle, that can link the poor and the marginalized across differences.

Closer to deconstructionist philosophy was the work of another Indian expatriate feminist, Gayatri Chakravorty Spivak (1988, 1999). Spivak's writings on feminism are in several genres and defy short summary. She would not think of herself as producing a 'theory of gender'; indeed she seems sceptical about any such project. Her most famous essay, 'Can the Subaltern Speak?', builds on the work of the radical Indian historians who founded the journal *Subaltern Studies*, but challenges their hope of rediscovering subaltern consciousness. Her most famous concept, 'strategic essentialism', adopts the deconstructionist critique of identity categories but then suggests there is value in those categories for practice. In the essay where this idea emerged, Spivak still performed the classic feminist move of pointing to the absence of women from a system of interpretation constructed by men. She consistently calls attention to women in poverty, in extremely marginalized situations, but emphasizes the dangers of intellectuals claiming to speak on behalf of dominated groups.

Spivak's virtuosity with the technique of deconstruction raises a difficult but vital question – the tension between coming oneself from the global periphery, and using concepts from the metropole. Paulin Hountondji (1997), a philosopher from Benin, has explored this issue in depth, speaking of the 'extraversion' that is characteristic of knowledge production in post-colonial countries. In a global division of scientific labour, the crucial step of theorizing occurs overwhelmingly in the global North. Intellectuals in the periphery are trained to look to the North for the source of their concepts, methods, equipment, training and recognition.

This is strikingly true of gender studies too. Most research and debate on gender questions around the global South draws on gender theory from Europe and the United States, and tries to combine it with local data or experience. This was, for instance, the structure of knowledge when the All-China Federation of Women sponsored a week-long symposium on 'theoretical studies on women' in 1984, in the early days of the Chinese government's turn towards capitalism. The idea of women's studies was borrowed from the United States, local statistics about the situation of women were compiled, and the result was an agenda for 'women's studies the Chinese way' – with a focus on women's relationship to the new economic policies (Shen 1987).

The problem of extraversion has concerned many gender researchers in the majority world. When gender research was launched in Africa in the 1970s, there was an attempt to locate it within African perspectives, though ideas and methods were adapted from the metropole (Arnfred 2003). There has been a sharp debate about whether the concept of gender itself can be applied in Africa. Some have argued that gender categories did not exist, or were not important, in pre-colonial times, i.e. that there was no social category corresponding to the Western category of 'women'. Western gender categories are therefore an intrusion, imposed on local people by colonialism (Oyěwùmí 1997). But other scholars do see pre-colonial gender patterns in the same culture (Bakare-Yusuf 2003). Colonialism certainly changed gender patterns, but did so by building on distinctions that already existed. In contemporary Africa, complex gender systems certainly do exist and have major consequences. Among them are the patterns of economic inequality, gender-based violence and sexuality that shape the HIV/AIDS crisis (Ampofo et al. 2004).

Most gender theorists in the global South have worked out their ideas in negotiation with theory from the North; the question is how deep the extraversion goes. The Uruguayan sociologist Teresita de Barbieri is one who found a convincing balance. In an ambitious essay 'Sobre la categoría género. Una introducción teórico-metodológica' ('On the Category of Gender: A Theoretical-Methodological Introduction') (1992), she offered a relational model of gender, based on the central idea of social control over women's reproductive power. This control involves a wide range of processes: 'practices, symbols, representations, values, collective norms'. De Barbieri emphasized that, though the figures of the woman as mother and the man as head of household are the nucleus of gender definitions in Latin America, gender is not a simple dichotomy. The gender system involves male/male and female/female relations as well as male/female – for instance, inequalities among women involving domestic service – and it involves life-cycle shifts. There are conflicts of interest within gender categories, such as men who support feminist demands. Building on Black feminist thought from Brazil, de Barbieri also emphasized how gender relations are interwoven with race relations and class divisions. She argued convincingly that gender research needed to include men. In the years after her paper was published, research on men and masculinities indeed become one of the features of Latin American gender studies (Gutmann and Viveros 2005).

Even more ambitious is the work of Bina Agarwal in India, who has a claim to be one of the most important modern theorists of gender. An economist by profession, Agarwal has been involved as a public intellectual in development policy debates, and makes use of the techniques developed by Northern economics. She has drawn together feminist studies of states, communities and households around Asia (Agarwal 1988). She is a patient empirical researcher, and her great book *A Field of One's Own* (1994) analyses the changing relations of women and men to the land in different regions of South Asia, via the intricate politics of families and livelihoods in rural society. Her second significant book, *Gender and Green Governance* (2010), explores the various conditions under which women's participation in forest management improves environmental and social outcomes. Agarwal uses quantitative and qualitative data to illustrate common patterns as well as considerable divergences in women's participation related to class, caste and other sources of social and economic difference. About half the world's populations still live in rural areas, including the majority of the world's poor. But that isn't the only reason Agarwal's work is important. Her detailed and sophisticated work exploring gender in environmental politics, and connecting environmental issues to social justice and land rights, is a major contribution to modern environmental thought (see chapter 7).

Gender theories have usually assumed well-integrated gender orders, with norms and hierarchies all complete. Yet thinking about the societies of the global periphery raises the question of how gender orders might be dis-integrated, how gender relations might *lack* order. Amina Mama (1997), one of the leading feminist thinkers from Africa, emphasizes that the high levels of gender-based violence in contemporary society are connected to the gendered violence of colonialism. Mai Ghoussoub (2000) speaks of a great cultural disturbance in the contemporary Arab world around the position and identities of men, 'a chaotic quest for a definition of modern masculinity'. Discussing masculinities and femininities in the 'water wars' in Bolivia, Nina Laurie (2005, 2011) forcefully argues that research on globalization processes in the South cannot presume a consolidated gender regime. Jane Bennett (2008) in South Africa makes a similar point about doing feminist research in conditions where 'relative chaos, gross economic disparities, displacement, uncertainty and surprise' are the norm not the exception.

It's unlikely, then, that theory can work exactly the same way in different global regions. We are not being homogenized, as popular theories of globalization suppose. But we don't live in a mosaic world where each culture is intact and separate. If such a world ever existed, five centuries of imperialism and a world economy have ended it. We need ways of talking to each other across distances and boundaries, in gender studies as in other fields.

In *Re-orienting Western Feminisms: Women's Diversity in a Post-colonial World* (1998), the Australian sociologist Chilla Bulbeck describes this problem and considers what is involved in moving beyond the Euro-centrism still common in feminist thought in the metropole. To respond adequately to the post-colonial and neo-colonial world is not just a matter of tacking a critique of racism on to gender analysis. It needs what Bulbeck calls a 'world-traveller perspective': learning to see oneself as others see one, learning to respect other experiences, and learning to work in coalitions.

It is encouraging that prominent gender theorists in the North as well as the South have begun doing that. Mohanty's *Feminism without Borders* has already been mentioned. Not long after that book came out, Sandra Harding, one of the founders of feminist science studies in the United States, published *Sciences from Below: Feminisms, Postcolonialities, and Modernities* (2008). This is an imaginative attempt to expand the Eurocentric vision, in an important area of gender theory, through perspectives from the global South. It's the kind of work that is now vital to the future of gender studies.

5

Gender relations and gender politics

Patterns in gender

The research projects discussed in chapter 2 included two studies of organizations, Barrie Thorne's study of American elementary schools and T. Dunbar Moodie's study of South African mines. Each of these organizations had a regular set of arrangements about gender: who was recruited to do what work (e.g. all of the mineworkers were men); what social divisions were recognized (e.g. creating 'opposite sides' in the playground); how emotional relations were conducted (e.g. the 'mine wives'); and how these institutions were related to others (e.g. the families of the workers).

Such a pattern in gender arrangements may be called the *gender regime* of an institution. Research has mapped the gender regimes of a very wide range of organizations – schools, offices, factories, armies, police forces, sporting clubs. An example is a study of 10 public sector workplaces in the state of New South Wales, Australia (Connell 2007). Well-defined gender regimes could be found in all of them: most managers were men, most technical workers were men, most clerical workers and human service workers were women. At the same time, change in gender patterns was going on. Widespread changes were the automation of masculinized industrial jobs, the disappearance of the 'secretary' as a well-defined occupation, and the acceptance of equal opportunity as a principle. A middle-aged man summed up his experience this way:

> I would like to think we are a little bit more enlightened now. I think
> it has been proven that women can do just about any job that a male

can do, that there are no male-dominated industries as such – maybe the construction industry is. But I think that from an Agency viewpoint and even from a workplace viewpoint now, it is accepted that we have got women [professional staff], they can come in and do just as good a job as what men can do.

Yet at the grassroots worksite level, every agency in the study remained gendered in substantial ways. How to understand both questions – structure and change – is the subject of this chapter.

When Thorne went into Oceanside Elementary School and found that most of the teachers were women, she was not surprised. Moodie was not astonished to find an all-male workforce at the Witwatersrand gold mines. The gender regimes of these particular organizations are part of wider patterns, which also endure over time. These wider patterns can be called the *gender order* of a society. The gender regimes of institutions usually correspond to the overall gender order, but may vary from it. Change often starts in one sector of society and takes time to seep through into others.

When we look at a set of gender arrangements, whether the gender regime of an institution or the gender order of a whole society, we are basically looking at a set of social *relationships* – ways that people, groups and organizations are connected and divided. 'Gender relations' are the social relationships arising in and around the reproductive arena discussed in chapter 3.

Gender relations are always being made and re-made in everyday life. This point is well established by ethnomethodology, a school of sociological research concerned with what we presuppose in everyday conduct. Candace West and Don Zimmerman, in a famous article called 'Doing Gender' (1987), analyse the way in which gender is constituted in routine interaction. People engaging in everyday conduct – across the spectrum from conversation and housework to interaction styles and economic behaviour – are held accountable in terms of their presumed 'sex category' as man or woman. The conduct produced in response to this accountability is not a product of gender – it is gender itself.

We make our own gender, but we are not free to make it however we like. Our gender practice is powerfully shaped by the gender order in which we find ourselves. That is what West and Zimmerman imply when they say we are 'held accountable' for our gendered conduct. Social theory has used the concept of *structure* to capture the fact of powerfully determined patterns in relationships. Relations among people would have little significance if they were randomly arranged. Patterns in these relations would have little significance if they were ephemeral. It is the enduring or extensive patterns among social relations that social theory calls 'structures'. Thus we speak of class structures, kinship structures, and so on.

The gender arrangements of a society are a social structure in this sense. For instance, if religious, political and conversational practices all place men in authority over women, we speak of a patriarchal structure of gender relations. Or if clans of men regularly marry each other's sisters, we speak of a kinship structure of exchange.

A structure of relations does not mechanically decide how people or groups act. That is the error of social determinism, and it is no more defensible than biological determinism. But a structure of relations certainly defines possibilities for action, and their consequences. In a strongly patriarchal gender order, women may be denied education and personal freedoms, while men may be cut off from emotional connections with children. In the gender order of modern Australia, Huey (Harriet) Brown (chapter 2) was given certain possibilities and not others. Those he took up – such as drag, prostitution and domestic partnership – had major consequences for the rest of his life.

In this sense, social structure conditions practice. Yet structure does not exist in a way that is somehow prior to everyday life. Social structures are brought into being by human activity, over time; they are historically created. Gender relations come into being as we continue to engage in 'gendered modes of behaviour', as Carol Hagemann-White (1987) puts it. Structure and change are not opposed; they are part of the same dynamic of our social life.

Gender relations in four dimensions

When the pioneering British feminist Juliet Mitchell published her famous article 'Women: The Longest Revolution' in 1966, she argued that women's oppression involves not one, but four structures: production, reproduction, socialization and sexuality. The British sociologist Sylvia Walby in *Theorizing Patriarchy* (1990) distinguished six structures in contemporary patriarchy: paid employment, household production, culture, sexuality, violence and the state. The Indian economist Bina Agarwal (1997) argued that gender relations are constituted within four interrelated arenas of contestation: the household/family, the market, the community and the state.

Why make such distinctions? Though gender theories have sometimes been one-dimensional, there are strong reasons for acknowledging multiple dimensions in the structure of gender relations. We often experience disparities and tensions, as if one part of our lives were working on one gender logic, and another part on a different logic.

For instance, the modern liberal state defines men and women as citizens, that is, as alike. But the dominant sexual code defines men and women as opposites. Meanwhile, customary ideas about the division of labour in family life define women as housewives and carers of children. Accordingly, women entering the public domain – trying to exercise their rights as citizens – have an uphill battle to have their authority recognized.

A striking illustration of these tensions is the story of Julia Gillard, Prime Minister of Australia from 2010 to 2013, the first woman to lead the national government. Her arrival in office, though it occurred by an intra-party manoeuvre, was celebrated by many, particularly by women. She held on to power at the following election. At the same time, her leadership was contested from many sides of politics. Conservative public figures and the opposition party bitterly opposed Gillard in the role. The hostility was often expressed in reference to her being an unmarried woman. Before she took office an opposition politician described Gillard as 'deliberately barren' and claimed that her choice not to have children made her unfit for leadership. People at protests opposing her government's carbon-trading scheme held signs reading 'Ditch the Witch', 'JuLIAR', and 'Bob Brown's Bitch'. (Bob Brown was the leader of the Greens party who negotiated with Labor to design the carbon-trading policy.) As well as constant commentary on Gillard's physical appearance and clothes, there were political cartoons featuring sexualized imagery of her, and some violent comments against her from radio presenters. In October 2012 she gave a passionate speech in Parliament arguing that the opposition leader and his party had made sexist public statements about her. The 15-minute video of the speech attracted global attention and is now known as the 'Misogyny Speech'. In July 2013, with an election looming and her poll numbers down, Gillard's own party ejected her from office.

There are various ways of mapping the multiple dimensions in gender. The model followed in this book is a fairly simple one, distinguishing four dimensions of the structure of gender relations: power, production, cathexis and symbolism. In each of these dimensions we can see a distinctive sub-structure of gender relations. This model is a tool for use, not a fixed philosophical scheme. So it is a practical question how useful it is, and how far in time and space it applies.

Power: direct, discursive, colonizing

Power, as a dimension of gender, was central to the Women's Liberation concept of 'patriarchy' – to the idea of men as a dominant 'sex class', the analysis of rape as an assertion of men's power over women, and the critique of media images of women as passive, trivial and stupid. The power of husbands over wives, and fathers over daughters, is an important aspect of the structure of gender. This is still an accepted idea in much of the world, even in modified forms such as the idea of the father as 'head of the household'. The continuing relevance of gendered power analysis is indicated by statistics of violence and abuse. For instance, a 2005 Australian Bureau of Statistics survey found 15 per cent of women reported being victims of intimate violence from a former partner, a far higher proportion than men (5 per cent). A recent World Health Organization multi-country study found that between 15 per cent (Japan) and 71 per cent (Ethiopia) of women reported physical and/or sexual violence by an intimate partner at some point in their lives – an average of about one-third of all women, worldwide.

Women's Liberation recognized that patriarchal power was not just a matter of direct control of women by individual men, but was also realized impersonally through the state. A classic example, analysed in a famous article by Catharine MacKinnon (1983), is court procedure in rape cases. Independent of any personal bias of the judge, the procedures by which rape charges are tried effectively place the complainant rather than the defendant 'on trial'. The woman's sexual history, marital situation and motives in laying a charge are all under scrutiny. Despite attempts at reform, it can still be a damaging experience for a woman to bring charges.

Another important case of direct power relations is bureaucracy. Clare Burton (1987), an Australian social scientist who served in public life as an equal opportunity commissioner, spoke of the 'mobilization of masculine bias' in selection and promotion of staff. By this she meant the pervasive tendency, in organizations dominated by men, to favour criteria and procedures that favour men. Since men do control most large-scale organizations in the world (as noted in chapter 1), this is a far-reaching process producing gender inequality. A major example is armies, which are basically bureaucracies that specialize in violence. Men, rather than women, control the means of force in every part of the contemporary world.

Power also emerged as a major theme in Gay Liberation writing such as Dennis Altman's *Homosexual: Oppression and Liberation* (1972). Here the focus was on power applied to a specific group of men, through criminalization, police harassment, economic discrimination, violence and cultural pressure. Gay Liberation theorists linked the oppression of gay men with the oppression of lesbians and the oppression of women generally. This argument laid the foundation for the analysis of gendered power relations among men, including violence. The same national

statistics that show women as more often the target of domestic violence show men as more often the target of other forms of crime – usually committed by other men. Public violence often involves challenges to masculinity and displays of masculine prowess or courage.

The approach to power popularized by the French historian Michel Foucault (1977) is sceptical of the idea that there is a unified agency of power in society. Rather, Foucault argued, power is widely dispersed, and operates intimately and diffusely. This post-structuralist approach appealed to many feminist as well as gay theorists, who saw a way of understanding the fine texture of power and its 'productiveness', the way power generates identities and practices. The discourse of fashion and beauty, for instance, positions women as consumers, subjects them to humiliating tests of acceptability, enforces arbitrary rules, and is responsible for much unhappiness, ill health, and even some deaths by starvation in countries that have giant food surpluses (when girls' dieting turns into anorexia). Yet there is no man with a gun compelling women to do all this.

The most sweeping exercise of power in the last 500 years, however, is not captured by either of these concepts. This is the creation of global empires, the invasion of indigenous land by the imperial powers – overseas mainly by Spain, Portugal, the Netherlands, France and Britain, overland by Russia and the United States – and the domination of the post-colonial world by economic and military superpowers.

As Valentine Mudimbe (1994: 140) says of the Congo, 'to establish itself, the new power was obliged to construct a new society'. Indigenous societies were pulverized, or mined for labour; and indigenous gender orders were transformed, by plantation economies, missions, population displacement, and other processes. Colonizing forces, overwhelmingly men from the metropole, seized women's bodies as well as the land. A fused gender/race hierarchy became a core feature of colonial society. It persists in the contemporary world.

Power is contested, and gender power relations are no more total than other kinds. Oppressive laws sparked campaigns for reform – such as the most famous of all feminist campaigns, the struggle for the vote. Domestic patriarchy may be softened quietly by the inhabitants of the 'red chamber' (as the classic Chinese novel put it), the women of the household. Discursive power can also be contested or transformed, as shown in the remarkable work of the Australian educator Bronwyn Davies. In *Shards of Glass* (1993) Davies shows how educators in the classroom can help children and youth gain control of gender discourses, and learn to shift between, or manoeuvre among, identities. Colonizing power too was always contested, and women played an important part

in colonial liberation struggles. Contemporary women's activism is found in every part of the world, and campaigns in different countries are increasingly connected (Moghadam 2005). As well as a concept of inequalities of power, then, we need a concept of equal power – of gender democracy (see chapter 8).

Production, consumption and gendered accumulation

The 'sexual division of labour' was the first dimension of gender to be recognized in social science, and remains the centre of most discussions of gender in anthropology and economics. In many societies, and in many situations, certain tasks are performed by men and others are performed by women. So, in the Aboriginal communities of the Australian central desert before colonization, hunting wallabies and kangaroos was undertaken by men, collecting root vegetables, seeds and small animals was mainly undertaken by women. In contemporary Europe and North America, computer software engineering is mainly done by men, while data entry is mainly done by women.

Such divisions of labour are common, perhaps even universal, through recorded history. But while gender divisions of labour are common, there is not exactly the same division in different cultures or at different points of time. The same task may be 'women's work' in one context, and 'men's work' in another. Agricultural labour – digging and planting – is an important example.

A striking modern case is secretarial work. Being a clerk was originally a man's job – as described in Herman Melville's dark short story 'Bartleby the Scrivener' (1853). With the advent of the typewriter and the growing scale of office work, clerical work increasingly involved women. In the mid-twentieth century it had became archetypal 'women's work', as Rosemary Pringle shows in *Secretaries Talk* (1989). Women continue to be crowded into clerical jobs, where they persist. The US Census found that between 2006 and 2010, 96 per cent of the 4 million workers with jobs that fell under the category 'secretaries and administrative assistants' were women. But with the advent of the personal computer and word processing programs, clerical work is again, increasingly, being done by men – though not as a separate job. Rather it is mixed in with other work. A corporate executive nowadays may read and type 60, 80 or 100 e-mails a day.

In the industrial and commercial society that has emerged over the last few hundred years, which we now call 'capitalism', gender divisions between different jobs are not the whole of the gender division of labour. We have to take account of the *total* social division of labour

(Glucksmann 2000). There is a larger division between 'work', the realm of paid labour and production for markets, and 'home', the realm of unpaid labour. The whole economic sphere is culturally defined as men's world (regardless of the presence of women in it), while domestic life is defined as women's world (regardless of the presence of men in it).

The Norwegian sociologist Øystein Holter (2005) argues that this division is the structural basis of the modern capitalist gender order. His point is not only that our notions of 'masculinity' and 'femininity' are closely connected with this division. Just as important, the social relations that govern work in these two spheres are different. In the economy, work is done for pay, labour-power is bought and sold, and the products of labour are placed on a market ruled by the logic of profit. In the home, work is done for love or mutual obligation, the products of labour are a gift, and the logic of gift-exchange prevails. From these structural differences, Holter argues, flow characteristically different experiences for men and women – and our ideas about the different natures of men and women.

This is not exactly a distinction between production and consumption, though that has been suggested by others as the economic core of the gender system. Domestic consumption requires work, just as much as factory-based production does. Whatever may happen on TV, real housewives do not spend their time lolling on couches and scoffing chocolates. Housework and childcare are hard work, even with vacuum cleaners and microwave ovens. But housework and job-work are done in different social relations, as Holter correctly observes, and consequently have very different cultural meanings.

The division of labour itself is only part of a larger pattern. In an industrial economy the shared work of women and men is embodied in every major product and service. Yet women and men are differently located in a *gendered accumulation process*. Maria Mies (1986), the German theorist who formulated this issue most clearly, suggested that the global economy developed through a double process of colonization and 'housewifization'. Women in the colonized world, formerly full participants in local non-capitalist economies, have been increasingly pressed into the housewife pattern of social isolation and dependence on a male breadwinner.

Three decades after Mies wrote, the picture looks more complex. There is more recognition of the significance of women's paid work, as a flexible, cheap labour force. Increased labour force participation for women has coincided with an increase in informal and unprotected forms of work in export-oriented industries such as manufacturing and monoculture farms producing cash crops. Heidi Gottfried's *Gender, Work and Economy* (2013) assembles a mass of research showing how

global manufacturing now crucially depends on women's low-wage labour in a global assembly line that is geographically spread out across hemispheres.

Accumulation in the global economy is mainly organized through large corporations and global markets. The gender regimes of these institutions make it possible for them both to use labour, and to apply the products of men's and women's joint work, in gendered ways. The way firms distribute corporate income – through wage structures and benefits packages – tends to favour men, especially middle-class men. Women workers in export-oriented industries continue to be concentrated in temporary and seasonal jobs, while the few permanent jobs in these sectors are reserved for men (Razavi et al. 2012). The products that corporations produce through gendered labour, when placed on the market, have downstream gender effects and gendered uses – from clothes to cosmetics to computers to machine guns.

The gendered accumulation process has many effects beyond the economy narrowly defined. For instance, where there is a gender division of labour in occupations – such as men being the majority in engineering and mechanical trades, women in arts-based and human service jobs – there will be a division in the education systems which prepare people for this work. It is very familiar to teachers that enrolments in high school and technical college courses in engineering and computing are mainly boys, while enrolments in fine arts and food preparation are mainly girls. As the British researchers Madeleine Arnot, Miriam David and Gaby Weiner show in *Closing the Gender Gap* (1999), the classic study of gender in a whole school system, strong differences in fields of study survive despite historic changes that have eliminated gender differences in school retention.

Cathexis: emotional relations

The importance of emotional attachment in human life was made clear a hundred years ago in the work of Sigmund Freud – and before him, by the poets. Borrowing ideas from literature and neurology but mainly learning from his own patients, Freud showed how charges of emotion – both positive and negative – were attached, in the unconscious mind, to images of other people. His famous analysis of the 'Oedipus complex', the psychological residue of a young child's powerful emotions towards mother and father, showed how important the patterning of these attachments might be. (Emotional attachment was called 'cathexis' by Freud's English translators. For careful definitions of these terms, see *The Language of Psycho-Analysis*: Laplanche and Pontalis 1973.) Freud's

psychology gradually influenced the social sciences, and so opened up for investigation the *social* structuring of emotional relations, attachments or commitments.

Emotional commitments may be positive or negative, favourable or hostile towards the object. For instance, prejudice against women (misogyny), or against homosexuals (homophobia), is a definite kind of cathexis, though a negative one. Emotional commitments are often, as Freud emphasized, both loving and hostile at once. That pattern he called 'ambivalence', and it is a useful idea for understanding the complexities of gender relations.

A major arena of emotional attachment is sexuality. Anthropological and historical studies have made it clear that sexual relations involve culturally formed relationships, not simple biological reflexes (Caplan 1987). Though sexuality cannot be reduced to gender, as Gary Dowsett (2003) correctly argues in relation to the HIV/AIDS epidemic, sexuality is often organized on the basis of gender.

The hegemonic pattern in the global North today assumes that sexual attraction goes across genders, i.e. involves a man and a woman. This assumption requires a sharp distinction between cross-gender (heterosexual) and same-gender (homosexual) cathexis. In fact this distinction is so important that it is commonly taken as defining different kinds of people, 'homosexuals' and 'heterosexuals'. Certain biologists go looking for a homosexual gene to explain the difference. (Curiously, no one has gone looking for the heterosexual gene.)

But cross-cultural research shows that many societies do not make these distinctions, or do not make them in the same way. In classical Greece, the hegemonic pattern of sexuality included strong attachments among men, especially between older men and male youth. More recently, the 'Sambia', a community in Papua New Guinea described in a well-known ethnography by Gilbert Herdt, *Guardians of the Flutes* (1981), treat same-gender sexuality as a ritual practice that all men are involved in at a particular stage of life. From a European point of view, all Sambia men are homosexuals at one age, and all switch over to become heterosexuals at another. That is absurd, of course. From a Sambia point of view, they are simply following the normal development of masculinity.

In contemporary metropolitan society, households are expected to be formed on the basis of romantic love, that is, a strong individual attachment between two partners. This ideal is the basis of most television soaps and Hollywood weepies, and its importance is confirmed by research with groups who might be thought sceptical of it. They include the American university students described ethnographically by Dorothy Holland and Margaret Eisenhart in *Educated in Romance* (1990).

Difficulties in attaining this ideal in one's life may vary. Sociologist Averil Clarke studied the pursuit of romantic relationships by college-educated African-American women in *Inequalities of Love* (2011). Compared to their white and Hispanic counterparts, college-educated black women's lives include less marriage and sex, and more unwanted pregnancy, abortion and unwed childbearing. Clarke argues that inequalities are produced through the pursuit of romantic love and formation of households, not just through the economy. As the ideal of romantic love is spread around the world by religion, advertising and other cultural pressures, it comes into conflict with other ways of forming new households, especially arranged marriages that represent alliances between kinship groups. That is a familiar tension as contemporary globalization impacts on family life.

The other crucial emotional connection in the household is between parent and child. This relationship too may be strongly gendered. In the globally hegemonic pattern, care and attachment to young children is the business of women, especially mothers, while fathers as breadwinners are expected to be emotionally distant. But this pattern is also under challenge, with 'new fatherhood' ideals spreading (see chapter 6). A recent study of the discourse of fatherhood in contemporary Japan by Taga Futoshi shows how difficult the emotional dilemmas can be. Whichever way fathers turn, the result can be conflict and a sense of guilt (Taga 2007).

Emotional relations are also found in the workplace. Arlie Hochschild's classic book *The Managed Heart* (1983) analyses emotional labour in the US economy. There are many jobs where producing a particular emotional relationship with a customer is central to the work being done. These are, typically, gender-typed jobs. Hochschild's main examples are airline hostesses, where workers are trained to produce sympathy and induce relaxation; and telephone debt collectors, where workers must display aggression and induce fear. Hochschild argues that this kind of labour is becoming more common with the expansion of service industries. If so, alienated relations based on commercialized feelings and gender stereotypes may be increasingly important in modern life.

Hostile emotional relationships are not only symbolic, like the ones enacted by Hochschild's debt collectors. They can be violent. Stephen Tomsen's (1998) study of homophobic killings in Australia shows two major patterns of conduct. One is gang attacks in public places by young men who go looking for gender deviants to punish, a process that depends on mutual encouragement in the group. The other is killings by individuals in private. Some of these involve a violent response to a sexual approach (and perhaps to the killers' own ambivalent desire) which is felt to be a threat to masculinity. Both patterns may result in killings of extreme brutality.

Symbolism, culture, discourse

All social practice involves interpreting the world. As post-structuralists observe, nothing human is 'outside' discourse. Society is a world of meanings. At the same time, meanings bear the traces of the social processes by which they were made. Cultural systems reflect particular social interests, and grow out of specific ways of life.

This point applies to gender meanings. Whenever we speak of 'a woman' or 'a man', we call into play a tremendous system of understandings, implications, overtones and allusions that have accumulated through our cultural history. The 'meanings' of these words are enormously greater than the biological categories of male and female. When the Papua New Guinea highland community studied by Marilyn Strathern (1978) say 'our clan is a clan of men', they do not mean that the clan entirely consists of males. When an American football coach yells at his losing team that they are 'a bunch of women', he does not mean they can now get pregnant. But both are saying something meaningful, and, in their contexts, important.

The study of cultural representations of gender, gendered attitudes, value systems and related problems has been probably the most active area of gender studies in the past two decades – in the rich countries of the global metropole. It is not so central in the developing world, where questions of poverty, power and economic change have higher priority. But even here it is relevant, as we see in Superna Bhaskaran's *Made in India* (2004), a lively discussion of beauty pageants and the internationalization of Barbie-doll femininity, discrimination against homosexuals, and gender images in Indian media.

The best-known model of the structure of symbolism in gender comes from the French psychoanalyst Jacques Lacan. Lacan's analysis of the phallus as master-symbol gave rise to a view of language as 'phallocentric', a system in which the place of authority, the privileged subjectivity, is always the masculine. The potentially infinite play of meaning in language is fixed by the phallic point of reference. In that case, culture itself embodies the 'law of the father'. And if that is so, the only way to contest patriarchal meanings is to escape known forms of language. Hence feminist thinkers such as Xavière Gauthier (1981) developed an interest in women's writing as an oppositional practice that had to subvert the laws of culture.

By the 1990s, escape from phallocentrism, and from rigid dichotomies of masculine and feminine, became a key form of gender politics in the metropole. Queer theory's critique of 'heteronormativity' – of which Lacan had been the great theorist – leads to a strategy of cultural disruption. In recent queer writing and politics there is an energetic celebration of diversity in sexual identities and self-presentations that takes pleasure in disrupting familiar gender categories (e.g. Bauer et al. 2007).

Though language – speech and writing – is the most analysed site of symbolic gender relations, it is not the only one. Gender symbolism also operates in dress, makeup, gesture, in photography and film, and in more impersonal forms of culture such as the built environment.

Rosa Linda Fregoso's *The Bronze Screen* (1993) illustrates some complexities of the cultural dynamics of gender. She studies films produced by Chicana/Chicano film-makers about the community of Mexican affiliation in the south-western USA, outside the Anglo-centric Hollywood orbit. Chicano (men) film-makers, Fregoso observes, have not demeaned their women characters, but they have not given them an active role in discourse. Only with the advent of woman film-makers was there exploration of generational difference, language, religion and relationships from women's standpoints. Elizabeth Ault (2014) makes a stronger criticism of *The Wire* (HBO, 2002–8), the critically acclaimed television crime drama set in Baltimore focused on institutions and structural dimensions of urban politics and problems. Ault argues that the few portrayals of African-American mothers in the drama exhibit a view of black motherhood as irresponsible, irrational and emasculating.

Gender symbolism is constantly deployed in social struggle. The politics of the anti-apartheid movement in South Africa show this, as different symbolic models of masculinity were put into play. One of the most formidable opponents of apartheid was the union movement, which constructed masculinity on a 'worker' model. A more ambiguous role was played by the Zulu-nationalist Inkatha movement, which tried to mobilize men around a 'warrior' image but stood for a conservative social order. In the aftermath of the armed struggle, the 'young lions' of the African National Congress's guerrilla forces lost their social respect, and often fell into unemployment and violent crime (Waetjen 2004; Xaba 2001).

Symbolic expressions of gender change over time, and so do attitudes to gender equality. In an extended analysis of survey data from Germany and Japan, Ulrich Mohwald (2002) shows a shift of attitudes in both countries towards gender equality, though the course of events was different. The breadwinner/housewife model, formerly unknown in Japan, was constructed in the late nineteenth and early twentieth centuries as a middle-class ideal. Following the Second World War, Japanese women endorsed both legal equality *and* this unequal nuclear-family model. Another shift of opinion followed the Women's Liberation movement, with increasing value placed on women's careers and sharing work in the home. In Japan this shift occurred in the attitudes of all generations. In Germany, however, the shift away from traditional gender attitudes involved a generational split – it mainly happened in the younger generation.

Interweaving and intersection

The four dimensions just discussed are tools for thinking; they are not separate institutions. Though a division of labour is a different thing from a symbolic representation, no division of labour could long be sustained without symbolic categories. Birgit Pfau-Effinger's (1998) very sophisticated cross-national analysis of gender arrangements in European labour markets turns on this point – different cultural models of gender underpin different divisions of labour. In real-life contexts, the different dimensions of gender constantly interweave, and condition each other.

Further, the structures of gender are interwoven with other social structures. Fregoso's analysis of gender in Chicana/o film would make no sense if it were not seen in the context of ethnic inequality in US society. Hochschild's analysis of gendered emotional labour and Pringle's analysis of secretarial work presuppose a class structure where groups of workers depend on capitalist corporations for their livelihood and have to deliver certain kinds of labour to get their wages.

This point has been emphasized in recent sociology under the heading of 'intersectionality'. American lawyer Kimberlé Crenshaw in 1989 coined the term to describe the ways race and gender interact to shape the experiences of black women in employment. Crenshaw rightly argued that attending to gender or race separately cannot capture their experiences. Sociologist Patricia Hill Collins (1991) took up the idea and applied it to all women, arguing that gender is always interrelated with other cultural patterns of oppression.

Intersectionality can be an unfortunate term, because it suggests social structures are rigid arrangements that we can understand by a kind of geometry. Good analyses of intersectionality will think in terms of the interplay between structures, i.e. the ways they change each other; and how actual social situations are produced out of that mutual conditioning. Ethnicity, for instance, is constantly defined through gender relations. The notion of an extended family is central to the rhetoric of ethnicity: 'our kith and kin', as the British used to say; 'brothers born of warrior stock', in the language of Zulu nationalism in South Africa (Waetjen and Maré 2001). Jill Vickers (1994) notes that male-dominated ethnic politics usually lays heavy emphasis on women's reproductive powers. Rod Earle and Coretta Phillips (2012) explored the ways masculinities and ethnicities mutually shape prison life in their ethnography of cooking practices in a UK prison.

For many purposes we need to treat gender as a structure in its own right. We should not collapse gender into other categories, or treat it as the effect of some other reality (as used to be done with class and is now sometimes done with discourse). But we must also remember that gender relations always work in context, always interact with other dynamics in social life. And from those interactions come many of the forces for change.

Change in gender relations

Why do gender arrangements change? Most explanations have focused on external pressures: new technology, urban life, mass communications, secularism, or just 'modernization'. It is true that social forces such as these can alter gender patterns. But gender relations also have internal tendencies towards change.

Gender theorists who have emphasized the discursive construction of gender have also noted that discourses are fluid. The uncertain and contested character of the category 'women' is a central theme of Judith Butler's extremely influential book *Gender Trouble* (1990), and also the feminist theorizing of Gayatri Chakravorty Spivak (1988). Gender identities are produced discursively, but meanings in discourse are not fixed. If we follow Derrida's analysis in *Of Grammatology* (1967), the founding text of postmodern philosophy, meanings are incapable of being fixed in any final way. Further, there is no fixed connection between discursive identities and the bodies to which those identities refer. People with male bodies can enact femininity, people with female bodies can enact masculinity. Gender identities can be played with, taken up and abandoned, unpacked and recombined.

But seeing change in gender relations as a result of generalized instability is not convincing. It is difficult to avoid the fact that in some historical situations gender identities and relations change slowly; in other situations they change explosively. Sylvia Walby's *Gender Transformations* (1997) suggests that distinct 'rounds' of restructuring can be identified in the metropole. Nor does a concept of generalized instability give any grip on why some people would want to change gender arrangements, while others would resist. Further, the idea of generalized instability of categories seems to have arisen in the global metropole, and perhaps captures something important about social life there. In other parts of the world, however, the idea seems less attractive. For instance, gender boundaries seem to have hardened in Iran and some Arab countries in the last generation (Moghadam 2002, 2013).

Thinking of gender as a social structure leads to another account of change. Structures develop *crisis tendencies*, that is, internal contradictions that undermine current patterns, and force change in the structure itself. This approach to change is inspired by German critical theory, especially the work of Jürgen Habermas (1976). It allows us to distinguish periods when pressures for change are only gradually building, from periods when they erupt into actual crisis and force rapid change. It also allows us to identify interests that can be mobilized for and against change.

Crisis tendencies can be identified in each of the four dimensions of gender relations defined earlier in this chapter. We will illustrate with one of them, production. The division of labour has been the site of massive change. Through the second half of the twentieth century there was a worldwide incorporation of women's labour into the market economy. The global labour force participation rate for women in 2012 was 51.1 per cent compared with men's 77.1 per cent. In rich countries the historical change took the form of growth in married women's workforce participation rates, i.e. movement from unpaid to paid work, especially in the service sector. In the developing world, the change took the form of an even more massive move into cities, into market-based agriculture and certain forms of industry. In the last decade the gender gap in labour force participation has remained constant overall. This remaining gender difference does not mean than women do less work than men; women have continued to do most of the domestic work and childcare.

There is an underlying contradiction between the roughly equal contribution to total social labour by women and men, and the gendered appropriation of the products of social labour. The gendered appropriation is seen in the unequal incomes of women and men as groups, the better conditions and career prospects that men generally have, and the patriarchal inheritance of wealth and organizational power. Women have a general interest in changing this, so many become active in trade unions, in community organizing, and in pressure groups concerned with taxation and benefits. But the turbulence of the gendered accumulation process, and its intersection with class relations, affect this. Economically privileged women (usually the most influential in politics) have an interest in resisting economic reforms that cut deeply into gender inequalities, because that would disturb the corporate system from which they benefit. So we do not see rich women on the picket lines supporting strikes at *maquiladora* factories or fast food outlets.

The analysis of contradiction works best if there is a coherent gender order within which crisis tendencies arise. But what if the gender order has been smashed, the intelligibility of the world broken? That is precisely what happened in imperial conquest, with the arrival of the colonizing power. A colonized society, as Georges Balandier (1955) argued in a penetrating analysis of change in central Africa, is a society in crisis. As we noted in chapter 4, a consolidated gender order cannot be presumed, in the colonized or post-colonial world.

Empire set about restructuring gender relations, and historians have traced the construction of gender orders in colonies. A powerful example is Robert Morrell's *From Boys to Gentlemen* (2001a), which documents the making of elite boys' schools in the British colony of Natal, intended to produce a form of masculinity capable of ruling a subject race. Morrell also traces the creation of a network of gendered institutions, including military forces and voluntary associations, through which the ruling was done.

Neoliberal globalization similarly restructures local gender orders, as well as being itself a deeply gendered process (as will be seen in chapter 8). A good deal of evidence about this is emerging in recent research on motherhood. In Nicaragua, following the election of a right-wing government led by Violeta Chamorro in 1990, a neoliberal agenda drove public sector cuts, privatized state agencies and reduced social services. Julie Cupples' (2005) interviews with single mothers in the town of Matagalpa show these changes reflected in mothers' loss of dignity and greater difficulty in making ends meet. But the women of Matagalpa responded actively. With the growth of an informal economy they moved into employment, however precarious, more confidently than the men – often reducing or abandoning their housework commitments to do so. Having to care for children obliged the women to generate a family income. Over time, Cupples suggests, paid work became consolidated as part of women's identity. Being a breadwinner is now part of motherhood, rather than being opposed to it.

Gender politics

If change in gender relations is possible, then it can become the goal of social action. This is a simple definition of gender politics – the struggle to alter a gender order, or to resist alteration.

Historically the most important movement in gender politics has been feminism. Feminist awareness and feminist campaigns are the sources of most of the gender theories discussed in chapter 4, most of the research discussed in chapter 3, and most of the agendas to be discussed in chapters 7, on environment, and 8, on large-scale politics.

It is necessary to say that not all political movements among women are feminist. Raka Ray's (1999) study of women's politics in India gives a classic example. The Communist Party of India (Marxist), the long-term governing party in the province of West Bengal, established a women's organization called Paschim Banga Ganatantrik Mahila Samiti. This functioned mainly to implement the official line coming down from the male leadership of the Party – a line that insisted on solidarity between working-class women and men, not on the specific interests of women. Consequently the women of the Samiti, while working for women's economic and educational advance, shied away from anything that implied a direct challenge to men – for instance, from making a public issue of gender-based violence, though that has been a central issue for feminists all over India.

Of course this pattern is not peculiar to India. Postwar Japan, for instance, saw a remarkable growth of women's organizations – women had gained the vote, and in the 1950s and 1960s were an important constituency. As Tanaka Kazuko (1977) describes, the men's parties set up women's auxiliaries to claim this constituency, and there were also big state-based women's organizations. But these organizations were tied to a patriarchal political system. When Women's Liberation arrived, it represented a radical break. As in the United States and Europe, the claim for *autonomous* women's organization was a vital departure – and from that, the shape of modern gender politics has developed.

Gay Liberation, emerging in the United States at almost the same time, similarly involved autonomous organization, combining the personal and the structural. Public demonstrations produced similar feelings of exhilaration and common purpose. Lesbian and gay politics, however, involved another dimension, the process of 'coming out'. Making a declaration to oneself, one's family, one's friends and workmates, can be difficult and takes time. Adjustments and realignments in everyday life have to be made. The collective process of establishing a community, an identity in the culture, and a presence in politics and economic life, both depends on the individual process and supports it.

There was an extra complication in gay politics, because a gender division ran down the middle of it. Lesbians and gay men are not in the same social situation, not even in the same political situation. Laws that criminalized homosexual sex for men, in many countries, ignored women. So did some gay male activists. Gay Liberation itself was mainly a men's movement – though the iconic action with which it began, the 1969 'Stonewall' anti-police riot in New York, was led by transsexual and transvestite sex workers.

A decade after the emergence of Gay Liberation, homosexual men's politics was transformed by the HIV/AIDS epidemic. A whole new set of relationships, with doctors and the state, had to be negotiated, while a hostile symbolic politics about infection, pollution and uncleanness, whipped up by religious leaders, politicians and the media, had to be dealt with. Both jobs had to be done in a context of illness, bereavement and fear. Gay communities in wealthy countries not only survived this terrible crisis, but also evolved new responses and community education approaches, creating AIDS support organizations and the 'safe sex' strategy (Kippax et al. 1993). In poor countries, men who have sex with men usually lack economic resources, and may also face homophobic governments. This is a serious problem in Africa, which has the highest burden of HIV infection and illness. Governments in Senegal, Zimbabwe and Uganda have made homosexual men targets for blame and persecution – which has disrupted AIDS prevention work. The attitude is not unknown in rich countries too. In the middle of a bushfire crisis in Australia in 2013, the national government turned its attention to trying to prevent marriage-equality ('gay marriage') laws being introduced by the city government of Canberra.

Some gender politics explicitly resists change, such as the charmingly named 'Women Who Want to be Women', which once existed in the United States, and 'REAL Women', a conservative lobby group that still exists in Canada campaigning against abortion and universal access to childcare. Small 'fathers' rights' groups arise in many countries, which are fiercely hostile to feminism, and accuse divorce courts of being biased against men. Anti-abortion movements, usually drawing on the membership of hard-line churches, have been the most successful anti-feminist campaigns of all, intimidating abortion providers, and capturing control of many international aid programmes via the US government. The biggest force of resistance to women's reproductive rights internationally has been the Catholic church. As Mala Htun's (2003) study makes clear, church intransigence prevented abortion reform right across Latin America for a generation. (The entirely predictable outcome is that rich women can get safe abortions, and poor women cannot.)

The defence of patriarchal gender orders has not, on the whole, required social movements among men. It has been accomplished by the normal functioning of patriarchal institutions – the state, the corporations, the media, the religious hierarchies. Certainly there is political intent. Most mass media in the world are persistently anti-feminist, some of them (such as the Murdoch media empire) strikingly so. But for the most part, no political campaign is needed; everyday sexist practice, e.g. the media's trivialization and sexualization of women, does the job.

Take, for example, military forces, which are easily recognized as patriarchal institutions. Frank Barrett (1996), researching gender patterns in US naval officer training, documents an oppressive but efficient regime emphasizing competition, physical hardness, conformity, and a sense of elite membership. This is designed to produce a narrowly defined hegemonic masculinity, and therefore it created serious problems for women trainees when they began to enter US military forces under 'equal opportunity' principles. Similar patterns are seen in Emma Sinclair-Webb's (2000) account of military training in Turkey, in Ruth Seifert's (1993) study of military training in Germany, and in other countries.

Not all men defend patriarchy. A 2009 CBS News Poll found 58 per cent of American men identified as feminist, and a smaller proportion (34 per cent) believed that a strong women's movement is still needed. A small number are building a men's feminist movement. One of the most interesting forms of gender politics in the last generation has been the emergence of gender-equality movements among heterosexual men (called 'pro-feminist' men in the United States). Tina Sideris (2005) describes an example in South Africa, where since the end of apartheid there has been a public principle of gender equality in tension with long-standing local patriarchies. A group of men in the rural Nkomazi region near the border with Mozambique are trying to move to a more respectful and gender-equal practice in their lives. All are married, with children. They are able to renegotiate the gender division of labour in their households, and adopt nonviolence. But they find it difficult to shift the meaning of masculinity away from being a head of household. In the Nkomazi gender regime, the authority dimension seems hardest to shift.

That is an informal movement; in other places gender-equality politics among men is more organized. Groups promoting gender justice have emerged in the United States, Scandinavia, Germany, Chile, Mexico, India and other countries. Indeed, there is now an international network of men's movements and NGOs supporting gender equality and opposed to gender violence, called MenEngage (www.menengage.org). Research and action programmes intended to reduce violence against women, and support engaged fatherhood, are now found in many countries and have support from the United Nations. Most remain small, compared to the scale of the problems (Connell 2005; Lang et al. 2008).

The struggle against gender-based violence is a central feature of gender politics, and involves decades of protest and advocacy by women and men. 'Reclaim the Night' protests held to contest violence against women have been held since 1975. The first was held in Philadelphia in response to the murder of Susan Alexander Speeth whilst walking home alone. These marches are often, but not always, organized and attended by women only, and involve a speak-out or candlelight vigil. A new iteration of these protests arrived in 2011 in Canada. Public protests called SlutWalks were organized in response to a Toronto Police officer's advice that to remain safe 'women should avoid dressing like sluts'. These rallies aim to subvert victim-blaming rhetoric and end the culture of fear and victimization. SlutWalks spread to cities including London, Chicago, Philadelphia, Bhopal, Delhi and São Paulo. They have sent ripples of debate through feminist networks over whether the concept of SlutWalks trivializes gender-based violence, or reflects Western, middle-class privilege to be able to call oneself a 'slut' without suffering discredit (Borah and Nandi 2012).

These kinds of tensions within social movements reflect the dynamic nature of gender. Whilst there are considerable continuities in the gender order, resistance, and the debate it inspires, contribute to change.

6

Gender in personal life

To most people, being a man or a woman is above all a matter of personal experience. It is part of the way we grow up, the way we conduct family life and sexual relationships, the way we present ourselves in everyday situations, and the way we see ourselves. This chapter examines some issues that arise in this realm of intimacy, and reflects on how to understand what happens here.

Personal politics

In 1997 Pam Benton, who had been Raewyn's partner for 29 years, died of breast cancer. Breast cancer is almost entirely a women's disease. The medical specialists who treat it, however, are mostly men – as medical specialists mostly are in Australia. And they, naturally enough, have many of the attitudes and styles of interaction that men in the professions are likely to have.

Early in the treatment, Pam was referred to a prominent Sydney oncologist. Oncology is specialization in cancer, especially in its treatment through chemotherapy, the use of toxic drugs. This gentleman delivered himself of the opinion that if women would use their breasts for what they were intended for, they would not have so much trouble. Pam was furious, and did not consult him again.

There is, as the oncologist well knew, research evidence that rates of breast cancer are lower in women who have had babies early in life and have breast-fed. That is, so to speak, impersonal fact. (Though even with impersonal fact, one may ask why researchers should have been concerned with that particular question rather than studying cancer-causing chemicals in the environment.) The oncologist made this research finding into a gender insult – which he probably did not even realize was offensive – by his bland presumption that what women are 'for' is bearing babies. To him, if they had a different pattern of life, they were asking for what they got.

The story suggests how intimate, and how unavoidable, gender politics is at a personal level. Some issues about power and inequality are mundane, such as who does the dishes, who puts out the garbage and who writes the shopping list. Some are life-and-death, such as how childbirth and cancer treatment are done. Pam had been an activist in the women's movement over 20 years. She could see the gender politics in cancer medicine, and was not willing to be put down again.

The first tumour, which Pam discovered through routine screening, was so advanced that it required a mastectomy, surgical removal of the whole breast. This is a frightening (though not in itself life-threatening) operation which leaves a long scar where the breast has been. Recovering from the operation, Pam made contact with the support services available to mastectomy patients. The main services provided were: supply of an artificial breast, in the appropriate size to replace the one that was lost; visits from women who came to give grooming and dress advice so that the patient could present a normal, attractive feminine appearance to the world; and advice on how to restore family normality, overcome a husband's (expected) sexual disgust at a mutilated body, and deal with children's anxiety about their mother's being taken away from them.

This, too, is political. It is about placing women back in the culture of heterosexual femininity. It is about denying that normality has been rent. It is about holding women responsible for other people's emotional needs. And – not least – it is about restoring normal services to men.

But this politics operates at so deep a level of emotion that it is hardly perceptible as politics unless one is already aware of gender issues. Many women dedicate their lives to making a family and seeing it through the life-cycle. A sense of having an attractive or at least presentable body is an important part of Australian culture's construction of womanhood. Women who are shocked by a major operation, and terrified by discovering they have a deadly disease, are unlikely to revolt against stereotyping, especially when it is presented to them as a form of care by other women.

Gender politics almost always has this dimension of intimacy, as well as involving the larger social relations discussed in chapter 5. That is one reason change in gender relations can be so threatening, to many women as well as to many men. Impending changes can upset people's cherished images of themselves, assumptions about personal relationships, their social embodiment and their habits of everyday conduct.

The personal politics of gender is found everywhere, so we will also give cases from other parts of the world. One comes from Costa Rica in central America, and is narrated by Susan Mannon (2006). Costa Rica is a banana and coffee exporter, vulnerable to price fluctuations; the Latin American debt crisis of the 1980s drove the country into a neoliberal restructuring, in which many men became unemployed. Mannon interviewed middle-aged married people in an urban area, and tells particularly about one couple, called Cecilia and Antonio, who lived through these events.

Their household had been set up on a breadwinner/housewife basis, though this was an anxious position as Antonio was an unskilled public sector worker. This gender division was not imposed on Cecilia; she was an active participant in creating demarcations between family roles. Economic need drove change. As inflation gripped, Cecilia, like other married women, returned to the money economy. She did this at first by renting out a room in their house, in effect commodifying her domestic work. In the 1990s the sharp breadwinner/housewife division began to blur – by Cecilia expanding her labour, not Antonio, who did not help around the house. He held on to authority in the family, with support from patriarchal norms in the society around; Cecilia did not use her new economic strength in bargaining with him. Too serious a challenge might have disrupted the social position of respectability that she was actually trying to protect. Patience and love won out.

In the Indian province of Andhra Pradesh there is a relatively high prevalence of HIV. This was recognized in the early 2000s and various public health initiatives have followed. A vigorous organizing project among local sex workers is called Project Parivartan. Most are women who come from working-class, lower-caste positions who are marginal in society; gender inequalities are deeply entrenched and sex work itself is stigmatizing. The power differentials, therefore, are steep. This is reflected inside the sex trade, where it is usually the privilege of male clients to decide whether or not to use a condom.

A project report (George and Blankenship 2007) relates experiences of activists in Parivartan when trying to protect themselves from the epidemic by insisting on condom use. In one case, when a customer had solicited the worker on the street and paid in advance, she took him to a rented room, where he refused to use a condom. A dispute arose about the money; the customer eventually 'threatened to shout and wake the neighbours, and put the house owner to shame'. The threat was effective, because this would reveal the woman's sex work and disrupt the arrangements under which she earned her living. Even so basic a change as introducing condom use involves struggle.

Chapter 2 described changes in gender symbolism in Soviet and post-Soviet Russia. Anna Temkina (2008) reports a life-history study with middle-class women in St Petersburg that takes the story one step further. Different sexual 'scripts' can be distinguished in their stories. The women who had grown up in the Soviet period had lives organized by marriage, usually placed themselves in a passive position in their narratives, and described themselves as objects of men's desire – all reasonably in accord with Soviet gender ideology. In short, Temkina observes, their sexual lives were ruled by others and by the surrounding conditions.

But this is not the dominant story among younger women, who have grown up in the turmoil of the 1990s and under the new capitalist regime. These women describe themselves as having agency in their sexual lives. They are more likely to emphasize seeking their own pleasure, or using their sexuality to gain benefits, i.e. bargaining with men. They are still under constraints, however. As the limited Soviet emancipation of women was rolled back, neo-traditionalist ideologies of gender emerged, and a new public patriarchy was constructed, now centred on Vladimir Putin. But the young women of the 2000s are making more conscious choices about sexuality, contraception and relationships, being more inclined to see their life as a project than as a destiny.

When activists in the Women's Liberation movement said 'the personal is political', they were making a point that still holds good. There is gender politics in our most intimate relationships and decisions. Struggles here are not susceptible to sweeping gestures; the complexities are many, the price of change can be high, and sometimes one is tired and just wants to forget it. But this intimate politics always underlies the more public politics and cannot be abandoned.

Growing up gendered: sex role socialization and psychoanalysis

When sex role theory provided the main framework of gender studies, there was a straightforward account of how people acquired gender. Babies were identified as either female or male and put in pink and blue clothes respectively. The blue babies were expected to behave rougher and tougher, to be more demanding and vigorous. In time they were given toy guns, footballs and computer games. The pink babies were expected to be more passive and compliant, also prettier. As they grew older they were dressed in frilly clothes, given dolls and makeup kits, told to take care of their appearance and be polite and agreeable.

Put more formally, the idea was that 'sex roles' were acquired by socialization. Various 'agencies of socialization', notably the family, the school, the peer group and the mass media, took the growing child in hand. Through an immense number of small interactions, these agencies conveyed to the girl or the boy the social 'norms' or expectations for behaviour. This could be done by imitating admired 'role models', such as a father might be for a boy; or it could be done piecemeal. Compliance with the norms would lead to rewards, or 'positive sanctions': smiles from mother, approval from friends, success in the dating game, appointment to a good job. Nonconformity or deviance would lead to negative sanctions, all the way from frowns to getting beaten up or sent to gaol.

With this mixture of positive and negative reinforcement, most children would learn the gender-appropriate behaviour, develop the traits the society thought appropriate for women or for men, and thus 'internalize' the norms. As fully socialized members of society, they would in turn apply negative sanctions to deviants, and convey the norms to the next generation. Of course the process could go wrong, for instance if fathers disappeared from families and boys lacked role models, which would probably lead to juvenile delinquency.

There is something to be said for this story of how gender is acquired, but there are also severe problems with it; so severe, in fact, that the socialization model should be abandoned.

First, it is too monolithic. The world does not consist of neatly homogeneous cultures. Cultures were smashed, fragmented and re-composed by conquest, colonization, migration, and contemporary globalization. The ethnic pluralism of modern societies mixes traditions. The model of sex role socialization mistakes what is dominant for what is normative. Further, multiple patterns arise within gender relations, through the contradictions and dynamics discussed in chapter 5. There are always multiple patterns of masculinity and femininity to complicate the picture of learning.

Second, the socialization model supposes that learning gender is a matter of acquiring traits, that is, regularities of character that will produce regularities of behaviour. Sex role theory, basically, is a version of the difference model of gender discussed in chapter 3. But as the research reviewed in chapter 3 shows, major differences in traits between women and men (or between girls and boys) are hard to detect.

Third, the socialization model pictures the learner as passive, the agencies of socialization as active. In real life, gender learning does not look like this. Consider the American elementary schools studied by Barrie Thorne (chapter 2). The boys and girls here are not lying back and letting the gender norms wash over them. They are constantly active. They sometimes accept gender divisions supplied by adults and sometimes don't. They set up their own gender divisions in the playground, and then disrupt them. They try out gendered self-presentations (e.g. the older girls putting on lip gloss); they complain, joke, fantasize and question about gender. Similar energy appears in other studies of schools, such as the British upper secondary students described by Máirtín Mac an Ghaill in *The Making of Men* (1994).

The socialization model seems to miss the pleasure that is obvious in much gender learning; the resistance which many young people put up to hegemonic definitions of gender; and the difficulty involved in constructing identities and working out patterns of conduct in a gender order marked by power, violence and alienated sexualities. James Messerschmidt's *Flesh and Blood* (2004), with vivid studies of the lives of American youth who have got in trouble with the law through violence, is full of evidence of this difficulty, and also of the resistance and the divergent trajectories that result.

Fourth, the socialization model recognizes just one dimension of learning – towards or away from the sex role norms. This makes it hard to understand the shifts of direction that often appear in a young person's life, coming apparently from nowhere. There can be a shift of attachment from mother to father, a new level of aggression, a sudden burst of sexual activity, a turning away from girls or boys. Rather than just failing to 'internalize' the gender patterns of her/his parents, a young person may vehemently reject them, criticize their political or human inadequacy, and launch out on a search for something different.

The contradictory character of human development is much better understood by psychoanalysis, though psychoanalysis is currently less influential in social science. Freud's case studies – Dora, Little Hans and the 'Wolf Man' are the most famous – emphasize conflict and contradiction. Freud recognized that a person is often developing in different directions at the same time, at unconscious and conscious levels. Psychoanalysis has been developing for a century, and contemporary schools remain deeply divided, but in virtually all of them, this insight remains important.

In Freud's account, gender development centred on the Oedipus complex – the emotional crisis of middle childhood in which the child's sexual desire, focused for the moment on mother and father, was repressed. This crisis set up an unconscious pattern of motivation, different for boys and girls, that continued to influence their mental life from the shadows, and in the normal case led to adult heterosexual attraction. Psychoanalysis thus offered an explanation of how a conventional gender pattern was transmitted from generation to generation with apparent ease, shaping the strongest desires of adult men and women. But it also showed that this effect was achieved through emotional contradictions and crises which could lead along other paths. Thus non-normative gender development could also be understood.

Psychoanalytic theories and methods have always been controversial. There is a strong tendency for psychoanalytic movements to turn into cult-like celebrations of a founding father (Freud, Jung, Adler, Lacan), and for some of the smaller sects, a founding mother (Klein). Yet there are powerful insights here, about the contradictory character of development, about the importance of bodily desire, and about unconscious motivation.

A better account: embodied learning

A good account of how we acquire gender must recognize both the contradictions of development, and the fact that learners are active, not passive. It must recognize the agency of bodies in the social world, since the active learner is embodied. It must recognize the power and the complexity of the institutions that occupy the learner's world. It must give an account of the gender competencies that are learned, and the different life projects in which they are used. And it must recognize historical change in all these respects.

The pleasure involved in learning gender is to some extent a bodily pleasure, pleasure in the body's appearance and the body's performance. Bodily changes such as menarche, first ejaculation, the 'breaking' of a boy's voice and the development of a girl's breasts are important, but their meanings remain ambiguous until they are given definition by the society's gender symbolism.

Because gender practice involves bodies but is not biologically determined, the learned behaviour may be hostile to bodies' physical well-being. Young men in rich countries such as the United States and Australia, enacting their fresh-minted masculinities on the roads, die in appalling numbers in traffic accidents, at a rate four times higher than young women. A large number of adolescent girls and young women go in for dieting, in an attempt to maintain their heterosexual attractiveness. For a smaller number this escalates into life-threatening anorexia. In poorer countries the circumstances are different but the stakes are also very high. In the Palestinian confrontation with Israeli military occupation, the intifada, most of the direct resistance has been carried out by very young men and boys. As Julie Peteet (1994) showed in a terrifying ethnography, being beaten or arrested by the Israeli army and police became a kind of rite of passage into masculinity for Palestinian youth; and some of them were killed.

Embodied learners encounter the gender regimes of the institutions they come in contact with. The socialization model was right about the importance of the family, the school, and the media in children's lives, but failed to recognize the internal complexity of the gender regimes of these institutions. In a school, teachers and peer groups present a range of different patterns of masculinity and femininity to the children. Differences among teachers are well shown in Mac an Ghaill's (1994) study. Differences in peer groups are a theme of Douglas Foley's (1990) ethnography of a high school in a Texas country town. Here the interplay of gender, class and ethnicity constructs several versions of masculinity. There is the dominant group of Anglo 'jocks', anti-authoritarian Mexican-American 'vatos', and the group which Foley calls ironically the 'silent majority'. In Julie Bettie's (2003) ethnography of a high school in California, the focus is on femininities; and again the ethnic hierarchies are important.

The diversity of gender patterns among children and youth shows up with particular clarity in research that looks across different social groups. Stephen Frosh, Ann Phoenix and Rob Pattman, in a very perceptive study called *Young Masculinities* (2002), report on 11- to 14-year-old boys in 12 secondary schools across London. They show that ethnic position is prominent in London boys' views about masculinity – Afro-Caribbean boys being thought high in masculinity and Asian boys low. Relationships with schools are ambivalent, academic success being both desired and thought feminine. Above all, this study shows that diversity in the boys' lives exists in tension with 'canonical narratives' of masculinity, i.e. a hegemonic pattern (an admired physical toughness, sports skills, heterosexuality). All boys acknowledge the hegemonic masculinity but most do not fully inhabit it. Rather, their adolescence is marked by a complex negotiation with definitions of gender, in which they may criticize some versions of masculinity as too tough, while rejecting others as effeminate.

Much of young people's learning about gender is learning what we might call gender competence. Young people learn how to navigate the local gender order and the gender regimes of the institutions they deal with. They learn how to adopt a certain gender identity and produce a certain gender performance – how to 'do gender', as West and Zimmerman (1987) famously put it. Young people also learn how to distance themselves from a given gender identity, how to joke about their own performance. Most boys and girls fail to match gender ideals of handsomeness, beauty, skill, achievement or recognition. But most of them cope.

Active learning means a commitment of oneself in a particular direction. The learner does not simply absorb what is to be learned, but engages with it, moves forward in life in a particular direction. The pleasure in gender learning is the pleasure of creativity and movement. Gender learning can occur at any moment that a person encounters gender relations in the course of everyday life. A lovely piece of research that shows this lifelong process is Wendy Luttrell's *Schoolsmart and Motherwise* (1997), based on interviews with African-American and white working-class women in adult education programmes in the United States, looking back down the years of their lives.

Gender learning takes definite shapes. From early in the process, what is learned is connected with other pieces of learning. Children learn about, and create in their own lives, the configurations of gender practice in personal life that we call 'femininity' and 'masculinity'.

Gender configurations, being patterns of activity, are not static. Masculinity and femininity are 'projects', to use a term suggested by the philosopher Jean-Paul Sartre (1968). They are patterns of a life-course projected from the present into the future, bringing new conditions or events into existence. Simone de Beauvoir's *The Second Sex* (1949) includes a long section that discusses alternative life projects for women as they existed in European society and history. There is likely to be overlap in the gender projects, a degree of social standardization of individual lives. These common trajectories of gender formation are what researchers pick up as patterns of masculinity or femininity in life-history and ethnographic research.

Gender projects are not one-dimensional or smooth, and may involve heavy costs. Any trajectory involves a number of distinct moments in which different gender commitments are made, different strategies are adopted, or different resolutions of gender issues are achieved. This can be seen in the lives of a group of men from the Australian 'green' movement (Connell 1995: ch. 5). Most of them grew up in homes with a conventional gender division of labour, and in childhood and adolescence began to make a commitment to hegemonic masculinity. But this moment of engagement was followed by a moment of negation, as they started to distance themselves from hegemonic masculinity, for a variety of reasons, including family conflict. Most then, in the counter-culture or in the green movement, encountered feminism and were obliged to confront gender issues head-on: this was a moment of separation from hegemonic masculinity. Some were still at this point when we interviewed them. Some, however, had moved on to a moment of contestation, starting a political project of reforming masculinity and committing themselves to gender equality.

The diversity of masculinities and femininities shown by a great deal of gender research implies different trajectories of gender formation. Class inequalities, ethnic diversity, regional difference, national origin and migration create different experiences of childhood. Major social changes may alter relations between parents and children.

The collapse of the Soviet Union and the formation of a new capitalism in the 1990s involved the most dramatic economic decline in recent world history. Jakob Rigi's (2003) heartbreaking ethnography traces the consequences in Kazakhstan. As in other post-Soviet republics, a few powerful families seized control of most public assets. Rich parents could buy both consumer goods and education for their children and find them good jobs in the new economy. However, the majority were thrown into poverty and insecurity. This drove a wedge between working-class parents and children. The parents, for the most part, held to the Soviet-era values of education and the work ethic. Youth, who had already in the late Soviet period been moving towards Western consumerism, saw that the old strategies no longer worked, and, in an environment of disillusion, casual employment and family quarrels, carved out new paths for themselves, which were often sharply gendered. Young men moved into crime or security work (or both), young women into prostitution or jobs where they could trade on their sexuality. A massive commodification of sexuality and collapse of women's rights was a feature of the famous 'transition to democracy'.

The diversity of trajectories is also shown in a British study, Gillian Dunne's *Lesbian Lifestyles* (1997). Some of the women she interviewed served an 'apprenticeship' to conventional femininity, some were tomboys; some grew up in families with a conventional division of labour, some in egalitarian homes. Dunne emphasizes the agency of the girls in responding to these experiences. But she also notes the intractability of the gender order. As they moved into adolescence, where the 'romance' and 'dating' culture ruled, many of the girls found the middle ground in gender relations, which they had previously occupied, disappearing beneath their feet. As one woman, Connie, recalls:

> The whole thing changed, suddenly they became totally different people. I thought what is this thing that happens to everyone else and doesn't happen to me? ... I didn't know how to behave, quite honestly. They all seemed to have this secret code that they all learned, and I didn't. They all knew how to behave at discos, and I would sit pinned to the wall terrified. Where did they learn this? I didn't have it. It was some sort of pattern of social behaviour that everyone fell into, and I didn't have it – God! ... The big 'goo goo' eyes came out, the painted faces, and the frocks, and all that stuff, and the act, the peacock act, basically attracting.

As the gender order changes, new trajectories become possible. In parts of the world influenced by the Women's Liberation movement, young women growing up in the following decades had their own dilemmas about jobs, marriage and children, as can be seen in the stories told in Chilla Bulbeck's three-generation study, *Living Feminism* (1997). But they did not face the same impasse as women of earlier generations. Belief in gender equality has also spread among younger men, in some places. Witness the national study of men in Germany by Paul Zulehner and Rainer Volz (1998), where men below 50 endorse a gender-equal model of family life, and reject 'traditional' norms, much more often than men above 50.

Discourse and identity

Perhaps the commonest way of understanding the presence of gender in personal life is through the concept of 'gender identity'. The term 'identity' shifted meaning during its long history; we pick up the story in the mid-twentieth century, when psychoanalytic insights became the basis of the most influential model of identity. Erik Erikson's famous *Childhood and Society* (1950) interpreted a range of modern personal, social and political problems as difficulties in achieving identity. 'The study of identity, then, becomes as strategic in our time as the study of sexuality was in Freud's time' (Erikson 1950: 242). But where Freud had focused on conflicts involving unconscious agencies of the mind (the 'id' and the 'superego'), Erikson emphasized the conscious agency, the 'ego'. The ego is the mental agency involved in transactions with the outside world, the agency where the conscious sense of self is located.

To Erikson the term 'identity' meant the coherence of the psychological mechanisms by which the ego handles the pressures that impinge on it – from the unconscious mind, on the one side, and the outside world, on the other. The question 'who am I?' is, in principle, answered by the ego's success in mastering the trials and tribulations of psychological development. This was, Erikson thought, a particularly important issue in adolescence.

The key application of this concept to gender was made by the American psychiatrist Robert Stoller (1968), who altered it in two ways. First, the 'core gender identity' that Stoller saw as the basis of adult personality was supposed to be formed very early in life, not in adolescence. Second, the concept of identity acquired a different frame of reference. Erikson referred to the integration of the ego as a whole. Stoller's conception was much more specific. To talk of 'gender identity' is to talk only of one aspect of the person – her or his involvement in gender relations or sexual practice.

To Stoller this narrower focus did not matter because he assumed that the integration of the personality as a whole was largely focused on the sense of being a male or a female. But on any other view of personality and social process, an exclusive focus on gender is a problem. We can speak just as meaningfully of 'racial identity', 'generational identity' or 'class identity'. If we acknowledge the 'constant interweaving' (Bottomley 1992) of these social relations, which is now common in discussions of intersectionality, we must attend to these other forms of identity in order to understand gender identity. The concept of 'gender identity' formulated by Stoller thus leads towards a conception of identity as inherently plural rather than unitary.

A model of identity built on gender dichotomy was easily accepted by the 1970s because American feminist research emphasized gender difference in the rearing of children. Nancy Chodorow in *The Reproduction of Mothering* (1978) linked the gender division of labour, which assigned the task of caring for babies and infants exclusively to women, with the paths of development for girls and boys that resulted from their different emotional situations in early childhood. Girls, brought up by a parent of their own gender, tend to have less distinct ego boundaries. When they grow up they have a stronger motivation for nurturing children. Boys, pushed towards separation from a mother who is responding to the gender distinction, tend to have an earlier discontinuity or break in development. They have more difficulty in establishing gender identity, and stronger boundaries to the self in adulthood.

Though it has been well established that men can 'mother' (Risman 1986), it is still the case that, in contemporary Western society, few of them do. But the reasons for this may be economic rather than psychological. Introducing paid leave for fathers of young children, in Scandinavia, has been a successful reform (Holter 2003). There has also been more recognition – by Chodorow (1994) among others – that we do not find dichotomous gender patterns in adult personalities. That of course was a major conclusion of the 'sex similarity' research discussed in chapter 3.

Variation within gender categories is plain in the recent research on masculinity. In contrast to the way 'the male role' was discussed in the 1970s, it has become common to speak of 'masculinities' in the plural. There is considerable diversity between societies in their constructions of gender for men. This can readily be seen by comparing descriptions of masculinities in Latin America (Gutmann and Viveros 2005), the Middle East (Ghoussoub 2000; Sinclair-Webb 2000) and Southern Africa (Morrell 2001b). There is also considerable evidence that there are multiple masculinities within the same society, even within the same institution, peer group or workplace.

The trend has therefore been to speak of multiple gender and sexual identities. Some psychologists, for instance, have mapped out the stages of acquisition of a 'homosexual identity' (Troiden 1989) as one among a number of possible sexual identities in modern society. The concept of identity has increasingly been used for claims made by individuals about who they are in terms of difference from other people.

This is closely related to the growth, especially in the United States, of identity politics. One becomes a member of a social movement by claiming the identity (as Black, as a woman, as lesbian, etc.) that the movement represents. Queer politics takes the process a step further. Queer activists have challenged taken-for-granted communities by emphasizing their diversity: highlighting the presence of Black lesbians in white-dominated lesbian communities, for instance. Yet the queer movement has, ironically, generated a spectacular new identity, LGBT (lesbian, gay, bisexual, transgender), sometimes expanded by adding TQI (transsexual, queer, intersex) and even others who can be assembled under the umbrella as 'sexual minorities'. LGBT persons, and the LGBT community, are now familiar entities in human rights talk and sexual politics.

Even the identities on which social movements have been based prove, on close examination, to be less solid than we might think. Arne Nilsson's (1998) beautifully crafted study of homosexual history in the Swedish city of Gothenburg identifies three ways of being homosexual: 'so', commonly a bit effeminate; 'real men', often working-class youth; and '*fjollor*', flamboyant queens. Three identities, perhaps? But Nilsson also shows how the patterns of homosexual life grew out of the structure of the industrial and maritime city. Among the conditions shaping sexuality were crowded housing, a sharp gender division of labour, high density of men in public spaces, a non-respectable working-class street life, connections to other cities via the shipping trade, certain patterns of policing, and the poverty of many young men, who might enter homosexual relationships for a period and then move on.

The distinctive forms of homosexual practice changed as these conditions changed. The 1950s saw rising affluence in Sweden, suburban working-class housing, the growth of the welfare state, and moral panics about the seduction of youth. A sharper cultural distinction between heterosexual and homosexual people followed the increasing privacy of sexual conduct itself. Thus the configurations of sexual and social practice which might easily be read as 'identities' were dependent on historically transitory social conditions, and for many participants were only a limited part of their whole sexual life-history.

One wonders, then, whether the term 'identity' for a configuration of gender or sexual practice may be actively misleading. Guy Hocquenghem (1972), one of the most brilliant theorists of Gay Liberation, argued that homosexual desire is in principle inchoate, anarchic, an impersonal flux not a personal unity. Homosexual desire is desire that escapes being 'oedipalized', that is, organized by the patriarchal social order. Homosexuality is, on this argument, the opposite of an identity, being desire and practice that cannot be welded into a unity.

A great deal of heterosexual desire also fails to be 'oedipalized'. Heterosexual desire, too, is often perverse, transitory, unbounded, and pushes against the social authority that constructs fixed positions and bounded identities in a heterosexual order. As Lynne Segal puts it in *Straight Sex* (1994: 254–5): 'Sexual relations are perhaps the most fraught and troubling of all social relations precisely because, especially when heterosexual, they so often threaten rather than confirm gender polarity.' For instance, it is precisely in sex that heterosexual men are most likely to experience dependence, uncertainty, passivity and – quite simply – shared experience with women.

In discursive psychology, the branch of psychology that looks at the way human subjectivities are constituted in culture and discourse, gender identity is not presumed to be a stable pattern of personality at all. It is, rather, a speaking position within a gender discourse, which a person can take up, or abandon, at different times.

Is a unified identity really so desirable? To weld one's personality into a united whole is to refuse internal diversity and openness, perhaps to refuse change. Major reform in gender relations may well require a loss of self, an experience of gender vertigo, as part of the process. This seemed common among the group of men in the Australian 'green' movement who were trying to change traditional masculinity. The American sociologist Barbara Risman (1998) has found a comparable experience in 'fair families' in the United States. But how far can changing gender configurations go? We now turn to the extreme cases recognized in gender studies.

Transition, transgender and transsexual

One of the most dramatic proofs of the importance of social processes in gender, and a familiar disproof of biological essentialism, is the fact that different societies have recognized different gender categories. There are not only women and men; there might also be third genders, or variations on two that seem to multiply the gender categories in which people can live.

This question has intrigued gender researchers, and there is a large ethnographic literature addressed to categories such as the *berdache*, the 'two-souled' people of indigenous cultures in the south-western region of North America (Williams 1986), who have male bodies, a social position closer to that of women than of men, and great spiritual power. Javanese society traditionally provided a space for *banci*, people with male bodies and women's dress who typically have sex with straight men. In Brazil there are *travesti*, often in poverty and making their living as sex workers, who are physically male but feel themselves feminine, and have sex with men within a sexual culture that makes a strong distinction between the insertive and the receptive partner.

These groups are all different from each other, and it is debated whether the idea of a 'third gender' makes sense for any of them. Certainly all such patterns can change, as shown in Thailand. In research by Peter Jackson (1997), the traditional Thai sex/gender categories for males were *phuchai* (man, mainly heterosexual) and *kathoey* (effeminate or cross-gender, receptive homosexual). Under the impact of international gay culture, these categories have not disappeared. Rather, they have been elaborated with a series of additions: *bai* (bisexual), *gay-king* (homosexual, preferring to be insertor), *gay-queen* (usually effeminate, preferring to be receptive) and *gay-quing* (masculine or effeminate, and sexually versatile).

Even within the gender order of the global North, which emphasizes a dichotomy of man and woman, there are opportunities for violating the boundaries, whether in a carnival mood or with great seriousness. A well-known study by Marjorie Garber, *Vested Interests* (1992), finds an astonishing range of cross-dressing practices, in theatre, film, the sex industry, religion, music, detective stories, television ... ranging from Marlene Dietrich's top hat to Boy George's dresses. People who somehow live across gender boundaries, who don't just dip in and out, have intrigued gender analysts within Western culture as much as 'third gender' categories have intrigued ethnographers.

From the earliest days of scientific research on sexuality and gender, such people have appeared in the pages of research monographs as a kind of intriguing monster. Richard von Krafft-Ebing, whose disdainful *Psychopathia Sexualis* (1886) was both a founding text of medico-legal sexology and a considerable under-the-counter best-seller, collected lurid cases of 'mental hermaphroditism'. The genial Havelock Ellis devoted over a hundred pages of his *Studies in the Psychology of Sex* (1928) to 'Eonism', his name for thorough-going gender inversion (after a French aristocrat, the Chevalier d'Eon, who had at different times presented as a man and as a woman). Even the great Sigmund Freud (1911) did it: his discussion of the case of Dr Schreber examines gender-change beliefs as part of an analysis of psychosis.

After psychoanalysis and the social science of gender were well developed, 'transsexuals', as such people came to be called in the 1950s, still appeared to psychiatrists and sociologists as a kind of natural experiment exposing the mechanisms of the gender system. The story of the creation of 'transsexualism' as a medical syndrome, the ambiguous role of doctors, and the controversy within the medical profession has been well told (Meyerowitz 2002; Stryker 2008), and interested readers can find many of the key documents in Susan Stryker and Stephen Whittle's admirable *Transgender Studies Reader* (2006).

With the rise of performative theories of gender there has been great interest in variations in gender and violations of norms. If normative gender is brought into being performatively, then by changing the performative actions, we should be able to create non-normative gender. This line of thought gave rise in the 1990s to a transgender movement influenced by queer theory, mainly in the United States, which has since had considerable impact across the world. This movement emphasized the instability of gender boundaries, rejected the 'binary' of male and female, and tried in various ways to live outside, or beyond, or across, gender categories. Kate Bornstein's *Gender Outlaw: On Men, Women and the Rest of Us* (1994) is perhaps the best-known statement from this movement.

The analysis of gender in the present book suggests an important difference between this transgender movement, focused on the symbolic dimension of gender and trying to break down or blur the symbolic categories of gender, and the projects of transition between locations in the gender order that since about 1950 have been called transsexual. Viviane Namaste in *Invisible Lives* (2000) challenges transgender discourse, urging attention to the real-life experiences, subjectivities and struggles of transsexual men and women that are 'erased' by queer theory as well as by government agencies. Simply accessing healthcare and social services, as Namaste's research in Canada shows, can be very difficult. Yet the state, and the world of institutions more widely, is critically important for transsexual women. Namaste's studies in her important book *Sex Change, Social Change* (2011) show the struggles for recognition and safety that have to be carried on – in prisons, in the media, in universities, in social services, in human rights forums.

The following account is based on the analysis in Raewyn Connell's paper 'Transsexual Women and Feminist Thought' (2012), where more detail will be found. Whereas transgender stories mostly emphasize the fluidity of gender, transsexual autobiographies mostly emphasize gender's stability, indeed its intransigence. This is abundantly clear in the best social-scientific study of gender transition, Henry Rubin's *Self-Made Men* (2003). The gender project, to use the term introduced earlier in this chapter, is consistent over time – however 'wrong' in terms of conventional social embodiment it may be.

Experiences of contradictory embodiment are central in transsexual women's lives. This is well shown in the survey undertaken by Claudine Griggs (1998) as well as autobiographies such as Katherine Cummings' *Katherine's Diary* (1992). Transsexual women describe these experiences in different ways: having a man's body and a woman's body at the same time, or one emerging from the other, or – the traditional one – being trapped in the wrong body. These figures of speech have aroused scorn, but they do highlight the importance of social embodiment. Transsexuality is best understood not as a syndrome nor as a discursive position, but as a bundle of life trajectories that arise from contradictions in social embodiment. Transsexual women's narratives speak of recognition: sometimes a dramatic moment, sometimes a gradually growing awareness, but centrally a matter of recognizing a fact about oneself, that one is a woman despite having a male body.

But this recognizing is a fearful thing, because the central contradiction in transsexuality is so powerful. This fact is totally at odds with what everyone around knows, and with what the transsexual woman knows too, being also recognizable as a man (or boy, since this often happens in youth). And there is no walking away from this terror: gender is intransigent, both as a structure of the society and as a structure of personal life. Some transsexual women try to keep the contradiction inside their skins, and ride out the terror. Some kill themselves; it's not clear how many, but there are high rates of attempted suicide. Moving towards transition is an attempt to end this precarious practice and achieve a settlement.

Because the contradiction is one of embodiment, transition now usually involves modifications to the body with medical aid. This involves a number of procedures: psychiatric screening, hormonal treatment (mainly oestrogen for transsexual women, testosterone for transsexual men), surgery ('top' and 'bottom' in different packages), electrolysis, vocal training, and sometimes others. The process is unavoidably traumatic, as shown in Griggs' (1996) superb narrative of reassignment surgery.

There is nothing pretty about gender reassignment; these are rough measures and have rough results. Though media and scholarly attention have focused obsessively on the surgery, that is only part of the medical treatment, and medical treatment is only part of transition. A huge amount of other work is to be done. This includes raising funds; getting personal support, post-operative care, legal documentation; finding housing; dealing with relationship crises; dealing with a workplace or finding work; dealing with bodily changes; gaining social recognition; and dealing with hostility. Any of these may be uppermost in turn.

This work, as the sociology of gender would lead us to expect, engages all the dimensions of the gender order; it is not only about sexuality or identity. It is structured by the inequalities of the gender order; the process is not the same for transsexual women and transsexual men. Transsexual women are shedding the patriarchal dividend that accrues to men as a group, in labour markets, finance markets (e.g. housing), family status, professional authority, and so on. A small but path-breaking econometric study by Kristen Schilt and Matthew Wiswall (2008) in the United States finds there is an economic penalty in transition for both men and women, but transsexual men eventually are better paid after transition than before, while transsexual women lose, on average, nearly one-third of their income.

A great deal rests on the responses of others. Transition puts partnerships, especially marriages, at acute risk: a wife's position in the gender order is seriously challenged, and may be traumatically undermined, by a husband's moves towards transition. With transsexual women's children, too, relationships may end at transition. Even when they continue, both child and parent have to handle the significant loss that occurs in transition. Gender relations are embodied; here it is embodied fatherhood being lost, and it is not only the transitioning woman who pays the price. These issues have become more prominent in autobiographies, such as the very readable account of transition by Jennifer Boylan (2003). As Boylan's story shows, families can be resilient, and partnerships and parent/child relationships can be re-woven. Indeed family members may be vital supports during transition.

Gatekeepers for jobs and housing have to be negotiated with. According to recent research by Schilt and Wiswall (2008) and Catherine Connell (2010) in the United States, transsexual women have different workplace strategies. Some respond by concealing their stories – the 'stealth' strategy – while others are not only open about their transition, but contest rather than conform to sexist conventions. These studies, however, had mainly middle-class samples. A lot of working-class transsexual women have always survived by sex work. As Harriet (chapter 2) found, there is a certain clientele of straight men who are excited by transsexual women. But this does not mean they respect them. Roberta Perkins' pioneering book presenting the voices of transsexual women in Sydney includes Naomi, a stripper who remarked:

> I think men have a definite dislike for women in general, that's why women are raped and bashed, and strippers are up there to provide an outlet for this dislike by the yelling of profanities at them. Transsexuals are lower down than women according to men, and look how many men sexually abuse transsexuals. (1983: 73)

For that kind of reason, sex work is likely to be a precarious milieu, exposing transsexual women to high levels of HIV infection and violence (Garofalo et al. 2006; Namaste 2009).

In the past, feminists have often held negative views of transsexual women. This is less common now, and some transsexual women are well-recognized feminists. Most transsexual women are not banner-bearers for any cause. Gender transition only happens through severe contradictions in personal life, which can be unbearable, and commonly absorb a great deal of energy simply to hold together. Transsexual lives can be made harder, as Namaste says, by denial of recognition from institutions or movements. Yet in some sense these lives do show the potentials for change that lie in the historical process of social embodiment, and they enrich the project of gender justice that feminism has launched.

7

Gender and environmental change

Today we are witness to an unprecedented period of environmental change. Since the industrial revolution, human populations, predominantly in the global North, have been burning fossil fuels, clearing land and consuming crops and animals at unsustainable rates. These biophysical changes signal that the Earth's ecological and geological systems are shifting out of 10,000 years of relative stability into a much more unstable climate.

Changes in 'Earth system processes' already exceed levels at which the planet can remain stable for humanity to exist into the future (Rockström et al. 2009). Natural scientists tell us that 'planetary limits' have been exceeded on at least three counts: climate change linked to increases in greenhouse gases in the atmosphere; loss of biodiversity and extinctions of species; and disruption of the nitrogen cycle through modern agriculture. We are also approaching boundaries for global freshwater use, change in land use, ocean acidification and interference with the global phosphorus cycle. Nobel prize-winning atmospheric chemist Paul Crutzen and his colleagues have argued that a new name is needed for this new geological era. With the term 'Anthropocene' they have captured the role of humans in propelling this transformation (Crutzen and Stoermer 2000).

Interpretations of what this new era means for society are sobering, and often alarming. Popular intellectuals have warned that climate changes, combined with other forms of environmental degradation, have the potential to disrupt established patterns of social relations profoundly (Lovelock 2006; Lynas 2007). By the end of this century, societies may look very different. Rising sea levels, increased environmental disasters, food and water shortages could lead to large death tolls, and, as resources deplete, to conflict and social instability.

Clearly, the arrival of the Anthropocene challenges our understanding of what it is to be human. Humankind as a whole is threatened, although there are much greater risks to poor people in the global South from environmental change. Across the history of imperialism, ecological disruptions have precipitated social conflicts and social conflicts have damaged environments. Indigenous peoples have been removed from lands they had managed for centuries – to make way for agriculture, urban expansion, mining and other extractive industries, and, ironically, to create conservation areas set up by Northern environmental organizations. Slavery and soil degradation are linked. Poor labour protections for workers are linked to polluting factories in the global South, and these inequalities and displacements are continuing (Merchant 2003).

A growing number of development practitioners make the case that women are particularly vulnerable to the effects of environmental change. This is due to their over-representation amongst those living in poverty, their social role as carers and providers of food, and their labour in agricultural production. So we can say that environmental change is a crisis for all humanity, but its impacts are highly uneven and strongly gendered.

Paying attention to the social causes of ecological crisis also raises questions about gender. Even the term 'Anthropocene' calls for attention. The word *anthropos* in Greek refers to a male human being, though it is also used for all humans, like the term 'mankind'. This invites us to ask about the role that gender plays in driving environmental exploitation.

Are ecological crises shaped by particular elements of gender hierarchies, such as particular masculinities? Is there a distinct role for women to play in social change for sustainability? And do gendered forms of environmental change intersect with class and race, and with the global transformations that have been propelled by colonialism and capital expansion? How does gender play out in the existing responses to crisis – in environmentalism, society and environmental management? Finally, what shifts in gender will be needed to make the transition to an ecologically sustainable society possible?

These questions have been debated by ecofeminist writers and feminist environmentalisms since the 1970s.

Ecofeminism: debating the nature of women

Ecofeminism is not a single theory on gender and the environment, but refers to a variety of perspectives. It has been broadly defined as 'the position that there are important connections between how one treats women, people of color, and the underclass on one hand and how one treats the nonhuman natural environment on the other' (Warren 1997: xi).

Ecofeminism has origins in the 1970s radical environmental movement in Europe, the United States and Australia. The term 'ecofeminism' is often attributed to French feminist writer Françoise d'Eaubonne in her 1974 book, *Le féminisme ou la mort* (Feminism or Death). Chiah Heller used the term 'social ecofeminism', also in 1974 (Biehl 1988; Mellor 1996). Another way to see the arrival of ecofeminism is as a movement that spontaneously developed in several parts of the world during a time when both radical feminism and environmentalism were on the rise (Salleh 1998).

One of the founding intellectuals of Western environmentalism was a woman who called the paradigm of scientific progress into question. Rachel Carson was an American marine biologist and conservationist who left her job in the US Bureau of Fisheries to become a full-time nature writer in the 1950s. She contributed greatly to reshaping concepts of human relationships with nature. Carson's first three books about marine life used notions of the Earth as home and haven, and nature as a mother caring for children, although she did not identify as a feminist writer. With rich examples Carson described the power of industrial fishing to dramatically reduce fish populations. At the same time, she illustrated the resilience of marine ecosystems, offering sophisticated insights into nature and human activity (Norwood 1987).

In her best-selling book *Silent Spring* (1962), Carson argued that synthetic pesticides like DDT, many of which had been developed through the military funding of science since the Second World War, were toxic to ecosystems and human health. The book is written in conversational prose, but filled with scientific data. (Its bibliography runs to over 55 pages.) *Silent Spring* revealed that chemical companies were actively spreading disinformation about the potential risks of pesticides, and brought to light the failings of the scientific establishment and governments charged with protecting human health.

The political impact of Carson's work was profound. A wave of environmental concern filtered through to the broader public, particularly women readers. The book also attracted a great deal of criticism that illustrates the gendered character of contestation over the environment. Carson was accused by corporate and government critics of writing in an emotional tone that played on fear rather than adhering to scientific methods (Oreskes 2004). Media reports persistently commented on her unmarried status in ways that discredited her authority (Corbett 2001). However, the backlash did not impede her intervention. President John

F. Kennedy moved quickly to investigate the risks of pesticides used in agriculture and installed a scientific committee that delivered a report in 1963 that supported her main claims. DDT was banned in 1972.

At the same time, unprecedented numbers of women were engaged in peace and anti-nuclear activism. Extensive nuclear weapons testing began after the Second World War in the United States, the USSR and colonized regions in West Africa, the Indian Ocean and the Pacific, creating public anxieties about nuclear war and contamination. Activists in the metropole began mobilizing in large numbers to oppose nuclear technology as a source of energy and as an instrument of war. In 1961, at the height of the Cold War, about 50,000 women participated in the Women Strike for Peace (WSP) march in 60 cities across the United States. They were demanding a ban on nuclear testing and an end to the Cold War. The WSP used the image of women as a moral force, drawing on traditional ideas of women's rights and responsibilities as mothers.

Placards at the strike read 'Save the Children', 'Testing Damages the Unborn', 'We Strike against Death, Desolation, Destruction and on Behalf of Life and Liberty', and 'Please No More Strontium 90'. (Strontium 90 is a hazardous radioactive isotope produced by nuclear fission, linked to childhood cancer; levels of strontium 90 in mother's milk had risen sharply since the atmospheric testing of nuclear bombs.) The WSP was overwhelmingly made up of white and middle-class women in their mid-thirties to late forties who were college educated and had participated in the workforce during the war period (Swerdlow 1993).

The WSP illustrates how feminists were able to use commonsense ideas about the role of women in reproduction and maternal nurturing as the basis for political power. However, concerns were raised within the movement that this view of women affirmed, rather than contested, patriarchal ideas about women and nature.

American librarian Elizabeth Gould Davis' book *The First Sex* (1972) was an early and influential example of feminist work that drew on ideas of female/male difference when discussing environmental problems. Davis argued that masculine power was the driving force behind environmental pollution and proposed that women were leaders of a potential new ecologism. Her description of masculinity and femininity is stark:

Man is the enemy of nature: to kill, to root up, to level off, to pollute, to destroy are his instinctive reactions to the unmanufactured phenomena of nature, which he basically fears and distrusts. ... Woman, on the other hand, is the ally of nature, and her instinct is to tend, to nurture, to encourage healthy growth, and to preserve ecological balance. She is the natural leader of society and of civilization, and the usurpation of her primeval authority by man has resulted in uncoordinated chaos. (Davis 1972: 335–6)

Mary Mellor (1996) calls this kind of reasoning about women and nature 'affinity ecofeminism'. The basis of women's power was often understood as a physiological and psychological connection with nature. Women are assumed to understand the workings of nature on the basis of their reproductive functions or an innate tendency towards nurturing and caring personalities.

Andrée Collard, a Belgian-born American feminist, wrote a book that is one of the best-known examples of direct affinity claims. In the *Rape of the Wild: Man's Violence against Animals and the Earth*, Collard (with Contrucci, 1989) argued that under patriarchy as a social order, nature, animals and women are objectified, owned and subject to male control over their reproductive systems. Men act on the basis of false beliefs in their 'natural' superiority compared to women and in men's separation from nature. As a counterpoint, Collard proposed women were a social class that modelled an alternative and more sustainable relationship to nature. The source of this agency was biological, according to Collard, who wrote that a woman's reproductive system enables her to 'share the experience of bringing forth and nourishing life with the rest of the living world' (Collard with Contrucci 1989: 102).

Feminist spirituality is a related theme, combining arguments about the connection between women and nature with the practice of alternate feminist spirituality. Feminist theologians and scholars of religion drew on old myths and legends as well as archaeological evidence to demonstrate the celebration of women's fertility and sexuality in ancient times (e.g. Daly 1973; Reed 1975; Stone 1976).

The American feminist theologian Mary Daly (see chapter 4) is the best-known author in this vein. She sought to reclaim women's spirituality from patriarchal theology. In her book *Beyond God the Father* (1973) Daly described patriarchal domination carried through Christian myths and symbols, such as the idea of 'original sin' committed when Eve and Adam disobeyed God in the Garden of Eden. Eve was tricked by the serpent into eating the forbidden fruit and then she gave some of the fruit to Adam to eat too. It is believed that when they did this they fell from perfection and brought evil into a perfect world. Some Christians believe that original sin explains the existence of war, conflict and immorality in the world, and why people need to have their souls 'saved' by God. Daly argues that this myth perpetuates ongoing social realities for women, who internalize blame for modem 'sins' in society such as sexism (1973: 48–9).

In *Gyn/Ecology* (1978) Daly elaborated her critique of patriarchal religion by extending her analysis to practices such as widow burning in India, foot binding in China, and female genital mutilation in Northern Africa. Daly's invented term 'gyn/ecology' is a nod to d'Eaubonne's 'ecofeminism', and combines the idea of interconnection between organisms and their environment with the critique of gynaecology (a branch of scientific medicine, mainly created by men, treating diseases particular to women). Daly says gyn/ecology is a process of developing understanding and articulating women's knowledge about and for themselves. As an alternative to patriarchal myths, Daly argued for a new form of feminist spirituality that could replace masculine symbolism and practices. She described it as including a less exploitative relationship to nature where 'we will look upon the earth and her sister planets and their being *with* us, not *for* us' (Daly 1973: 178).

There are significant criticisms of these early ecofeminist works, as there have been of other feminist theories, concerning race, sexuality and class within the gender order (see chapter 4). Davis was criticized by many, particularly Black feminists, for omitting Black women's history (Mellor 1996). American feminist poet and essayist Adrienne Rich suggested that Davis was engaged in 'myth making' about a universal matriarchy that preceded modern society, and that her book contained historical and analytical inaccuracies (Rich 1976: 86–93). Caribbean-American writer and civil rights activist Audre Lorde made similar arguments in a letter to Mary Daly in 1984. Lorde was responding to *Gyn/Ecology*, and argued that Daly generalized too much about women and created 'myths' about women of colour.

Few ecofeminists then agreed with the strong claims about women's biological affinity with nature, and almost none do so now. However, the criticisms of patriarchal social relations and their simultaneous oppression of women and nature are more widely shared.

Another current of affinity ecofeminism is focused less on the 'natural' basis for women's agency and more on social dynamics linking women and nature. Feminist theorists writing in this vein argue that gendered power over nature is real, but is social and dynamic rather than biologically fixed. Women's understanding of nature is based on their experience of exploitation, which is always changing across different places and historical moments.

For instance, Françoise d'Eaubonne (1974) drew on Marxist as well as feminist theory. She argued that patriarchal control over women's sexuality produced two interconnected crises: surplus production through commercialized agriculture; and overpopulation enforced by patriarchal religious institutions (she took particular issue with the Catholic church).

In a similar vein, Carolyn Merchant in *The Death of Nature* (1980) maintained that 'capitalist patriarchy' was the underlying cause of environmental problems. Men take part in the public sphere of commodification and women in the domestic sphere of unpaid labour. It is the public sphere of production that alienates us humans from nature as it transforms, degrades and pollutes ecosystems. Merchant's feminist history also illustrates that the type of rationality developed in the seventeenth-century European scientific revolution reflects masculine ideals.

How society could change to sustainable social organization was a tricky problem for these social ecofeminist writers. D'Eaubonne (1980) argued that 'patriarchal man' must be replaced with an egalitarian, environmentally sustainable process of provisioning, and that we need a 'planet in the female gender'. At another point, however, she was careful to say that 'power-to-women' was not a satisfactory alternative to patriarchy. An egalitarian sustainable society would need to be non-gendered.

What green societies, which are non-capitalist and non-patriarchal, could look like is debated within feminist circles working in Marxist and anarchist traditions. Anarchist ecofeminist Ynestra King was open about the political usefulness of pursuing a brand of affinity politics. King agreed that in patriarchal society women were ideologically presented as being closer to nature. Women could choose to foster this connection as an alternate political project that would bridge the gendered dualisms of nature and culture, spirit and matter, reason and intuition (King 1981). Carolyn Merchant (1980) tried to avoid pure social construction in her work. She proposed an expanded definition of reproduction to include the biological and social reproduction of human and nonhuman life.

The themes in these early debates are still relevant. By the 1980s, ecofeminism had become a 'fighting word' (Seager 2003). Heated debates blazed over the image of the Goddess and all variants of affinity claims. In this same decade, a new wave of economic globalization saw the expansion of environmentally destructive industries into new areas of social and ecological life, particularly in the global South. These problems were met with new movements opposing harmful development projects and capital expansion.

Feminist environmentalists in the South reinvigorated discussions about the nature of ecological crisis and the prospects for global environmental justice. Global environmental justice is defined in different ways by various social movement groups and official organizations. A common starting point is recognizing that environmental harms impact the poor, people of colour, women, indigenous and other minority groups most seriously. Feminist scholars, often from the global South, have debated the precise causes and impacts of global environmental *in*justice.

In this discussion, the affinity debate has continued. These discussions have extended feminist engagements with post-colonial and Marxist theories of underdevelopment and uneven development.

Gender, development and environmental justice

When the Ok Tedi gold mine in Papua New Guinea (PNG) was under construction in 1982, the tailings dam failed, and mining company BHP sent the poisonous mine waste directly into the creeks that run into the Ok Tedi and Fly Rivers, the main water system of south-western PNG. By the year 2000, more than 250 tonnes of waste had flowed into the rivers, contaminating drinking water and local agriculture and killing the forests along the flood plain. The contamination was disastrous for the Yonggom people living downstream.

BHP attempted to pull out of the project following revelations of the scale of the impacts, but at the behest of the PNG government the mine was kept open. For most of the 70,000 people living along the Ok Tedi and Fly Rivers, compensation has become the main source of income. In the long negotiation over community compensation for the continuation of Ok Tedi mine, women's groups have a seat at the table and have had some success in achieving compensation and benefits.

Two years after the Ok Tedi contamination, the worst industrial accident the world has ever seen occurred at the Union Carbide pesticide plant in Bhopal, India. During the night of 2 December 1984, toxic gas leaked from the plant and killed 7,000–10,000 people and injured or disabled up to 200,000 others. Poor communities in shanty towns nearby were some of the hardest hit by this disaster, which has created a long legacy of ill health, environmental contamination and disadvantage for victims. Women's organizations have been the largest groups representing victims in legal proceedings and nonviolent demonstrations. The struggle continues. Today, 30 years later, 350 tonnes of untreated toxic waste remains inside the plant.

These zones of industrial contamination in the global South are dramatic examples of a larger environmental crisis spreading across the world from the 1980s. Transnational corporations, facilitated by host governments, began a rapid process of installing mass industrial centres, building 'mega' hydroelectric dams, and digging huge holes to retrieve minerals. Much of this has happened in post-colonial societies where cheap labour is plentiful and social protections are minimal compared to most areas of the global North.

Significant social transformations are bound up with these environmental changes, often with gendered effects. For example, polluted or depleted aquatic ecosystems and forests can create economic stress and health risks for women, who are often responsible for gathering water and firewood. In locations like south-western PNG and Bhopal, transnational social movement networks emerged to fight for justice, and local women's groups were key participants in the struggles. These groups make claims on both transnational corporations and home governments. In negotiating environmental justice in contexts like these, women in the South are challenging gender structures on multiple scales.

Debates arose over how to understand these events in the global South. The most famous feminist environmental activist and writer giving voice to movements for environmental justice is Vandana Shiva from India. Shiva left a career as a nuclear physicist in order to campaign against ecologically destructive industries arriving in the South under the rubric of development. In her book *Staying Alive* (1989), Shiva described a process of 'maldevelopment'. Maldevelopment is the North's imperialist imposition of 'modernity' and capitalist expansion on the global South. It is justified by ideologies of economic growth and scientific knowledge. A key example of maldevelopment in Shiva's writing and activism is the expansion of industrial agriculture, where monocultures and genetically modified seeds owned by global corporations replace traditional farming techniques and create loss of diversity in plant and animal life as well as human cultures.

Shiva's critique of development and call for global environmental justice is feminist. She argues maldevelopment is violence against nature and women 'built into the very mode of perceiving both, and forms the basis of the current development paradigm' (Shiva 1989: xvi). She also argues that a new source of male–female inequality is the worldview of development economists, who define development in terms of participation in the male-dominated sphere of commercial production. Shiva was influenced by German sociologist Maria Mies in making this argument.

Mies' book *Patriarchy and Accumulation on a World Scale* (1986) used the metaphor of an iceberg for the global economy. Icebergs are huge pieces of floating ice that have broken off from glaciers. Only one ninth of an iceberg's full mass is usually visible above water. For Mies, the iceberg tip is the visible economy of capital and wage labour. Below the water in the invisible economy is housework, labour performed in unregulated informal sectors, work in the colonies, and the 'work' of nature (Mies 1986: xi). Although invisible in the formal model of the economy, the productive and reproductive capacities of women, people in the global South and nature constitute the base of the whole.

Shiva and Mies argue that these economic relations symbolically and materially exclude and threaten women's subsistence practices. As a counter-project, they have put forward a 'subsistence perspective' that connects political and spiritual aspects of sustainability (Mies and Bennholdt-Thomsen 1999; Mies and Shiva 1993). Shiva draws on the concept of *prakriti* (nature) and *Shakti* (the feminine) drawn from ancient Indian cosmology. She calls for a return to the 'feminine principle' – a 'category of challenge which locates nature and women as the source of life and wealth, and, as such, active subjects, maintaining and creating life-processes' (Shiva 1989: 46). The feminine principle is not exclusively the domain of women, rather a broader idea of activity and creativity in nature. Shiva states it is a 'non-patriarchal, non-gendered category of creative non-violence' (1989: 52).

Australian ecofeminist Ariel Salleh uses similar ideas in her work, which is best described as feminist ecological Marxism. Salleh (1998) argues that people located in the peripheries of the global economy are a potential source of social change. For Salleh, the agents of history in the era of global ecological crisis are 'meta-industrial workers' a previously unnamed class that performs reproductive labour at the interface of humanity and nature (Salleh 2000). She describes meta-industrial workers as operating outside of capitalism. They are peasants, gatherers and parents in the global South. Salleh draws on examples from indigenous cultures in Australia and elsewhere. She states their practices create a good 'metabolic fit' between human growth and ecological growth (Salleh 2010: 212). Salleh draws on statements made by social movement coalitions that mirror these ideas. However, there are few signs of a shared identity and social base to bring her vision alive.

Australian environmental philosopher Val Plumwood took up themes of Western imperialism, gender, race and class in more cultural terms. Plumwood was involved in Australian forest movements in the 1970s and 1980s. Her intellectual work dealt with the ethics of humanity's relationship to nature. In a well-read book titled *Feminism and the Mastery of Nature* (1994), she argued that nature needed to be incorporated as a fourth category of analysis in feminist theory addressing race, gender and class. She also argued that Western culture has produced a 'hyper separation' of nature and humanity. Dualism is the central mechanism for domination of nature and the Other. Plumwood uses the same fundamental argument as Shiva and Mies, that domination is produced through the master rationality of Western culture. Plumwood's work, however, has value in illuminating the instrumental rationalities creating nature, women and subaltern classes as Other (see also Plumwood 2002). Instrumental rationality assumes that nonhuman systems should serve human society's purposes. Not only does this justify destructive behaviour towards nonhuman animals and ecosystems, it also neglects the intrinsic value in nonhuman nature.

The material bases for sustainability are less clearly stated in Plumwood's work than in that of Shiva and Mies. She points to 'social formations built on radical democracy, co-operation and mutuality' but identifies no geographical or political sources of agency (Plumwood 1994: 196). The overall emphasis from Plumwood is on the battle of ideas.

These new more global claims about a common connection to nature, and collective agency for women and others in the global South, have also been questioned. In a UN-funded book called *Women, the Environment and Sustainable Development* (1994), Rosi Braidotti and colleagues argue that Shiva and Mies are overly critical of Western institutions and less so towards traditional cultures and economics. Indian economist Bina Agarwal wrote a widely cited article called 'The Gender and Environment Debate: Lessons from India' (1992). She called for attention to relations of power, privilege and property, before colonial rule as well as after. Agarwal argues that the role of imperialism in producing gendered environmental inequalities is exaggerated in the work of Shiva, King, Merchant and Salleh.

To avoid sweeping generalizations about Women (including Third World Women), Agarwal argues, a more detailed account of the material sources of dominance over women and nature is needed. While colonial rule clearly disrupted environmental and social stability, the gender division of labour already existing in pre-colonial societies remains important in the historical lineage of environmental change. Agarwal's rich empirical work (see also chapter 4), most fully presented in the book *A Field of One's Own* (1994), involves numerous case studies across India that illustrate how the women/environment link is mediated through structures of class, caste, race and ethnicity over time. Further, different combinations of state control over forest land and increased private ownership shape the gender effects of environmental degradation in post-colonial nations.

Agarwal has skilfully demonstrated ways to clarify the complexity of gender/race/class relations in environmental change with her empirical political-economy approach. The political project she proposed is 'feminist environmentalism'. Political action, in her view, should be based on 'struggles over resources *and* meanings', based on understanding the material and specific character of women's and men's relationship to nature (Agarwal 1992: 126–7).

Gender and environmental management

As environmental problems have commanded the world's attention, the range and complexity of government regulations to 'manage' or 'solve' environmental problems have escalated. For instance, at the Rio Earth Summit of 1992, three separate United Nations Conventions on Biodiversity, Desertification and Climate Change were created. Each of these conventions is now a huge process of negotiation between nation-states who meet each year to negotiate policy frameworks, environmental targets, timetables for action, and North–South burden-sharing arrangements.

Parallel to transnational politicking, new industries for 'green' products have arrived to meet public and consumer demand for sustainable energy, transport and consumables. Energy-saving light bulbs, organic foods, recycled paper, bio-degradable cleaning products, and more, now line supermarket shelves. Markets for energy alternatives like wind and solar technology, as well as more questionably sustainable sources like biofuels, gas and nuclear energy, have all grown in response to environmental regulation and public pressure. Finally, public policy has itself produced new markets that change nature–society relations. Derivative markets for trade in 'ecosystem services', and 'carbon markets' (effectively trade in pollution permits), have grown rapidly in the last 20 years.

The arrival of global institutions for environmental management is a transformation in both understandings of sustainability and distributions of power. A new workforce of environmental managers now inhabit government and intergovernmental institutions like the World Bank and the Intergovernmental Panel on Climate Change, as well as corporations and environmental advocacy organizations. These experts have been trained through specialist degree programmes in environmental and development economics, science, law, management and engineering.

Michael Goldman (1998), a sociologist who has done extensive ethnographic work in the World Bank, argues that this elite takes a managerial and technocentric approach to global environmental problems, and so has contributed to significant changes in how ecology–society relations are understood and acted upon. For instance, a shift in thinking about land in the South is evident. Expert reports use scientific and economic models to describe land in terms of its global ecological function. The Amazon has become the 'lungs of the Earth' in need of protection; 'World Heritage Areas' have been declared through international law for the global common good. The reform agenda from 'commons professionals' is routinely used to establish property rights over environmental resources, land enclosure for conservation, and public policy for population control.

A small but growing number of gender theorists have contributed to our understanding of global environmental management. Political scientist Karen Litfin (1997) formulated a feminist critique of the way power operates through scientific knowledge and policy paradigms. She was particularly interested in the increasing use of earth satellite observations for environmental monitoring in the 1990s. The heightened awareness of global climate change prompted the United States to invest heavily in atmospheric monitoring technologies (but not in technologies to reduce greenhouse gas emissions). Litfin criticized the assumption that scientific knowledge is neutral and the source of rational policy choices (1997: 33–4). Echoing ecofeminists such as Joni Seager (1993), she argued that the planetary gaze of satellite technology reflects masculine ideals of rationality and objectivity towards nature. This develops the line of thought begun by Merchant.

The new global data on greenhouse gas emissions have created a hierarchy of knowledge about environmental change that separates environmental management from social experience (see also Jasanoff 1994, 2010). Data about biophysical and chemical properties of the Earth supersede knowledge of local social processes where people are both the cause and object of change. In practice, the science-based way of knowing the Earth does not solve existing conflicts over responsibility for global environmental change. A key example is a dispute between environmental NGOs over the way emissions data are reported. The Washington-based World Resources Institute published a report on national greenhouse emissions (WRI 1990). The figures for national greenhouse accounts established that China, India and Brazil were in the top five nations responsible for climate change. Indian researchers Anil Argarwal and Sunita Narain criticized these claims in a counter-report titled *Global Warming in an Unequal World* (1991). They used the same figures to show that when emissions are recorded over time, and on a per person basis, Western nations still have primary responsibility. Agarwal and Narain argued that the WRI report falsely equated 'survival emissions' of the poor with 'luxury emissions' of the rich.

British social scientist Sherilyn MacGregor (2009: 128) argues that the new hegemonic approach to climate change signals a gendered political transformation, a 'masculinization of environmentalism'. Climate change is understood as a techno-scientific problem best addressed through technological innovation, and increasingly as a *security* issue that may require militarized responses. MacGregor argues that environmentalism was once a 'soft' political issue, but it has become 'hardened' by threats to global social order predicted by experts and decision-makers on climate change – who are most often men.

Some new research illuminates gender dynamics in elite climate politics in more detail. Canadian Marxist geographer Scott Prudham (2009) has looked at the British billionaire entrepreneur Richard Branson as an example of the 'green capitalist'. Green capitalism refers to an ideological belief that environmental problems can be resolved within the 'free

market', by market-based programmes, enclosure of land for conservation, capital investment and entrepreneurial innovation. Branson's very
public communications and actions perform this worldview. His public
identity is splashy and ambitious. Advertisements for Branson's travel
company often involve sexuality and are widely known for masculinized
and (hetero)sexualized themes, as in advertisements featuring men ogling
Virgin corporation's flight attendants, or Branson himself surrounded by
attractive women. In 2012, a subsidiary firm in the Virgin group was
criticized for making light of rape in an advertisement featuring a man
presenting a surprise present to a woman. A text caption on screen read:
'The gift of Christmas surprise. Necklace? Or chloroform?'

Branson's recent green efforts signal the fusion of capitalist entrepren-
eurialism and environmentalism. Branson was knighted in 2000 for
'services to entrepreneurship'. In September 2006 he pledged approxi-
mately £1.6 billion of his profits from Virgin air and rail interests to
develop alternative fuels made from plant products (often food products
like corn, sugar, soy and palm oil). In 2007 he announced the 'Virgin
Earth Challenge', a $25 million prize for researchers who develop tech-
nologies to 'remove' greenhouse gases from the atmosphere. In 2010 he
held a 'Creating Climate Wealth' conference and launched a 'Carbon
War Room' website. Both brought together business leaders to 'acceler-
ate profitable, entrepreneurial solutions that reduce carbon emissions at
gigaton level'. The vision is global, and in some ways the faith in entre-
preneurialism to steer a global environmental response is a departure
from the state-funded managerialism criticized by Litfin in the late 1990s.

Prudham (2009) argues that Branson's initiatives reflect an underlying
contradiction of green capitalism. More sustainable futures cannot be
secured within a growth-based economy. The methods of emissions
management in which Branson and his network invest are controversial.
They are an 'end of pipe' approach to pollution. That is, they target
environmental problems after they have arisen, and do nothing about
their causes, such as unsustainable production and consumption. There
is concern amongst environmentalists that these technologies at best will
not work, and at worst will create additional environmental and social
impacts. Vast areas of forests and agricultural land are being cleared to
farm biofuels in the South. The application of biochar (charcoal) to soils
on a large scale is now being debated as a means to increase carbon
sequestered in the land. This may lead to displacement of rural communities, and there is inadequate knowledge about the long-term effects on
land ecosystems.

The Branson case illustrates the ways entrepreneurial subjects contribute to the cultural legitimation of capitalism. 'Entrepreneurial subject' is
a term used to describe the type of identity associated with neoliberalism.

The role of business leaders in addressing social and environmental problems is celebrated much more now than it was in the mid-twentieth century. Prudham (2009) extends his ecological Marxist framework to include ideas from gender and cultural theory. Drawing on Judith Butler (1990) and Donna Haraway (1997), he argues that green capitalism is constituted by interwoven material–semiotic dimensions. Central to the normalization of green capitalism are the iterative 'performances' of the entrepreneurial subject as an environmental crusader. Branson and other celebrity entrepreneurs perform an 'already-existing, virulent, muscular neoliberal, masculinist subjectivity reworked to fit the green capitalist agenda' (Prudham 2009: 1607).

Expressions of masculinity in environmental politics are not fixed, as Martin Hultman (2013) shows in his case study of former Hollywood action man turned green Governor, Arnold Schwarzenegger. Hultman uses the biography of Schwarzenegger to comment on parallel changes in environmental politics and hegemonic masculinities. Across the star's film career, there has been a shift from highly violent and barely verbal 'cowboy' parts to roles that include strong elements of compassion and care (consider *The Terminator* versus *Kindergarten Cop*). In his political career in California, Schwarzenegger installed a market-based policy for greenhouse gas emissions and promoted green technological innovation, including funding to develop biofuels and hydrogen fuel cell technology for vehicles. Yet the film star is famous for driving a petrol-guzzling Hummer, which has become a symbol of consumer excess and American masculinity. Hultman (2013: 88) argues that Schwarzenegger's version of green 'ecomodern masculinity' combines values of economic growth with sustainability in the same way his movie roles began combining violence and caring themes.

These examples illustrate that elite responses to environmental crisis reflect continuities as well as change in the gender order (see also Alston 2011; Hemmati and Röhr 2009; Wamukonya and Skutsch 2002). Hegemonic masculinities are central in the contestation over global environmental change and the prospect of energy transition. Gender research into environmental politics shows that a masculine God-like view of the global problem has merged into technocratic, marketized 'solutions' to environmental crisis.

Continuing the search for feminist sustainability

The project of gender theory about the environment is not just critique; it is to build forms of knowledge that can revise and displace the current forms of environmental management. In her essay on global environmental knowledge, Karen Litfin did not conclude with a call for ecofeminist localism. She warns against the uncritical deployment of science, but notes that environmentalists, women and indigenous groups are seeking to integrate their knowledges with earth science, and so reclaim environmental science from a white male elite (Litfin 1997: 41–3).

Feminists have made a number of different responses to technocentric and market-oriented environmental management. Gender research about, and sometimes for, environmental management has diversified considerably. In just about every field of environmental concern – including food crises, community forestry, fisheries and disaster responses – there have been attempts to measure gender impacts and to 'mainstream' gender into policy. Feminist ecological economics is a fledgeling discipline seeking to bring alternative valuation methods into economic models (Nelson 1997, 2008; Power 2004).

Quantitative social science has produced evidence that greenhouse gas emissions per person are lower in nations where women have higher political status. Nations with higher proportions of women in Parliament are more likely to ratify environmental treaties than other nations (Ergas and York 2012). Dealing with the gendered impacts of climate change is now an established field for development practitioners, who have made some progress towards gender-sensitive climate policies (see Masika 2002; Terry 2009).

New frontiers of gender theory in the global North concern questions about nature. Donna Haraway, a pioneering US scholar of science and technology studies, has written a number of texts bringing together science and feminism, including her creative and much-debated essay called 'A Manifesto for Cyborgs: Science, Technology, and Socialist Feminism in the 1980s' (1987). Haraway proposed the cyborg (a cybernetic organism that is hybrid machine and organism) as an identity for feminist eco-socialism that is capable of subverting dualisms of domination: human/machine, nature/culture, subject/object, and so on. Her concern is to transcend political identification with Mother Earth and to subvert the ideas in women's movements about a return to an original unity with nature or universalized claims about 'women's experience'.

Haraway argues that the cyborg is a creature of fiction *and* a social reality of the 1980s: 'Late-twentieth-century machines have made thoroughly ambiguous the difference between natural and artificial, mind and body, self-developing and externally designed, and other distinctions that used to separate organisms and machines. Our machines are disturbingly lively, and we ourselves frighteningly inert' (1987: 5). She describes the cyborg as a creature of the non-gendered world and the 'illegitimate offspring of militarism and patriarchal capitalism' (1987: 4). Rather than taking an oppositional stance to technoscience, Haraway explores the possibilities of embracing technology, and argues that seeing ourselves as machines may enliven greater responsibility. The cyborg's field of action is the material (social-natural) world. Haraway and those who have followed her seek to build a theory of gender and the nonhuman that establishes a hybrid but monistic understanding of the world.

A field of feminist theory has recently emerged in the global North called 'new materialism' (Coole and Frost 2010), or 'material feminisms' (Alaimo and Hekman, 2008). Scholars in this field consider that their approach takes nonhuman matter and its agency in shaping 'social' life and gender more seriously than previous feminist theories did. In her book *The Nick of Time*, Elizabeth Grosz wrote: 'Biology does not limit social, political, and personal life: it not only makes them possible, it ensures that they endlessly transform themselves and thus stimulate biology into further self-transformation' (2004: 1). American political philosopher Jane Bennett uses similar language to convey connection between the human and nonhuman world. Her book *Vibrant Matter: A Political Ecology of Things* (2010) seeks to account for the active agency of nonhuman matter. In her words, materiality 'is a rubric that tends to horizontalize the relations between humans, biota, and abiota' (Bennett 2010: 112). Put more simply, new materialism tries to avoid being anthropocentric by seeing the nonhuman and human as equally important in shaping our experience. Its proponents criticize feminist theories that arguably produce a division and hierarchy between the human and nonhuman worlds.

Lena Gunnarsson (2013) argues that these works overemphasize the dynamic and unbounded qualities of nature. She claims that they overlook the constraining effects of biophysical properties on gender and other social relations. Global climate change is an important example of an environmental limit. The capacity of the Earth to absorb or balance out our fossil fuel emissions is being tested. If we continue along this trajectory, major species extinction is likely, and human development will be undermined. Overall, we can say that material feminist theory revives attention to the nonhuman world at an important point in history. However, this tradition has little to say about the political aspects of reorganizing society and the gender order so as to live within the Earth's limits.

Perhaps the best work in this field is research where feminist materialism is combined with analysis of green political projects and movements. Feminist economic geographers Kathy Gibson and the late Julie Graham wrote together under the name J.K. Gibson-Graham in a project theorizing alternatives to capitalist development. They described their intellectual work as 'deconstructing existing local economies to reveal a landscape of radical heterogeneity' (Gibson-Graham 2011: 2). In their book *The End of Capitalism (As We Knew It)* (2011), Gibson-Graham argued that global capitalism is not a given. What we understand as a capitalist system is in fact an assemblage of capitalist and non-capitalist enterprises, various forms of finance and property relations, and market and non-market relations.

In their last article written together, Gibson-Graham outlined a feminist economic ethics of belonging in the time of the Anthropocene, as discussed at the beginning of this chapter. Investigating non-capitalist social relations is the other side to their deconstructionist method. For Gibson-Graham, deconstruction is a 'reading practice' that criticizes all theories that assume binary oppositions such as human/nonhuman, man/woman, masculinity/femininity. They describe their work as applying 'a feminist political imaginary' to environmental social practices in order to discover new 'assemblages that are experimenting with new practices of living and being together' (Gibson-Graham 2011: 4). They use academic research methods to record and facilitate local sustainable economies. They use local initiatives (employee-owned businesses that contribute to local sustainability, and alternative currency projects in the United States, and a local fresh produce co-operative in Australia) to illustrate connection to the nonhuman world and alternative development pathways.

Feminist studies on environmental problems show that gender is inexorably part of environmental change. Critiquing and transcending modern science and its claims to be value-neutral has been a focus for feminists in the North and South. Feminists concerned with maldevelopment and colonialism have revealed the connections among gender, capitalism and imperialism in producing environmental problems, on local and global scales. Influential theorists in this field draw on perspectives from the global South and variants of ecological Marxism and social ecology.

In the new millennium, there is even greater need for gender understandings of environmental change. Gendered patterns of power are visible in new global environmental management and the new influence of wealthy entrepreneurs. The increasing intensity and scale of environmental problems point to the challenge of understanding human societies in relation to the nonhuman world. This is a challenge for social theory in general. Feminist environmental philosophers and cultural theorists have been working creatively to integrate the nonhuman into our understandings of the gendered world.

8

Economies, states and global gender relations

Most discussions of gender concern the personal, such as identities, motherhood, child rearing, family life, and sexuality; and the pathologies of personal life, such as prejudice, domestic violence and rape. To understand personal relations, as we saw in chapter 6, we must take into account institutions, economies, ideologies and governments. Chapter 5 set out a way of understanding the structures of gender relations: they are multidimensional, they take shape as gender regimes and gender orders, they are open to change and become the focus of politics and social contestation. These features are found in organizations as well as personal life. This chapter examines corporations, states and the global economy, showing how we can understand gender relations and their politics on the largest scale.

Gendered corporations

The corporation is the key institution of developed capitalism. There were 7.4 million corporations in the United States in 2010, according to taxation statistics. Most were small, but more than 2,000 held assets of $2.5 billion or more each. Transnational corporations are the main players in the international economy. The biggest have workforces in the hundreds of thousands, such as Toyota with 331,000 workers in 2013. They have profits (and sometimes losses) in the tens of billions, such as Exxon Mobil with $44.9 billion profit in 2012; and annual revenues bigger than the entire national product of small countries.

Corporations are gendered institutions, with a gendered history. 'Companies' of merchants in early modern Europe were entirely composed of men. When ownership began to be divided up and became itself a kind of commodity, with the creation of joint-stock companies and the first stock exchanges in the seventeenth and eighteenth centuries, these too were socially defined as men's institutions.

The gendered character of corporations only came into focus in the wake of the Women's Liberation movement, when the new feminism challenged organization theory. The change is marked by the work of Rosabeth Kanter in the United States, whose *Men and Women of the Corporation* appeared in 1977. Kanter criticized the absence of gender awareness in organization research, and showed how gender issues mattered, even for the minority of women who did make it into the corporate hierarchy.

Over the next three decades, social research on corporate life built up. Some of the studies have already been mentioned· Hochschild's (1983) research on 'emotion work' in airlines and debt agencies; and Pringle's (1989) study of secretaries. Some of the best research has focused on manual workers in large-scale industries.

The sociologist Miriam Glucksmann (using the pen-name Ruth Cavendish) wrote a wonderful account of British factory life in *Women on the Line* (1982). This was based on seven months' participant observation in a motor vehicle component assembly plant, and gives a vivid picture of the corporate hierarchy, daily life on the shop floor, and the connections with home life. There was a rigid gender division of labour in this plant. Women were employed in the low-paid routine jobs only, their promotion was blocked, while men could get twice the wage for doing easier jobs. 'It was obvious that the only qualification you needed for a better job was to be a man.' The women were disillusioned about men, and supported each other in daily conflicts with male supervisors. But their poverty, fatigue, household demands, and the gender segregation of working-class life made effective organizing almost impossible.

Gender divisions are also strong in corporate agriculture, which is now transforming rural life across the world. A fascinating oral history study in Chile by Heidi Tinsman (2000) describes the export-oriented fruit industry created under the Pinochet dictatorship. The companies engaged in this business recruited women workers on a large scale. But the consequences were not as expected. Rural women's command of an income and ability to make shopping trips and purchasing decisions changed the balance of power with husbands. The segregated work groups created by the employers provided an alternative to domestic isolation, and led to new relationships among women. In both ways the process eroded the dictatorship's official ideology, which defined women basically as mothers.

As this research built up, a theory of gendered organizations emerged in the work of Joan Acker in the United States, Peta Tancred in Canada, Claire Burton in Australia, and British researchers such as the Collinsons and Jeff Hearn. The writing of this school is collected in Mills and Tancred's book *Gendering Organizational Analysis* (1992). The key idea was that gender discrimination is not an accidental feature of bureaucracy, which can be fixed by changing a few attitudes. Gender is a structural feature of corporate life, linked to gender relations in other sectors of society. Gender shapes job definitions, understandings of 'merit' and promotion, management techniques, marketing and a whole lot more.

The analysis of gender in workplaces has become steadily more sophisticated since those beginnings. There is increasing attention to the extent of unintentional gendering, and the dynamic character of gender in personal interactions within organizations (Martin 2006). Sylvia Gherardi and Barbara Poggio (2001) provide a telling example in their study of Italian corporations. Women were arriving at a management level here. But as they did, a 'dance' of adjustment and compromise occurred, and the gender order seemed to close around them.

In the United States significant numbers of women have now reached middle management, and there is endless discussion of the 'glass ceiling' which prevents their getting into top-level management. In 1991 the US Congress set up a 21-person Glass Ceiling Commission to investigate the problem. They found that among the biggest corporations in the United States at the time, 97 per cent of senior managers were white, and 95 to 97 per cent were men. Of the top 1,000 companies, two had women CEOs. This was thought to be progress.

Gender issues are usually thought to be about women, but with this kind of imbalance, the idea gradually dawned that these were also issues about men. Managerial masculinities emerged as a research field in the 1990s, and remain an active field of study. It is clear, for instance, that managerial masculinities change over time. The British historian Michael Roper, in a fascinating book called *Masculinity and the British Organization Man since 1945* (1994), traces changes in the management of British manufacturing firms. An older generation of managers had a hands-on relation with the production process, identified themselves closely with the firm and the quality of the product, and took a paternalistic interest in the engineering workers. With the growing power of finance capital in the British economy, a new cadre of managers has appeared. They are also men, but are more oriented to accountancy and profit, less interested in technology and the product, and not very much interested in the workers. A more generic, and more ruthless, managerial masculinity has taken over.

Capitalism is a turbulent economic system; markets expand and collapse, industries rise and fall, corporations restructure themselves in search of profit. The neoliberal economy of our generation is more open to individual promotion for a minority of women, but also seems to foster a more aggressive masculinity in management. An aggressive and competitive masculinity appears in studies of financial trading floors, though, as Peter Levin (2001) notes, it is expressed in different ways depending on fluctuations in the pace of work.

When Rosabeth Kanter studied women in corporations in the 1970s, she found that social pressures tended to reinforce traditional femininity. When Judy Wajcman studied women managers in globally oriented high-technology firms in the 1990s, she found they were under heavy pressure to act like the men. They had to work the long hours, fight in the office wars, put pressure on their subordinates, and focus on profit. In order to survive in this world, women managers had to re-structure their domestic lives so they, like men, could shed responsibilities for childcare, cooking and housework. Wajcman found no truth in the widespread belief that women coming into management would bring a more caring, nurturant or humane style to the job. It is not surprising that she called her book *Managing Like a Man* (1999).

As the economy globalizes, what are the implications for managerial masculinity? A disturbing answer is given by a study of an international merger of finance companies in Scandinavia, where gender orders are among the most egalitarian on earth. Janne Tienari and colleagues (2005) conducted interviews with the top executives of the merged firm, and found a remarkable situation. The senior managers were overwhelmingly men, and basically did not want to hear about gender-equality problems. They took management to be naturally men's business, 'constructed according to the core family and male-breadwinner model'. The researchers think that the conditions of transnational business intensify the discourse of managerial masculinity as competitive, mobile and work-driven – overriding Scandinavian societies' discourse of gender equality. If they are right, the outlook for gender relations in the wider world of transnational corporations is not good.

What about the situation lower down, among the people who actually do the corporations' work? Here gender relations are more diverse, as corporations have assembled large and socially complex workforces. The world-wide review of ethnographies of workplace gender by Winifred Poster (2002), and the ambitious attempt by Heidi Gottfried (2013) to analyse gender in the global economy as a whole, show not only the use of gender division and gender stereotyping as means of control, but also the great variety of situations in which gender is constructed. Racial hierarchies, sexualization and class distinctions all affect the making of workplace masculinities and femininities. Women are more likely than men to be concentrated in the informal sectors of the global economy, where their work is precarious, worse paid, and often dangerous. That was horribly shown in 2013 by the Rana Plaza clothing factory collapse in Bangladesh, with an official death toll of 1,219 and twice that number injured.

What of the institutions that represent workers' interests in battles with corporate power – the unions? Here too we find mostly patriarchal organizations. Though there have been some famous episodes in union organizing among women, such as the London matchgirls' strike in 1888, union membership has remained mainly men, and union leadership overwhelmingly men. It has been difficult to establish a voice for women through the unions, even in a country like Australia where both unionism and feminism have been strong. Resistance from men who embody an old, combative style of working-class masculinity has been a constant problem.

Yet as economies have changed, women have been a rising proportion of union membership. Three recent presidents of the Australian Council of Trade Unions (the unions' peak organization) have been women, and a former union lawyer, Julia Gillard, became Prime Minister in 2010. Recent research by an Australian/US team (Franzway and Fonow 2011) traces the details of feminist politics in world-wide labour movements, and, while documenting all the difficulties, sees this as a hopeful arena for change.

Gendered states

Most of the world's presidents, prime ministers, cabinet ministers, generals and civil service managers are men. Women gained legal status, and the right to vote, later than men – and in some parts of the world still do not have legal equality. In the 1970s and 1980s, feminists in the metropole made a number of attempts to formulate a theory of the state as a patriarchal institution. Its main themes were that: the state is the core of power relations in gender; the state has a well-marked internal gender regime; the state makes policies with gender effects; the state constitutes gender categories and relations; the state is the key target in gender politics; and the state as the heart of gendered power is liable to crisis and change (Connell 1990). These conclusions were drawn from extensive research on politics and bureaucracies, and they have a certain solidity and realism. But they also have limitations, which are easier to see now.

From a broader gender perspective, the state is only one of society's centres of power. A traditional definition of the state is the institution that holds a monopoly of the legitimate use of force in a given territory. That definition supposes that there is agreement across the society on what is 'legitimate', and ignores other kinds of force such as domestic violence.

Husbands' beating of wives to enforce obedience is a widespread practice that used to be broadly legitimate, in many places still is, and only recently has been publicly challenged. Can we regard husbands as a 'power'? Conventional political analysis does not; but husbands' interests in their wives' sexual and domestic services have been institutionalized in law, religion and custom. This is a power to which state agencies have repeatedly accommodated. Wendy Hollway (1994) gives an example in a study of Tanzanian civil service employment, where women civil servants were sent on training programmes only if their husbands had given approval. 'Applications without a husband's permission were treated as if [official] permission had been withheld.'

Another kind of power has emerged in the form of security companies. There are said to be more private security agents in the United States now than there are official police. Increasing numbers of the affluent, even in rich countries, live in gated communities, housing complexes with fences patrolled by security employees, designed to keep out the poor, the black and the card-less. These private security systems are strongly gendered: controlled by men, mostly employing men, and, in the case of the gated communities, en-gating women. A substantial part of the armed force used in the US occupation of Iraq consisted of 'security contractors' – between 20,000 and 30,000 mercenary soldiers employed by corporations such as Blackwater Worldwide. Sandra Via (2010) argues that Blackwater's operations for the US government in Iraq and in New Orleans reflect hypermasculine ideas of 'cowboy' heroism, security and protection that are positioned against racialized Others. Blackwater rebranded itself as Xe in 2009 using more 'feminine' language after controversy over its responsibility for 17 civilian deaths and 20 more injured in Baghdad in 2007.

The main weakness of the old model of the gendered state, however, was that it emerged from the nation-states of the North and did not think beyond them. The state as an empire, the post-colonial state, the transnational state as a part of the global economy, were not part of the analysis. But those states have come more and more into focus. The gender dynamics of the imperial state have been explored in many colonies of the old empires – in studies of gender legislation in Bengal (Sinha 1995), military power in Natal (Morrell 2001a), convicts, work and sexuality in Van Diemen's Land (Reid 2007), and more.

Post-colonial states have also come in for close attention, such as the withering critique of corrupt and violent rule in Achille Mbembe's celebrated book *On the Postcolony* (2001). In parts of the world such as central and western Africa, the state structure left by colonialism, lacking legitimacy and often cutting arbitrarily across geographical and cultural landscapes, has been racked with conflict that has turned into military coups and internal war. The heavily masculinized military forces of the colonial era provided the core of many post-colonial state elites – notably in the richest country in the region, Nigeria.

In cases like Vietnam, Algeria, Zimbabwe and Cuba, the leadership of guerrilla forces gained control of the post-colonial state and set up authoritarian regimes. Even where a civilian leadership remained in control, as in India, the attempt to hold together a new republic and the drive for economic development valorized a hegemonic masculinity that was focused on authority and rational calculation, suppressed emotions, and was capable of rolling over local communities and traditions (Nandy 1983).

The Turkish state, the first modern republic in the Islamic world, was an important model for post-colonial regimes. General Mustafa Kemal, a hero of the First World War, came to power at a time of absolute crisis, and drove out occupying forces in what amounted to a war of independence. He then led a modernizing elite in setting up a secular state. Emancipation of women was famously on Kemal's agenda, and women still have a presence in Turkish public life greater than in most Sunni-majority countries. Yet until the current neoliberal-Islamist regime of Recep Tayyip Erdoğan's Justice and Development Party (AKP), a masculinized army remained the dominant force in the republic. As Emma Sinclair-Webb (2000) shows in a very interesting ethnographic study, military service in Turkey is a rite of passage into manhood, connected with national identity. But it is also a site of tension: professional soldiers, especially the officers, regard the conscripts as poor material. The army, that is to say, does not rely on an already-established masculinity, but tries to shape young men in a new mould. The army's capacity to impose its agenda, however, has run into difficulty – partly because it could not defeat the long-running Kurdish rebellion, partly from the rise of political Islam, and partly from cultural change among youth.

A comparative study of Nigeria and Chile by Philomina Okeke-Ihejirika and Susan Franceschet (2002) points to specific conditions for the success of 'state feminism'. In Chile, women were prominent in the struggle against the Pinochet dictatorship. Feminists gained access to the top levels of state power during the transition to democracy. (And in 2006 Michelle Bachelet, a social democrat who had been part of the resistance, was elected President; she returned to office following the 2013 election.)

But in Nigeria, though women were involved in the struggle for independence, and though feminist groups have persisted, the post-independence military regimes had no place for feminist ideas. Instead, they promoted tame women's organizations led by the wives of the real rulers – borrowing the US idea of the 'first lady' – which pursued a mild welfare agenda and a conservative view of women's place.

It was common that anti-colonial, nationalist or revolutionary movements mobilized women's support. The Chinese revolution is perhaps the best-known case. The Maoist slogan 'women hold up half the sky' was part of an attack on feudal attitudes and laws which had enforced the subordination of women (Stacey 1983). But establishing a post-colonial or post-revolutionary regime has often meant installing a revised version of patriarchy. Women have been recruited to the labour force, not necessarily to the political leadership. In the capitalist China ruled by Mao's successors, domestic servants known by the euphemism *baomu* ('protecting mother') have reappeared in great numbers, often poor women migrating from the countryside; their story is told in Yan Hairong's *New Masters, New Servants* (2008). In neighbouring Nepal, when the government of the new republic came into existence in 2008, it was eerie to see posters showing the genealogy of the ruling Maoist party: a row of male faces from Marx via Stalin to Mao. Not a woman among them. This is despite the critical role women played in the Maoist revolution. Rita Manchanda (2004) describes women's participation within this militarized culture as a paradox for women seeking emancipation and a new social agenda through the Party.

In some cases the exclusion of women is explicit. Yemen has been described as the most oppressive country in the world for women, though Saudi Arabia and the Vatican run close. The Wahhabi sect of Islam that predominates in the Arabian peninsula is as implacably opposed to women having authority as the Catholic sect of Christianity is. Nayereh Tohidi's (1991) narrative of feminist politics in Shi'ite Iran shows how assertive attitudes among women there were seen as evidence of the corruption of religion and culture by Western influences. In other cases the exclusion of women is a matter of practice, not dogma. Most post-colonial states have been dependent on multinational corporations, so have been operating in an economic environment dominated by wealthy and powerful men. Singapore, one of the striking success stories of dependent capitalist development, has also created one of the most monolithic patriarchies in post-colonial government.

Yet the current is not all one way. There is also a vibrant history of women's activism in post-colonial states, not least in the world's biggest Muslim-majority country, Indonesia (Robinson 2009). From Chile and Brazil to Pakistan and Indonesia, women have become prominent political leaders and heads of government. The post-colonial state in India has provided an environment in which a strong feminist movement could develop, and non-feminist women who had elite connections could rise to power. It is striking that of the five successor states to the British Indian Empire, four have had women prime ministers and the fifth nearly did (Burma with Aung San Suu Kyi). We should not forget that Sirimavo Bandaranaike, who became Prime Minister of Sri Lanka in 1960, was the first elected woman head of government in the world.

Women have long been part of the state's workforce, though initially in routine and low-paid jobs. Rising levels of women's education world-wide have made possible a growing role in administration and policy-making, even a feminist presence in the bureaucracy. In Australia, where this has been a major strategy of gender politics, the officials responsible for gender equality were known charmingly as 'femocrats'. Their story is entertainingly told in *Inside Agitators* (1996) by Hester Eisenstein, who spent some time as a femocrat herself. An early approach was to create special units within government departments that were responsible for women's affairs and gender equity.

In the 1990s another strategy became influential, especially in the European Union: 'gender mainstreaming', where all parts of government were supposed to implement gender policies in the course of their regular work. This was taken up by the United Nations, and has become wide-spread, for instance in the form of 'gender budgets'. A recent report on this process in the Philippines suggests the difficulties faced by gender mainstreaming: small budgets, lack of interest by senior bureaucrats, and widespread failure to report. In the agriculture sector, for instance, '[i]t was ... observed that men still dominated decision making in the politi-cal spheres, rural development agencies, rural organizations and even the homes' (Illo 2010: 149).

An important element of state policy is about controls over women's bodies. Mala Htun (2003), in a study of gender politics in Argentina, Brazil and Chile, shows that while women's rights fluctuated under the dictatorships and with the transition to democracy, in no case were abor-tion rights improved. Such experiences rub up against the theory of the 'woman-friendly state' advanced by some feminist theorists in Scandin-avia. Anette Borchorst and Birte Siim (2002), reviewing this theory, note the break from feminist pessimism about the state. A combination of feminist mobilization from below, and laws mandating gender equity from above, can produce a regime much more favourable to women's interests. Politics does matter.

This is the starting point for a striking initiative that came from Chile. The Grupo Iniciativa Mujeres developed the idea of a 'social watch' instrument, described by Teresa Valdés (2001), the project co-ordinator, as 'a strategy for citizen monitoring of gender equity'. The ICC – *Indice de compromiso cumplido* (index of achieved commitments) – is not based on an abstract definition of gender equity but on actual local policy commitments, embedded in national legislation, administrative rules or adoption of international agreements. It has three kinds of indicators: measures of 'political will', such as enactment of gender quota laws; measures of 'process', such as municipal programmes for domestic violence victims; and measures of 'result', such as the ratio between men's and women's incomes. In a second stage of this project, feminists from 18 Latin American countries, with the aid of UNIFEM (United Nations Development Fund for Women), worked on a combined ICC and published a continent-wide report tracing changes over an eight-year period (Valdés et al. 2003).

Another notable example of reform involving the state is the involvement of heterosexual men in achieving gender equality. Scandinavian countries have most experience with this, and their story is told in Øystein Holter's *Can Men Do It? Men and Gender Equality – The Nordic Experience* (2003). Only a few generations ago, the Nordic countries were socially conservative places with economies dominated by heavily masculinized industries – fishing, timber, mining – resulting in a stark gender division of labour. Gender relations have changed; Scandinavia now leads the world in women's representation in the public realm, men's involvement in childcare, and other measures. The state's role in that change has been crucial, for instance in providing financial support for fathers' involvement in the care of young children. Men do change, Holter argues, when the surrounding conditions allow it, and public policy can make the difference.

But the state has been changing recently, in ways that make power less accountable to women. Neoliberal 'reforms' have privatized many state services, and make remaining public services operate more like corporations. Women's increased presence in the public realm is now counterbalanced by a decline of the public realm itself – as Rachel Simon-Kumar (2004) puts it, a tendency for the state and the market to blur into each other. The key neoliberal policies – deregulating markets, reducing taxes and government services, transferring resources to private business – transfer power into institutions dominated by men. The state, in both metropole and periphery, is increasingly oriented towards the world of global capitalism.

These trends also signal the gendered relations between society and nature that underpin state-led privatization. The case of water privatization in post-colonial states has been well documented by feminists, who argue that neoliberal policies commodify water ecosystems and are implemented through development practices tied to particular forms of managerial masculinity (Larner and Laurie 2010; Laurie 2005). The 'social turn' within privatized water governance, which was supposed to include women, reaffirms neoliberal individualism rather than contesting it (Roberts 2008).

The stakes in gender politics

What is at stake in these struggles? Generally speaking, the people who benefit from inequalities have an interest in defending them, while those who bear the costs have an interest in ending them. Gender inequalities are usually expressed in terms of women's lack of resources relative to men's. For instance, chapter 1 cited statistics that show women's average wages, world-wide, are 18 per cent less than men's average wages. These figures compare the median earnings of full-time employed men and women, and are only one way to measure the surplus of resources made available to men. 'Gender gaps' exist in the quality and quantity of (paid) work women participate in. For instance, women are more likely to be in informal employment, including unpaid work for family businesses, and unemployment rates for women have increased since the financial crisis (ILO 2012).

This surplus can be called the *patriarchal dividend*: the advantage to men as a group from maintaining an unequal gender order. Of course, money income is not the only kind of benefit. Others are authority, respect, service, safety, housing, access to institutional power, emotional support, sexual pleasure and control over one's own body.

The patriarchal dividend is the benefit to men *as a group*. Some men get more of it than others, other men get less, or none, depending on their location in the social order. A wealthy businessman draws large dividends from the gendered accumulation process in advanced capitalism. On a world scale, the dividends may be almost in the realm of fantasy – consider the fortunes of Carlos Slim Helú ($73 billion), Bill Gates ($67 billion) and Amancio Ortega ($57 billion), the three richest humans in 2013. By contrast, an unemployed working-class man may draw no patriarchal dividend in an economic sense at all. Specific groups of men may be bluntly excluded from parts of the patriarchal dividend. Homosexual men, in most parts of the world, are excluded from the authority and respect attached to men who embody hegemonic forms of masculinity; though they may, and in rich countries often do, share men's general economic advantages over women.

Some women participate in the patriarchal dividend, generally by being married to wealthy men or inheriting fortunes from their fathers. Such women draw from the gendered accumulation process, i.e. live on a profit stream generated in part by other women's underpaid work. Wealthier women are able to benefit directly from poor women doing the housework and childcare. A multi-lateral trade in domestic labour has now developed: Peruvian women to Chile, Filipina women to East and South Asia, while other women travel from Moldava in Eastern Europe to domestic service in Turkey (Chang and Ling 2000; Keough 2006). This trade has allowed many middle-class women to move into professional or business careers, without putting pressure on middle-class *men* to raise their share of domestic labour.

The patriarchal dividend is the main stake in contemporary gender politics. Its scale makes patriarchy worth defending. The small band of sex role reformers in the 1970s who attempted to persuade men that Women's Liberation was good for them were undoubtedly right about the costs of hegemonic masculinity. But the same reformers hopelessly underestimated the patriarchal dividend. They missed what very large numbers of men stand to gain from current arrangements in terms of power, economic advantage, authority, peer respect, sexual access, and so on.

The harm of gender is most obviously the system of inequality in which women and girls are exploited, discredited, and made vulnerable to abuse and attack, for instance in rape, sexual harassment, sexualized imagery in the media, and sexual abuse of girls. Gender harm is also found in the effects of specific gender patterns. Femininities that make adolescent girls so anxious and self-conscious about their bodies that they develop anorexia are harmful in the same way cigarettes are. Contemporary hegemonic masculinities are dangerous to others when they promote inter-personal violence, occupational stress, arms races, strip mining and deforestation, hostile labour relations, and the abuse of technologies. Such masculinities are harmful to men themselves.

But if gender in these respects is harmful, it is in other respects a source of pleasure, creativity and other things we greatly value. Gender organizes our sexual relationships, and our relations with children, which are sources of personal delight and growth. Gender is integral to the cultural riches of most regions in the world, from *Noh* plays to reggae and hiphop. It is difficult to imagine Shakespeare's plays, Homer's *Iliad*, Joyce's *Ulysses*, Rumi's poetry, the *Ramayana* or Bergman's films without gender. The joys, tensions and complications of gender relations are among the most potent sources of cultural creation.

It is an attractive feature of recent queer politics that it has rediscovered the energy of gender practices, by shifting them off their conventional axes. Starting with the US direct action group Queer Nation in 1990, a great deal of creativity has been unleashed. Pleasures in gender display, in erotic inventiveness, in alternative embodiments, in games with gender language, are very evident. In the elementary schools studied by Barrie Thorne (chapter 2), the children took pleasure in learning to do gender. The lifelong gender projects discussed in chapter 6 are not tales of woe; for great numbers of people they are complex and satisfying accomplishments. But moments where the integrity of a gender project is lost, moments of gender vertigo, can be extremely distressing.

The stakes in gender politics, then, include the value of gender as well as its harm. Given these possibilities, 'gender politics' has to be understood as more than an interest group struggle over inequalities. In the most general sense, gender politics is about the *steering* of the gender order in history. It represents the struggle to have the endless re-creation of gender relations turn out a particular way.

It is often clear what gender reform movements are fighting against – discriminatory laws, gender-based violence, social oppression. But what are they fighting for? Where do they want to steer society, in the long run?

Many feminists think that gender is inherently about inequality. They see the patriarchal dividend as the core of the gender order, and gender harm as unavoidable in any gender system. Logically, then, they aim at the abolition of gender. A clear statement of this view is offered by the US sociologist Judith Lorber in *Breaking the Bowls: Degendering and Feminist Change* (2005). Recognizing that gender, however interwoven with other social structures, 'still exerts an enormous organizing, socializing and discriminatory power', Lorber sees two possible responses: acts of individual rebellion, or a strategy of de-gendering. She argues for de-gendering families, workplaces and politics, for seeking the abolition of gender wherever it is found, and for defining 'a world without gender' as the goal.

But there is another possibility: a strategy of gender democracy. This seeks to equalize gender orders, rather than shrink them to nothing. Gender does not, in itself, imply inequality. The fact that there are gender orders with markedly different levels of inequality is some evidence in support. That democratization is a practicable strategy is shown by the many social struggles that have actually changed gender relations towards equality. The Nordic policy regime just mentioned is an example on the large scale; the intimate politics that went into producing the American 'fair families' described by Barbara Risman (1998) is an example on the small scale.

A strategy of gender democratization, rather than gender abolition, has some points to recommend it. It allows us to preserve gender good – the many pleasures, cultural riches, identities and other practices that arise in gender orders and that people value. Democratizing gender does not require isolating the reproductive arena from social structures and institutions, but, rather, organizing on equal and inclusive lines the social processes involved in conception, birth, baby care and child rearing, as well as paid labour and political representation. This strategy connects gender reform with the ideals and practices of democratic struggle in other spheres of life. The ecological question, for instance, is an increasingly pressing arena of social struggle. Democratized gender relations will contribute to sustainable forms of social and political organization. Struggles against the expansion of corporate globalization are also an arena where gender justice is crucial, if any future alternate economic organization is going to address deep inequalities. No strategy of gender reform will be easy – on that, everyone agrees – but these look like significant advantages.

Gender in world society

Connections between gender relations in different parts of the world are not new. Kartini in Java, at the beginning of the twentieth century, could rely on support from women in the Netherlands (chapter 4). International women's organizations existed for most of the twentieth century, including the Women's International League for Peace and Freedom, founded during the First World War and still going today.

However, there has been much more attention to this question since the United Nations Decade for Women (1975–85). A series of high-profile world conferences on women created a global forum for these concerns and crystallized a policy agenda around women's interests (Bulbeck 1988). This reflects an important reality in gender relations today. There are significant features of the gender order which cannot be understood locally, which *require* analysis on a global scale.

The process that Sarah Radcliffe, Nina Laurie and Robert Andolina (2004) call 'the transnationalization of gender' is happening in all the dimensions of gender relations defined in chapter 5. The economic relations between women and men can hardly avoid being transnational, in a time when large percentages of national economies are owned by foreigners, large sections of industry are dependent on foreign trade, and major investment decisions are made by transnational corporations. Power relations are affected when global competitiveness is pursued via state restructuring and privatization of public services, and when masculinized military, paramilitary, spy and police institutions are linked internationally. Emotional relations and sexuality are impacted by migration, population policies and international travel – the international dimension of gender in the HIV/AIDS pandemic is impossible to miss (Mane and Aggleton 2001). The symbolism of gender is affected, as images of masculinity and femininity circulate on a vast scale in global media (fashion, music, 'celebrities', professional sports), while gender ideologies from different cultures are interwoven by migration, marriage and missionaries.

The connections seem to be of two basic types: interaction between local gender orders, and the creation of new arenas of gender relations.

Imperial conquest, neo-colonialism and the current world systems of power, investment, trade and communication have brought very diverse societies in contact with each other. Consequently the gender orders of those societies have been brought into contact with each other.

This has often been a violent and disruptive process. Imperialism included an assault on local gender arrangements which did not fit the colonizers' templates. Missionaries, for instance, tried to stamp out the third-gender '*berdache*' tradition in North America, and what they saw as women's promiscuity in Polynesia. The '*muu-muu*' dresses sold to thousands of tourists in Hawai'i are far from being an indigenous tradition; they are the legacy of male religious authorities' attempts to cover up women's bodies. Local gender arrangements were overthrown by slavery, indentured labour, land seizure and resettlement. In the contemporary world, the institutions of masculine violence in different parts of the world are linked by a global arms trade that amounted to at least $43 billion in 2011 (Stockholm International Peace Research Institute 2011).

An essay by Mai Ghoussoub (2000) on masculinity in Arab media, especially in Egypt, illustrates the turbulence of these large-scale changes in gender relations. She starts with two strange episodes: rumours about an Israeli-invented chewing gum that makes Arab men impotent; and the sudden popularity of mediaeval courtship manuals that celebrate sex in the name of Islam. (One is well-known in English translation as *The Perfumed Garden*.) Ghoussoub interprets these episodes as signs of a deep cultural disturbance about masculinity in the post-colonial Middle East. The context is slow economic modernization, political turbulence and the military weakness of Arab states in the face of Israel and the United States. The increasing economic and social status of women in Arabic-speaking societies has posed dilemmas for men whose identities are still founded in traditional gender ideologies. The old sex manuals emphasize women's active sexuality; and mass culture also portrays powerful women, such as the heroine of a popular film, *Mission to Tel Aviv*, who turns the tables on the Israelis. There are many signs, Ghoussoub argues, of 'a chaotic quest for a definition of modern masculinity'.

The flow of influence in imperialism and globalization is not all one-way. Ashis Nandy (1983) shows that British rule in India changed masculinities among the British, as well as among the Indians. There is an interesting historical literature on the 'imperial pioneer and hunter' as a masculine model (MacKenzie 1987). Yet there is no question that the pressure of the metropole on the gender orders of the global periphery is stronger than pressure the other way.

Imperialism and globalization have also created new institutions that operate on a world scale. These institutions all have internal gender regimes, and each gender regime has its gender dynamic – interests, gender politics, processes of change. World-spanning institutions thus create new arenas for gender formation and gender dynamics. They include transnational corporations, the international state, global markets and global media.

Corporations operating in global markets, such as Toyota, Microsoft, Shell, Glencore Xstrata and Allianz, are now the most powerful business organizations on the planet. They typically have a marked, though complex, gender division of labour in their workforces, and a strongly masculinized management culture. In the past, these corporations have provided relatively secure employment for a mostly male workforce in a primary labour market. Under neoliberalism they are organizationally more tightly integrated, through computerized management systems, but their workforces are less secure. Smaller companies, which supply the majors or operate in the niches they leave open, operate in informal labour markets and account for most of women's industrial employment.

The old empires were themselves a kind of transnational state. Since they passed from the scene (apart from a few remnants, such as the Pacific islands where France conducted nuclear tests), there has been a striking growth of agencies that link territorial states without themselves having a territorial base. They include the International Labour Organization, the League of Nations, the United Nations and its agencies such as the World Bank and the International Monetary Fund, and the Organization for Economic Co-operation and Development. There are also regional unions of states, some tight and some loose: the European Union, the African Union, Mercosur and others.

Mostly their gender regimes copy those of the conventional states that gave rise to them. Being an outgrowth of diplomacy, they are mainly staffed and run by men, as Cynthia Enloe's (1990) study of the diplomatic world showed. Yet women have been moving into the world of international diplomacy: since Enloe's book was written, the United States has had three women as Secretary of State – Madeleine Albright, Condoleezza Rice and Hillary Clinton. The United Nations organizations adopted the 'femocrat' strategy and set up several agencies to pursue gender equality, which were merged in 2010 into UN Women.

Aid agencies now generally have women's or gender programmes, and many NGOs do the same. There are widely known policy documents, especially CEDAW, the 1979 UN Convention on the Elimination of All Forms of Discrimination against Women, and the 1995 Beijing Declaration adopted by the Fourth World Conference on Women.

We can say the international state has some commitment to gender equality; we certainly cannot say that about international media. Multinational media corporations circulate film, video, music and news on a very large scale. There are also more decentralized media (post, smart phones, the internet) and their supporting industries. All contain gender arrangements and circulate gender meanings, and most of these are far from gender-equal. The internet has a huge supply of pornographic sites that present women as objects of male desire and consumption. The celebrity culture that is a staple of media for women is relentlessly heteronormative. Sports programming presents a monotonous diet of competitive, muscular masculinity. The modest excursions into change represented by programmes such as *Queer Eye for the Straight Guy* seem marginal in comparison.

International markets – capital, commodity, service and labour markets – have an increasing reach into local economies. Like international media, they are now weakly regulated. Recent research has shown the gendered character of markets as social institutions, with an aggressive, misogynist culture in areas such as commodities, energy, stock and futures trading (Ho 2009; Levin 2001). Here is a passage from an interview with an Australian finance company executive, one of the few women who actually worked as a trader in the 'very macho culture of the dealing room' (Connell 2012):

> In the dealing rooms, oh, full of the macho bravado, and the liar's-poker type environments. Where, you know, they're [saying] how big their positions are – the bragging, the womanizing, the whole bit. And all of which is entirely forgiven because they make a load of money ... it attracts a certain type of person. [How did you survive in this environment?] I ran a futures book. Futures isn't sexy these days, but they were [then] at the sexy end of the market, they were sophisticated, and people didn't really understand what you were doing. ... So they could have thought I was a green tree frog, I knew I was making money. So to that extent the simplicity of the performance criteria goes your way. But the culture was very very hostile. ... You'd get the whole kit-and-caboodle, you know: the nude posters went up, and all this sort of stuff, the comment on everything you wore, and everything you did.

In these various arenas we can see some outlines of an emerging world gender order. We cannot assume that there already is a global gender system, as earlier feminist theories of universal patriarchy did. There is enormous diversity still in local gender orders. But the links between them, and the transnational institutions just outlined, are already an important presence. Their weight in our lives will undoubtedly grow.

Gender politics on the world scale

Democratizing gender relations in global institutions is straightforward in concept though difficult in practice. It means getting wage equality in transnational corporations, ending the misogyny and homophobia in international media, gaining equal representation of women and men in international forums, ending gender discrimination in international labour markets, and creating anti-discrimination norms in the public culture.

A world-wide agency of change is already in existence, in the international state agencies just described. Feminist movements have a presence in international meetings (Stienstra 2000). There is also some presence of gay and lesbian movements, particularly in human rights agencies and UNAIDS, the Joint United Nations Programme on HIV/AIDS. The United Nations set up a Commission on the Status of Women as early as 1946. Article 2 of the 1948 Universal Declaration of Human Rights banned discrimination on the basis of sex, as well as race, religion, and so on. The human rights agenda has been more effective than the pro-feminist men's movement in winning support for gender equality from men such as the UN Secretaries-General – support that has been important in opening the spaces in which women's groups have operated.

It is not only through state institutions that gender equity is pursued internationally. Millie Thayer (2010) speaks of a 'feminist counterpublic', vast and heterogeneous, that exists on an international scale. Regional and global networks have some capacity to hold diverse groups together, and they are increasingly common. Valentine Moghadam (2005) describes transnational networks that address issues ranging from the gender dimensions of structural adjustment and trade, to the position of women in Muslim-majority countries. Other networks deal with gay and lesbian rights, and the role of men in gender equality.

The most important effects of this pressure have been on development agendas. From the 1940s to the 1960s a global apparatus of development aid was created (both driven, and distorted, by Cold War politics). Improving the literacy, skills and knowledge of girls and women was seen as a key move in economic and social development. Consequently, in most parts of the world a vast social investment was made in elementary education for girls and literacy programmes for rural and working-class women. In time, this effort took on gender-equality goals. One of the current UN Millennium Development goals, adopted in 2000, is to promote gender equality and empower women, with a specific target of eliminating gender disparities at all levels of education around the world by 2015. It won't happen, but it is notable that the goal was announced.

Beyond the education agenda, aid agencies funded dams, machinery, fertilizers, roads and other tools of economic growth. Before long it became obvious that not only were men in control of the aid programmes, but also most of the benefits went to men. Often women's lives were most disrupted, particularly in rural areas where development projects mean environmental damage. The response was the 'Women in Development' agenda, which feminists urged on aid agencies from the 1970s, to expand the funds directed towards women in poor countries.

In the 1990s a major debate occurred around this agenda. Some argued that a focus on women alone was ineffective, that men too had to become change agents if gender equality was to be achieved. A 'Gender and Development' strategy was proposed, including men and masculinities. Others argued that bringing men into the only part of the global development agenda where women had actually gained control would reinforce patriarchy, not challenge it (Chant and Gutmann 2002; White 2000).

Similar issues arose in the 'gender mainstreaming' debates. It became important, therefore, to look at the specific role of men in international gender politics. This issue was raised in very general terms at the 1995 Beijing World Conference on Women. A more serious examination was launched in UN forums in the late 1990s and early 2000s, using the new research on masculinities that had emerged since the 1980s. This culminated in a policy document, 'The Role of Men and Boys in Achieving Gender Equality', adopted by the 2004 meeting of the UN Commission on the Status of Women, the first broad international agreement on this issue (Lang et al. 2008).

The forces pushing for gender democracy in global arenas are still weak in relation to the size of the problem. They have little influence on transnational corporations and global markets. Obedience to anti-discrimination laws in head office does not prevent transnational corporations behaving badly in the 'global factory', as the scandals about Nike show. Transnational corporations' search for cheap labour around the world often leads them, and their local suppliers, to exploit the weak industrial position of women. This is especially the case where unions are hammered down, as in free-trade zones that governments have set up to attract international capital (Marchand and Runyan 2011).

Even in the United Nations system there is no unified force for change. The World Conferences on Women were vital, but among the delegations attending were some from conservative Catholic and conservative Muslim governments, opposed to gender equality. So these conferences have seen sharp conflict over issues such as abortion, contraception and lesbianism. Even the concept of 'gender' was under attack at Beijing, because it was supposed by right-wing forces to be a code word for feminism (Benden and Goetz 1998). Largely because of these conflicts, the conferences have now ended – a significant win for conservatives.

During the 1980s, differences between the gender patterns and gender beliefs from different parts of the globe were widely canvassed. The idea of 'third world feminism' emerged. While equality between women and men could be seen as a mark of modernity, it could also be seen as Western cultural imperialism. Even within the metropole, versions of feminism which emphasized women's autonomy aroused opposition from women of ethnic minorities who valued solidarity with the men of their communities in struggles against racism and colonial or neo-colonial domination (Bulbeck 1988; Mohanty 1991).

The issues here are difficult. The modern international order came, historically, from a violent system of imperialism. A democratic agenda must contest the legacy, the inequalities between the global North and the global South. The colonial system of the past, and the globalized world economy of the present, are based on the institutionalized power of men. But the anti-colonial struggle, too, was almost everywhere led by men and often valorized violent masculinities.

In post-colonial regimes, the men of local elites have often been complicit with businessmen from the metropole in the exploitation of women's labour. Multinational corporations could not operate as they do without this co-operation. In places like the Philippines, Thailand and Mexico, men of local elites have created international sex trade destinations. Arms trafficking similarly involves alliances between the men who control local military forces and the men who run arms manufacturing corporations in the metropole. Post-colonial regimes have generally been patriarchal, and sometimes deeply misogynist or homophobic. Defending 'Asian values' or 'African culture' or 'religion' can be the rhetorical ploy of privileged men clinging to power. But there are also many men of the popular classes, and many women, who value their own cultural traditions and have little enthusiasm for change. As we saw in chapter 5, change in gender arrangements is disturbing and often contested.

A successful response to these problems will ultimately come not from 'the West' or from international organizations, but from the gender theorists of the majority world, discussed in chapter 4; from the social movements they speak to; and from the networks and counter-publics that link them. General declarations, such as the Universal Declaration of Human Rights and CEDAW, get read in different ways, but with enough overlap to allow many practical measures to be taken.

Efforts at 'globalization from below' by feminist movements in different parts of the world involve the same logic. Without exact agreement on concepts or even goals, enough overlap can be found to make practical action possible. In an essay called 'Transnational Solidarity' (2002), Manisha Desai finds several common themes in women's resistance to neoliberal restructuring: asserting a right to work, struggling for a better quality of life, and sustainability. These issues can be the basis of South/ South connections that are still difficult to organize, but immensely important for the future of gender justice on a world scale.

Coda

This book has traced the numerous ways in which the gender order impacts social life, on local and global scales. We began with the observation that noticing gender is easy, but understanding it is a great challenge. Having come to the end of this book, we hope you now see great gains in the project of understanding gender.

Gender theory and empirical research from all over the world have developed our knowledge of gender relations profoundly. A rich body of data now exists. Informed by this developing knowledge, feminists have articulated powerful criticisms of the gender order. And at key points in history, these theorists and practitioners have changed the material and social situations of women in general, and lesbian, gay, bisexual and transgender people, in the North and South. They have also dealt head on with very difficult political and theoretical questions about the relationships between gender, sexuality, race, class, disability and more. We hope you come away from reading this book with a sense of the significance of these questions and the collective process of developing answers.

Debates and contestations within gender theory are incredibly important, not least because the gender order continues to be unequal. Gender theorists have struggled to articulate a body of thought to support practice that transforms the oppressive and unjust dimensions of the gender order. What is to be done?

In the final chapter we argued against a 'de-gendering' project for feminism on the basis that such a goal too quickly assumes gender must mean inequality, and that it undervalues cultural and social diversity. Our preference is for a democratization of gender relations – and of gender theory.

The criterion of democratic action in the world gender order must be what democracy always means: moving towards equality of participation, power, resources and respect. In global spaces, this criterion applies at the same time to relations within any gender order and to relations between gender orders. Contradiction can't be avoided. The conflicts at the World Conferences on Women illustrate the point. Migratory domestic labour illustrates the point. The sex trade illustrates the point. The dilemmas of homosexual men under homophobic regimes illustrate the point. Debate over the social basis for feminist environmentalism illustrates the point. Yet progressive movements cannot evacuate these arenas simply because democratic practice is difficult. Anti-democratic forces are certainly not evacuating them.

Gender analysis is work for many hands. It requires the capacity to listen carefully. It requires ways of giving recognition without falling into separatism. Given the history of colonization and the huge inequalities of the contemporary world, solidarity can be extraordinarily difficult, as Aileen Moreton-Robinson (2000) documents in her critique of white feminism in Australia. Myths about women's solidarity are common (Cornwall et al. 2008). It is the business of theory to think beyond what appears to be given, to dig through the myths and grapple with the inequalities, to find effective bases of solidarity, however provisional they may be.

As feminism has found, knowledge about gender has to be reconsidered again and again, in the light of the changing gender dynamics that appear in world gender politics. Given this willingness to learn, we are convinced that gender theory and research can play a significant role in making a more democratic world.

References

Adler, Alfred. 1927. *Understanding Human Nature*. Oxford: Oneworld.

Agarwal, Bina. 1988. *Structures of Patriarchy: State, Community, and Household in Modernising Asia*. New Delhi: Kali for Women (1992 edition).

Agarwal, Bina. 1992. 'The gender and environment debate: Lessons from India', *Feminist Studies* 18 (1): 119–58.

Agarwal, Bina. 1994. *A Field of One's Own: Gender and Land Rights in South Asia*. Cambridge: Cambridge University Press.

Agarwal, Bina. 1997. '"Bargaining" and gender relations: Within and beyond the household', *Feminist Economics* 3 (1): 1–51.

Agarwal, Bina. 2010. *Gender and Green Governance: The Political Economy of Women's Presence within and beyond Community Forestry*. Oxford: Oxford University Press.

Agarwal, Anil, and Sunita Narain. 1991. *Global Warming in an Unequal World*. New Delhi: Centre for Science and Environment.

Ahmed, Sarah. 2008. 'Open forum: Some preliminary remarks on the founding gestures of the "New Materialism"', *European Journal of Women's Studies* 15 (1): 23–39.

Alaimo, Stacey, and Susan Hekman, eds. 2008. *Material Feminisms*. Bloomington: Indiana University Press.

Alexievich, Svetlana. 1992. *Zinky Boys: Soviet Voices from the Afghanistan War*. New York: W.W. Norton & Co.

Alston, Margaret. 2011. 'Gender and climate change in Australia', *Journal of Sociology* 47 (1): 53–70

Altman, Dennis. 1971. *Homosexual: Oppression and Liberation*. New York: Outerbridge & Dienstrey.

Ampofo, Akosua Adomako, Josephine Beoku-Betts, Wairimu Ngaruiya Njambi and Mary Osirim. 2004. 'Women's and gender studies in English-speaking sub-Saharan Africa: A review of research in the social sciences', *Gender & Society* 18: 685–714.

Arnfred, Signe. 2003. 'African gender research: a view from the North', *CODESRIA Bulletin* 1: 6–9.

Arnot, Madeleine, Miriam David and Gaby Weiner. 1999. *Closing the Gender Gap: Postwar Education and Social Change*. Cambridge: Polity.

Ault, Elizabeth. 2014. '"You can help yourself/but don't take too much": African American motherhood on *The Wire*', *Television & New Media* 14 (5): 386–401.

Australian Schools Commission. 1975. *Girls, School and Society: Report by a Study Group to the Schools Commission*. Canberra: Australian Schools Commission.

Badran, Margot. 1988. 'The feminist vision in the writings of three turn-of-the-century Egyptian women', *British Journal of Middle Eastern Studies* 15 (1–2): 11–20.

Bakare-Yusuf, Bibi. 2003. '"Yorubas don't do gender": A critical review of Oyèrónkẹ́ Oyěwùmí's *The Invention of Women: Making an African Sense of Western Gender Discourses*', *African Identities* 1: 121–43.

Balandier, Georges. 1955. *The Sociology of Black Africa: Social Dynamics in Central Africa*. London: André Deutsch (1970 edition).

Banner, Lois W. 1983. *American Beauty*. Chicago: University of Chicago Press.

Barrett, Frank J. 1996. 'Gender strategies of women naval officers', in *Women's Research and Education Institute: Conference on Women in Uniformed Services*. Washington, DC: Women's Research and Education Institute.

Bauer, Robin, Josch Hoenes and Volker Woltersdorff, eds. 2007. *Unbeschreiblich Männlich: Heteronormativitätskritische Perspektiven*. Hamburg: Männerschwarm.

Bebel, August. 1879. *Women under Socialism [Die Frau und der Sozialismus]*. New York: Schocken Books (1971 edition).

Bell, Diane. 1983. *Daughters of the Dreaming*. Melbourne: McPhee Gribble/Allen & Unwin.

Bem, Sandra L. 1974. 'The measurement of psychological androgyny', *Journal of Consulting and Clinical Psychology* 42: 155–62.

Benden, Sally, and Anne-Marie Goetz. 1998. 'Who needs [sex] when you can have [gender]? Conflicting discourses on gender at Beijing', in *Feminist Visions of Development: Gender, Analysis and Policy*, edited by Cecile Jackson and Ruth Pearson. London: Routledge.

Bennett, Jane. 2008. 'Editorial: Researching for life: Paradigms and power', *Feminist Africa* 11: 1–12.

Bennett, Jane. 2010. *Vibrant Matter: A Political Ecology of Things*. Durham, NC: Duke University Press.

Bettencourt, B. Ann, and Norman Miller. 1996. 'Gender differences in aggression as a function of provocation: A meta-analysis', *Psychological Bulletin* 119: 422–7.

Bettie, Julie. 2003. *Women without Class: Girls, Race, and Identity*. Berkeley: University of California Press.

Bhaskaran, Suparna. 2004. *Made in India: Decolonizations, Queer Sexualities, Trans/national Projects*. New York: Palgrave Macmillan.

Biehl, Janet. 1988. 'What is social ecofeminism?', *Green Perspectives: Newsletter of the Green Program Project* 11: 1–8.

Blamires, Alcuid, ed. 1992. *Woman Defamed and Woman Defended: An Anthology of Medieval Texts*. Oxford: Clarendon Press.

Borah, Rituparana, and Subhalakshmi Nandi. 2012. 'Reclaiming the feminist politics of "SlutWalk"', *International Feminist Journal of Politics* 14 (3): 415–21.

Borchorst, Anette, and Birte Siim. 2002. 'The women-friendly welfare states revisited', *NORA* 10: 90–8.

Bornstein, Kate. 1994. *Gender Outlaw: On Men, Women, and the Rest of Us*. New York: Routledge.

Bottomley, Gillian. 1992. *From Another Place: Migration and the Politics of Culture*. Cambridge: Cambridge University Press.

Boylan, Jennifer Finley. 2003. *She's Not There: A Life in Two Genders*. New York: Broadway Books.

Braidotti, Rosi, Eva Charkiewicz, Sabine Hausler and Saskia Wieringa. 1994. *Women, the Environment and Sustainable Development: Towards a Theoretical Synthesis*. London: Zed Books.

Brooks, Robert. 2011. *Sex, Genes and Rock 'n' Roll: How Evolution Has Shaped the Modern World*. Sydney: New South Books.

Bulbeck, Chilla. 1988. *One World Women's Movement*. London: Pluto Press.

Bulbeck, Chilla. 1997. *Living Feminism: The Impact of the Women's Movement on Three Generations of Australian Women*. Cambridge: Cambridge University Press.

Bulbeck, Chilla. 1998. *Re-orienting Western Feminisms: Women's Diversity in a Postcolonial World*. Cambridge: Cambridge University Press.

Burton, Clare. 1987. 'Merit and gender: Organisations and the mobilisation of masculine bias', *Australian Journal of Social Issues* 22: 424–35.

Butler, Judith. 1990. *Gender Trouble: Feminism and the Subversion of Identity*. New York: Routledge.

Caplan, Pat, ed. 1987. *The Cultural Construction of Sexuality*. London: Tavistock.

Carson, Rachel. 1962. *Silent Spring*. Boston: Houghton Mifflin.

Chang, Kimberly A., and L.H.M. Ling. 2000. 'Globalization and its intimate other: Filipina domestic workers in Hong Kong', in *Gender and Global Restructuring*, edited by Marianne H. Marchand and Anne Sisson Runyan. London: Routledge.

Chant, Sylvia, and Matthew C. Gutmann. 2002. '"Men-streaming" gender? Questions for gender and development policy in the twenty-first century', *Progress in Development Studies* 2: 269–82.

Chapkis, Wendy. 1997. *Live Sex Acts: Women Performing Erotic Labor*. New York: Routledge.

Chodorow, Nancy. 1978. *The Reproduction of Mothering: Psychoanalysis and the Sociology of Gender*. Berkeley: University of California Press.

Chodorow, Nancy. 1994. *Femininities, Masculinities, Sexualities: Freud and Beyond*. Lexington: University Press of Kentucky.

Clarke, Averil. 2011. *Inequalities of Love: College-Educated Black Women and the Barriers to Romance and Family*. Durham, NC: Duke University Press.

Collard, Andrée, with Joyce Contrucci. 1989. *Rape of the Wild: Man's Violence against Animals and the Earth*. Bloomington: Indiana University Press.

Collins, Patricia Hill. 1991. *Black Feminist Thought: Knowledge, Consciousness, and the Politics of Empowerment*. New York, NY: Routledge.

Connell, Raewyn. 1987. *Gender and Power: Society, the Person and Sexual Politics*. Cambridge: Polity.

Connell, Raewyn. 1990. 'The state, gender, and sexual politics', *Theory and Society* 19 (5): 507–44.

Connell, Raewyn. 1995. *Masculinities*. Cambridge: Polity.

Connell, Raewyn. 2000. *The Men and the Boys*. Cambridge: Polity.

Connell, Raewyn. 2005. 'Change among the gatekeepers: Men, masculinities, and gender equality in the global arena', *Signs* 30: 1801–25.

Connell, Raewyn. 2006. 'Glass ceilings or gendered institutions? Mapping the gender regimes of public sector worksites', *Public Administration Review* 66: 837–49.

Connell, Raewyn. 2007. *Southern Theory: The Global Dynamics of Knowledge in Social Science*. Cambridge: Polity.

Connell, Raewyn. 2010. 'Inside the glass tower: The construction of masculinities in finance capital', in *Men, Wage Work and Family*, edited by Paula McDonald and Emma Jeanes. London: Routledge.

Connell, Raewyn. 2012. 'Transsexual women and feminist thought: Toward new understanding and new politics', *Signs* 37 (4): 857–81.

Coole, Diana, and Samantha Frost. 2010. *New Materialisms: Ontology, Agency, and Politics*. Durham, NC: Duke University Press.

Corbett, Julia. 2001. 'Women, scientists, agitators: Magazine portrayal of Rachel Carson and Theo Colborn', *Journal of Communication* 51 (4): 720–49.

Cornwall, Andrea, Elizabeth Harrison and Ann Whitehead. 2008. *Gender Myths and Feminist Fables: The Struggle for Interpretive Power in Gender and Development*. Oxford: Blackwell.

Crenshaw, Kimberlé. 1989. 'Demarginalizing the intersection of race and sex: A Black feminist critique of antidiscrimination doctrine, feminist theory and antiracist politics', *University of Chicago Legal Forum*: 139–67.

Crutzen, Paul, and Eugene Stoermer. 2000. 'The Anthropocene', *Global Change Newsletter* 41 (1): 17–18.

Cummings, Katherine. 1992. *Katherine's Diary: The Story of a Transsexual*. Melbourne: Heinemann.

Cupples, Julie. 2005. 'Love and money in an age of neoliberalism: Gender, work, and single motherhood in postrevolutionary Nicaragua', *Environment and Planning A* 37: 305–22.

Daly, Mary. 1973. *Beyond God the Father: Toward a Philosophy of Women's Liberation*. Boston: Beacon Press.

Daly, Mary. 1978. *Gyn/Ecology: The Metaethics of Radical Feminism*. Boston: Beacon Press.

Darwin, Charles. 1859. *The Origin of Species*. London: Dent (1928 edition).

Davies, Bronwyn. 1993. *Shards of Glass: Children Reading and Writing beyond Gendered Identities*. Sydney: Allen & Unwin.

Davis, E. Gould. 1972. *The First Sex*. Baltimore: Penguin.

de Barbieri, Teresita. 1992. 'Sobre la categoria género. Una introducción teórico-metodológica', *Revista Interamericana de Sociología* 6: 147–78.

de Beauvoir, Simone. 1949. *The Second Sex*. Harmondsworth: Penguin (1972 edition).

de Pizan, Christine. 1405. *The Book of the City of Ladies*. London: Pan Books (1983 edition).

d'Eaubonne, Françoise. 1974. *Le féminisme ou la mort*. Paris: Pierre Horay.

d'Eaubonne, Françoise. 1980. 'Feminism or death', in *New French Feminisms: An Anthology*, edited by Elaine Marks and Isabelle de Courtivron. Amherst: University of Massachusetts Press.

Delphy, Christine. 1970. 'The main enemy', in *Close to Home: A Materialist Analysis of Women's Oppression*. London: Hutchinson.

Derrida, Jacques. 1976. *Of Grammatology*. Baltimore: Johns Hopkins University Press.

Desai, Manisha. 2002. 'Transnational solidarity. Women's agency, structural adjustment, and globalization', in *Women's Activism and Globalization: Linking Local Struggles and Transnational Politics*, edited by Nancy Naples and Manisha Desai. New York: Routledge.

Donaldson, Mike. 1991. *Time of Our Lives: Labour and Love in the Working Class*. Sydney: Allen & Unwin.

Dowsett, Gary W. 1996. *Practicing Desire: Homosexual Sex in the Era of AIDS*. Stanford, CA: Stanford University Press.

Dowsett, Gary W. 2003. 'Some considerations on sexuality and gender in the context of AIDS', *Reproductive Health Matters* 11: 21–9.

Dull, Diana, and Candace West. 1991. 'Accounting for cosmetic surgery: The accomplishment of gender', *Social Problems* 38: 54–70.

Dunne, Gillian A. 1997. *Lesbian Lifestyles: Women's Work and the Politics of Sexuality*. Basingstoke: Macmillan.

Eagly, Alice H. 1987. *Sex Differences in Social Behavior: A Social-Role Interpretation*. Hillside, NJ: Lawrence Erlbaum.

Eisenstein, Hester. 1996. *Inside Agitators: Australian Femocrats and the State*. Sydney: Allen & Unwin.

Earle, Rod, and Coretta Phillips. 2012. 'Digesting men? Ethnicity, gender and food: Perspectives from a "prison ethnography"', *Theoretical Criminology* 16 (2): 141–56.

Ellis, Havelock. 1928. *Eonism and other Supplementary Studies. Studies in the Psychology of Sex*, vol. VII. Philadelphia, PA: F.A. Davis.

Engels, Friedrich. 1884. The Origin of The Family, Private Property and the State, in *Marx/Engels Selected Works*. Moscow: Progress Publishers (1970 edition).

Enloe, Cynthia. 1990. *Bananas, Beaches and Bases: Making Feminist Sense of International Politics*. Berkeley: University of California Press.

Epstein, Cynthia Fuchs. 1988. *Deceptive Distinctions: Sex, Gender and the Social Order*. New Haven, CT: Yale University Press.

Epstein, Cynthia Fuchs. 2007. 'Great divides: The cultural, cognitive, and social bases of the global subordination of women', *American Sociological Review* 72: 1–22.

Ergas, Christina, and Richard York. 2012. 'Women's status and carbon dioxide emissions: A quantitative cross-national analysis', *Social Science Research* 41 (4): 965–76.

Erikson, Erik H. 1950. *Childhood and Society*. London: Imago.

Fausto-Sterling, Anne. 2000. *Sexing the Body: Gender Politics and the Construction of Sexuality*. New York: Basic Books.

Firestone, Shulamith. 1970. *The Dialectic of Sex: The Case for Feminist Revolution*. New York: Morrow.

Foley, Douglas. 1990. *Learning Capitalist Culture: Deep in the Heart of Tejas*. Philadelphia: University of Pennsylvania Press.

Foucault, Michel. 1977. *Discipline and Punish: The Birth of the Prison*. New York: Pantheon.

Franzway, Suzanne, and Mary M. Fonow. 2011. *Making Feminist Politics: Transnational Alliances between Women and Labor*. Champaign: University of Illinois Press.

Fraser, Nancy. 1989. *Unruly Practices: Power, Discourse and Gender in Contemporary Social Theory*. Cambridge: Polity; Minneapolis: University of Minnesota Press.

Fregoso, Rosa Linda. 1993. *The Bronze Screen: Chicana and Chicano Film Culture*. Minneapolis: University of Minnesota Press.

Freud, Sigmund. 1900. *The Interpretation of Dreams*, in *Complete Psychological Works*, vols 4–5. London: Hogarth (1953 edition).

Freud, Sigmund. 1905a. 'Fragment of an analysis of a case of hysteria ("Dora")', in *Complete Psychological Works*, vol. 7. London: Hogarth (1953 edition).

Freud, Sigmund. 1905b. *Three Essays on the Theory of Sexuality*, in *Complete Psychological Works*, vol. 7. London: Hogarth (1953 edition).

Freud, Sigmund. 1911. 'Psycho-analytic notes on an autobiographical account of a case of paranoia (dementia paranoides)', in *Complete Psychological Works*, vol. 12. London: Hogarth (1958 edition).

Freud, Sigmund. 1918. 'From the history of an infantile neurosis', in *Complete Psychological Works*, vol. 17. London: Hogarth (1955 edition).

Freud, Sigmund. 1930. *Civilization and Its Discontents*, in *Complete Psychological Works*, vol. 21. London: Hogarth (1961 edition).

Frosh, Stephen, Ann Phoenix and Rob Pattman. 2002. *Young Masculinities: Understanding Boys in Contemporary Society*. Basingstoke: Palgrave.

Garber, Marjorie. 1992. *Vested Interests: Cross-Dressing and Cultural Anxiety*. New York: Routledge.

Garofalo, Robert, Joanne Deleon, Elizabeth Osmer, Mary Doll and Gary W. Harper. 2006. 'Overlooked, misunderstood and at-risk: Exploring the lives and HIV risk of ethnic minority male-to-female transgender youth', *Journal of Adolescent Health* 38 (3): 230–6.

Gauthier, Xavière. 1981. 'Is there such a thing as women's writing?', in *New French Feminisms: An Anthology*, edited by Elaine Marks and Isabelle de Courtivron. London: Harvester.

Geary, David C. 1998. *Male, Female: The Evolution of Human Sex Differences*. Washington, DC: American Psychological Association.

George, Annie, and Kim Blankenship. 2007. 'Challenging masculine privilege: An unintended outcome of HIV prevention and sex worker empowerment interventions'. Paper to 'Politicising Masculinities: Beyond the Personal' conference, Dakar, October.

Gherardi, Silva, and Barbara Poggio. 2001. 'Creating and recreating gender order in organizations', *Journal of World Business* 36: 245–59.

Ghoussoub, Mai. 2000. 'Chewing gum, insatiable women and foreign enemies: male fears and the Arab media', in *Imagined Masculinities: Male Identity and Culture in the Modern Middle East*, edited by Mai Ghoussoub and Emma Sinclair-Webb. London: Saqi Books.

Gibson-Graham, J.K. 2006. *The End of Capitalism (As We Knew It): A Feminist Critique of Political Economy*. Minneapolis: University of Minnesota Press.

Gibson-Graham, J.K. 2011. 'A feminist project of belonging for the Anthropocene', *Gender, Place and Culture* 18 (1): 1–21.

Gilligan, Carol. 1982. *In a Different Voice: Psychological Theory and Women's Development*. Cambridge, MA: Harvard University Press.

Glass Ceiling Commission. 1995. A Solid Investment: Making Full Use of the Nation's Human Capital. Recommendations. Washington, DC: Federal Glass Ceiling Commission.

Glucksmann, Miriam [writing as Ruth Cavendish]. 1982. *Women on the Line*. London: Routledge & Kegan Paul.

Glucksmann, Miriam. 1990. *Women Assemble: Women Workers and the New Industries in Inter-war Britain*. London: Routledge.

Glucksmann, Miriam. 2000. *Cottons and Casuals: The Gendered Organisation of Labour in Time and Space*. Durham: sociologypress.

Goldberg, Steven. 1993. *Why Men Rule: A Theory of Male Dominance*. Chicago: Open Court.

Goldman, Michael. 1998. 'Inventing the commons: Theories and practices of the commons professional', in *Privatizing Nature: Political Struggles for the Global Commons*, edited by Michael Goldman. London: Pluto Press/Transnational Institute.

Gottfried, Heidi. 2013. *Gender, Work, and Economy: Unpacking the Global Economy*. Cambridge: Polity.

Griggs, Claudine. 1996. *Passage through Trinidad: Journal of a Surgical Sex Change*. Jefferson: McFarland & Co.

Griggs, Claudine. 1998. *S/he: Changing Sex and Changing Clothes*. New York: Bloomsbury.

Grosz, Elizabeth. 1994. *Volatile Bodies: Towards a Corporeal Feminism*. Sydney: Allen & Unwin.

Grosz, Elizabeth. 2004. *The Nick of Time: Politics, Evolution and the Untimely*. Durham, NC: Duke University Press.

Gunnarsson, Lena. 2013. 'The naturalistic turn in feminist theory: A Marxist-realist contribution', *Feminist Theory* 14 (1): 3–19.

Gutmann, Matthew C., and Mara Viveros Vigoya. 2005. 'Masculinities in Latin America', in *Handbook of Studies on Men & Masculinities* edited by

Michael S. Kimmel, Jeff Hearn and Raewyn Connell. Thousand Oaks, CA: Sage.

Habermas, Jürgen. 1976. *Legitimation Crisis*. London: Heinemann.

Hacker, Helen Mayer. 1957. 'The new burdens of masculinity', *Marriage and Family Living* 19: 227–33.

Hagemann-White, Carol. 1987. 'Gendered modes of behavior – a sociological strategy for empirical research'. Paper presented at 3rd International Intradisciplinary Congress on Women, Dublin, July. Published by Berliner Institut für Sozialforschung und Sozialwissenschaftliche Praxis.

Halpern, Diane F., and Mary L. LaMay. 2000. 'The smarter sex: A critical review of sex differences in intelligence', *Educational Psychology Review* 12: 229–46.

Haraway, Donna. 1987. 'A manifesto for cyborgs: Science, technology, and socialist feminism in the 1980s', *Australian Feminist Studies* 2 (4): 1–42.

Haraway, Donna. 1997. Modest_Witness@Second_Millennium. FemaleMan© _Meets_OncoMouse™. London: Routledge.

Harcourt, Wendy. 2009. *Body Politics in Development: Critical Debates in Gender and Development*. London: Zed Books.

Harding, Sandra. 1986. *The Science Question in Feminism*. Ithaca, NY: Cornell University Press.

Harding, Sandra. 2008. *Sciences from Below: Feminisms, Postcolonialities, and Modernities*. Durham, NC: Duke University Press.

Hairong, Yan. 2008. *New Masters, New Servants: Migration, Development and Women Workers in China*. Durham, NC: Duke University Press.

Harper, Catherine. 2007. *Intersex*. Oxford: Berg.

Hemmati, Minu, and Ulri Röhr. 2009. 'Engendering the climate-change negotiations: Experiences, challenges, and steps forward', *Gender and Development* 17 (1): 19–32.

Herdt, Gilbert H. 1981. *Guardians of the Flutes: Idioms of Masculinity*. New York: McGraw-Hill.

Hird, Myra. 2009. 'Feminist engagements with matter', *Feminist Studies* 35 (2):329–56.

Hird, Myra. 2013. 'Waste, landfills, and an environmental ethic of vulnerability', *Ethics & the Environment* 18 (1): 105–24.

Ho, Karen. 2009. *Liquidated: An Ethnography of Wall Street*. Durham, NC: Duke University Press.

Hochschild, Arlie Russell. 1983. *The Managed Heart: Commercialization of Human Feeling*. Berkeley: University of California Press.

Hocquenghem, Guy. 1972. *Homosexual Desire*. London: Allison & Busby (1978 edition).

Holland, Dorothy C., and Margaret A. Eisenhart. 1990. *Educated in Romance: Woman, Achievement, and College Culture*. Chicago: University of Chicago Press.

Hollway, Wendy. 1994. 'Separation, integration and difference: Contradictions in a gender regime', in *Power/Gender*, edited by H. Lorraine Radtke and Henderikus J. Stam. London: Sage.

Holmes, Morgan, ed. 2012. *Critical Intersex*. Farnham, Surrey: Ashgate Publishing.

Holter, Øystein Gullvåg. 2003. *Can Men Do It? Men and Gender Equality – the Nordic Experience*. Copenhagen: Nordic Council of Ministers.

Holter, Øystein Gullvåg. 2005. 'Social theories for researching men and masculinities: Direct gender hierarchy and structural inequality', in *Handbook of Studies on Men and Masculinities*, edited by Michael S. Kimmel, Jeff Hearn and Raewyn Connell. Thousand Oaks, CA: Sage.

hooks, bell. 1984. *Feminist Theory: From Margin to Center*. Boston: South End Press.

Hountondji, Paulin J. 1997. 'Introduction: Recentring Africa', in *Endogenous Knowledge: Research Trails*, edited by Paulin J. Hountondji. Dakar: CODESRIA.

Htun, Mala. 2003. *Sex and the State: Abortion, Divorce, and the Family under Latin American Dictatorships and Democracies*. Cambridge: Cambridge University Press.

Hultman, Martin. 2013. 'The making of an environmental hero: A history of ecomodern masculinity, fuel cells and Arnold Schwarzenegger', *Environmental Humanities* 2: 83–103.

Hyde, Janet S. 1984 'How large are gender differences in aggression? A developmental meta-analysis', *Developmental Psychology* 20: 722–36.

Hyde, Janet S. 2005. 'The gender similarities hypothesis', *American Psychologist* 60 (6): 581–92.

Hyde, Janet S., and Nita M. McKinley. 1997. 'Gender differences in cognition: results from meta-analyses', in *Gender Differences in Human Cognition*, edited by Paula J. Caplan, Mary Crawford, Janet Shibley Hyde, and John T.E. Richardson. New York: Oxford University Press.

Illo, Jeanne Frances I. 2010. *Accounting for Gender Results: A Review of the Philippine GAD Budget Policy*. Quezon City: Women and Gender Institute, Miriam College.

ILO. 2012. *Global Employment Trends for Women*. Geneva: International Labour Office.

Inter-Parliamentary Union. 2013. 'Women in national parliaments: Situation as of 1 July', http://www.ipu.org/wmn-e/world.htm (accessed 20 March 2014).

ITUC. 2012. *Frozen in Time: Gender Pay Gap Unchanged for 10 Years*. Brussels: International Trade Union Confederation.

Irigaray, Luce. 1977. *This Sex Which is Not One*. Ithaca, NY: Cornell University Press (1985 edition).

Jackson, Peter A. 1997. '*Kathoey*><Gay><Man: The historical emergence of gay male identity in Thailand', in *Sites of Desire, Economies of Pleasure*, edited by Lenore Manderson and Margaret Jolly. Chicago: University of Chicago Press.

Jaffee, Sara, and Janet S. Hyde. 2000. 'Gender differences in moral orientation: A meta-analysis', *Psychological Bulletin* 126 (5): 703–26.

Jasanoff, Sheila. 1994. *The Fifth Branch: Science Advisers as Policymakers*. Cambridge, MA: Harvard University Press.

Jasanoff, Sheila. 2010. 'A new climate for society', *Theory, Culture & Society* 27 (2–3): 233–53.

Jeffords, Susan. 1989. *The Remasculinization of America: Gender and the Vietnam War*. Bloomington: Indiana University Press.

Jewkes, Rachel, and Robert Morrell. 2010. 'Gender and sexuality: Emerging perspectives from the heterosexual epidemic in South Africa and implications for HIV risk and prevention', *Journal of the International AIDS Society* 13 (1): http://archive.biomedcentral.com/content/pdf/1758-2652-13-6.pdf (accessed 20 March 2014).

Kanter, Rosabeth. 1977. *Men and Women of the Corporation*. New York: Basic Books.

Karkazis, Katrina. 2008. *Fixing Sex: Intersex, Medical Authority, and Lived Experience*. Durham, NC: Duke University Press.

Kartini. 2005. *On Feminism and Nationalism: Kartini's Letters to Stella Zeehandelaar, 1899–1903*. Clayton: Monash University Press.

Kemper, Theodore D. 1990. *Social Structure and Testosterone: Explorations of the Socio-bio-social Chain*. New Brunswick, NJ: Rutgers University Press.

Keough, Leyla J. 2006. 'Globalizing "postsocialism": Mobile mothers and neoliberalism on the margins of Europe', *Anthropological Quarterly* 79: 431–61.

King, Ynestra. 1981. 'Feminism and the revolt of nature', *Heresies* 13: 12–6.

Kippax, Susan, Raewyn Connell, Gary W. Dowsett and June Crawford. 1993. *Sustaining Safe Sex: Gay Communities Respond to AIDS*. London: Falmer Press.

Kirkwood, Julieta. 1986. *Ser Política en Chile: Las Feministas y los Partidos*. Santiago de Chile: FLACSO.

Klein, Alan M. 1993. *Little Big Men: Bodybuilding Subculture and Gender Construction*. Albany, NY: State University of New York Press.

Kling, Kristen, Janet Shibley Hyde, Caroline J. Showers and Brenda N. Buswell. 1999. 'Gender differences in self-esteem: A meta-analysis', *Psychological Bulletin* 125: 470–500.

Komarovsky, Mirra. 1946. 'Cultural contradictions and sex roles', *American Journal of Sociology* 52: 184–9.

Kondo, Dorinne. 1999. 'Fabricating masculinity: Gender, race, and nation in a transnational frame', in *Between Woman and Nation: Nationalisms, Transnational Feminisms, and the State*, edited by Caren Kaplan, Norma Alarconó and Hinoo Moallam. Durham, NC: Duke University Press.

Krafft-Ebing, Richard von. 1886. *Psychopathia Sexualis*, 12th edition. New York: Paperback Library (1965 edition).

Kristeva, Julia. 1974. *Revolution in Poetic Language*. New York: Columbia University Press (1984 edition).

Lang, James, Alan Greig and Raewyn Connell, in collaboration with the Division for the Advancement of Women. 2008. 'The Role of Men and Boys in Achieving Gender Equality'. 'Women 2000 and Beyond' series. New York: United Nations Division for the Advancement of Women/Department of Economic and Social Affairs. Electronic version at: http://www.un.org/womenwatch/daw/public/W2000andBeyond.html (accessed 20 March 2014).

Laplanche, Jean, and Jean-Bertrand Pontalis. 1973. *The Language of Psycho-Analysis*. New York, NY: Norton.

Larner, Wendy, and Nina Laurie. 2010. 'Travelling technocrats, embodied knowledges: Globalising privatisation in telecoms and water', *Geoforum* 41 (2): 218–26.

Laurie, Nina. 2005. 'Establishing development orthodoxy: Negotiating masculinities in the water sector', *Development and Change* 36: 527–49.

Laurie, Nina. 2011. 'Gender water networks: Femininity and masculinity in water politics in Bolivia', *International Journal of Urban and Regional Research* 35 (1): 172–88.

Levin, Peter. 2001. 'Gendering the market: Temporality, work, and gender on a national futures exchange', *Work and Occupations* 28: 112–30.

Lindberg, Sara M., Janet S. Hyde, Jennifer L. Petersen and Marcia Linn. 2010. 'New trends in gender and mathematics performance: A meta-analysis', *Psychological Bulletin* 136 (6): 1123–35.

Litfin, Karen. 1997. 'The gendered eye in the sky: Feminist perspectives on earth observations satellites', *Frontiers* 18 (2): 26–47.

Lloyd, Moya. 2007. *Judith Butler: From Norms to Politics*. Cambridge: Polity.

Lorber, Judith. 2005. *Breaking the Bowls: Degendering and Feminist Change*. New York: Norton.

Lovelock, James. 2006. *The Revenge of Gaia: Why the Earth is Fighting Back and How We Can Still Save Humanity*. London: Allen Lane.

Luttrell, Wendy. 1997. *Schoolsmart and Motherwise: Working-Class Women's Identity and Schooling*. New York: Routledge.

Lynas, Mark. 2007. *Six Degrees: Our Future on a Hotter Planet*. London: Fourth Estate.

Mac an Ghaill, Máirtín. 1994. *The Making of Men: Masculinities, Sexualities and Schooling*. Buckingham: Open University Press.

Maccoby, Eleanor E., and Carol Nagy Jacklin. 1975. *The Psychology of Sex Differences*. Stanford, CA: Stanford University Press.

MacGregor, Sherilyn. 2009. 'A stranger silence still: The need for feminist social research on climate change', *The Sociological Review* 57: 124–40.

MacGregor, Sherilyn. 2010. 'Gender and climate change: From impacts to discourses', *Journal of the Indian Ocean Region* 6 (2): 223–38.

MacKenzie, John M. 1987. 'The imperial pioneer and hunter and the British masculine stereotype in late Victorian and Edwardian times', in *Manliness and Morality*, edited by J.A. Mangan and James Walvin. Manchester: Manchester University Press.

MacKinnon, Catharine A. 1983. 'Feminism, Marxism, method and the state: Towards feminist jurisprudence', *Signs* 8: 635–58.

Malinowski, Bronisław. 1927. *Sex and Repression in Savage Society*. London: Routledge & Kegan Paul.

Malos, Ellen, ed. 1980. *The Politics of Housework*. London: Allison & Busby.

Mama, Amina. 1997. 'Heroes and villains: Conceptualizing colonial and contemporary violence against women in Africa', in *Feminist Genealogies, Colonial Legacies, Democratic Futures*, edited by M. Jacqui Alexander and Chandra Talpade Mohanty. New York: Routledge.

Manchanda, Rita. 2004. 'Maoist insurgency in Nepal: Radicalizing gendered narratives', *Cultural Dynamics* 16 (2–3): 237–58.

Mane, Purnima, and Peter Aggleton. 2001. 'Gender and HIV/AIDS: What do men have to do with it?', *Current Sociology* 49: 23–37.

Mannon, Susan E. 2006. 'Love in the time of neo-liberalism: Gender, work, and power in a Costa Rican marriage', *Gender & Society* 20: 511–30.

Marchand, Marianne H., and Anne Sisson Runyan, eds. 2011. *Gender and Global Restructuring: Sightings, Sites and Resistances*, 2nd edition. London: Routledge.

Martin, Patricia Yancey. 2006. 'Practising gender at work: Further thoughts on reflexivity', *Gender, Work & Organization* 13: 254–76.

Masika, Rachel. 2002. 'Editorial: Climate change', *Gender and Development* 10 (2): 2–9.

Mbembe, Achille. 2001. *On the Postcolony*. Berkeley: University of California Press.

Mead, Margaret. 1935. *Sex and Temperament in Three Primitive Societies*. New York: William Morrow (1963 edition).

Mellor, Mary. 1996. 'The politics of women and nature: Affinity, contingency or material relation?', *Journal of Political Ideologies* 1 (2): 147–64.

Melville, Herman. 1853. 'Bartleby the scrivener', in *Alienation: A Casebook*, edited by David J. Burrows and Frederick R. Lapides. New York: Crowell (1969 edition).

Merchant, Carolyn. 1980. *The Death of Nature: Women, Ecology, and the Scientific Revolution*. New York: Harper & Row.

Merchant, Carolyn. 2003. 'Shades of darkness: Race and environmental history', *Environmental History* 8 (3): 380–94.

Mernissi, Fatima. 1975. *Beyond the Veil: Male–Female Dynamics in Modern Muslim Society*. London: Saqi Books (1985 edition).

Messerschmidt, James. 2004. *Flesh and Blood: Adolescent Gender Diversity and Violence*. Lanham, MD: Rowman & Littlefield.

Messner, Michael. 2007. *Out of Play: Critical Essays on Gender and Sport*. Albany: State University of New York Press.

Meyerowitz, Joanne. 2002. *How Sex Changed: A History of Transsexuality in the United States*. Cambridge, MA: Harvard University Press.

Mies, Maria. 1986. *Patriarchy and Accumulation on a World Scale: Women in the International Division of Labour*. London: Zed Books.

Mies, Maria, and Veronika Bennholdt-Thomsen. 1999. *The Subsistence Perspective: Beyond the Globalised Economy*. Melbourne: Spinifex Press.

Mies, Maria, and Vandana Shiva. 1993. *Ecofeminism*. London: Zed Books.

Mill, John Stuart. 1869. 'The subjection of women', in *J.S. Mill: Three Essays*. London: Oxford University Press (1912 edition).

Mills, Albert J., and Peta Tancred, eds. 1992. *Gendering Organizational Analysis*. Newbury Park, CA: Sage.

Mitchell, Juliet. 1966. 'Women: The longest revolution', *New Left Review* 40: 11–37.

Mitchell, Juliet. 1974. *Psychoanalysis and Feminism*. New York: Pantheon Books.

Moghadam, Valentine M. 2002. 'Islamic feminism and its discontents: Toward a resolution of the debate', *Signs* 27 (4): 1135–71.

Moghadam, Valentine M. 2005. *Globalizing Women: Transnational Feminist Networks*. Baltimore, MD: Johns Hopkins University Press.

Moghadam, Valentine M. 2013. 'What is democracy? Promises and perils of the Arab Spring', *Current Sociology* 61 (4): 393–408.

Mohanty, Chandra Talpade. 1991. 'Under Western eyes: Feminist scholarship and colonial discourses', in *Third World Women and the Politics of Feminism*, edited by Chandra Talpade Mohanty, Ann Russo and Lourdes Torres. Bloomington: Indiana University Press.

Mohanty, Chandra Talpade. 2003. *Feminism without Borders: Decolonizing Theory, Practicing Solidarity*. Durham, NC: Duke University Press.

Mohanty, Chandra Talpade, Ann Russo and Lourdes Torres, eds. 1991. *Third World Women and the Politics of Feminism*. Bloomington: Indiana University Press.

Mohwald, Ulrich. 2002. *Changing Attitudes towards Gender Equality in Japan and Germany*. Munich: Iudicium.

Moodie, T. Dunbar, with Vivienne Ndatshe. 1994. *Going for Gold: Men, Mines and Migration*. Johannesburg: Witwatersrand University Press.

Morgan, Robin, ed. 1970. *Sisterhood is Powerful: An Anthology of Writings from the Women's Liberation Movement*. New York: Vintage.

Morgan, Robin, ed. 1984. *Sisterhood is Global: The International Women's Movement Anthology*. New York: Feminist Press at the City University of New York.

Morrell, Robert. 2001a. *From Boys to Gentlemen: Settler Masculinity in Colonial Natal 1880–1920*. Pretoria: University of South Africa.

Morrell, Robert, ed. 2001b. *Changing Men in Southern Africa*. London: Zed Books.

Moreton-Robinson, Aileen. 2000. *Talkin' Up to the White Woman: Indigenous Women and Feminism*. St Lucia: University of Queensland Press.

Mudimbe, Valentine. 1994. *The Idea of Africa*. Bloomington: Indiana University Press.

Namaste, Viviane K. 2000. *Invisible Lives: The Erasure of Transsexual and Transgendered People*. Chicago: University of Chicago Press.

Namaste, Viviane K. 2009. 'Undoing theory: The "transgender question" and the epistemic violence of Anglo-American feminist theory', *Hypatia* 24 (3): 11–32.

Namaste, Viviane K. 2011. *Sex Change, Social Change: Reflections on Identity, Institutions, and Imperialism*. Toronto: Canadian Scholars' Press.

Nandy, Ashis. 1983. *The Intimate Enemy: Loss and Recovery of Self under Colonialism*. New Delhi: Oxford University Press.

Nelson, Julie. 1997. 'Feminism, ecology and the philosophy of economics', *Ecological Economics* 20 (2): 155–62.

Nelson, Julie. 2008. 'Economists, value judgments, and climate change: A view from feminist economics', *Ecological Economics* 65 (3): 441–7.

Newman, Meredith A., Robert A. Jackson and Douglas D. Baker. 2003. 'Sexual harassment in the federal workplace', *Public Administration Review* 63: 472–83.

Ng, Janet, and Janice Wickeri, eds. 1996. *May Fourth Women Writers*. Hong Kong: Chinese University of Hong Kong.

Nilsson, Arne. 1998. 'Creating their own private and public: The male homosexual life space in a Nordic city during high modernity', *Journal of Homosexuality* 35: 81–116.

Norwood, Vera. 1987. 'The nature of knowing: Rachel Carson and the American environment', *Signs* 12 (4): 740–60.

Novikova, Irina. 2000. 'Soviet and post-Soviet masculinities: After men's wars in women's memories', in *Male Roles, Masculinities and Violence: A Culture of Peace Perspective*, edited by Ingeborg Breines, Robert Connell and Ingrid Eide. Paris: UNESCO Publishing.

Okeke-Ihejirika, Philomina E. and Susan Franceschet. 2002. 'Democratisation and state feminism: Gender politics in Africa and Latin America', *Development and Change* 33: 439–66.

Oreskes, Naomi. 2004. 'Science and public policy: What's proof got to do with it?', *Environmental Science & Policy* 7: 369–83.

Oyěwùmí, Oyèrónké. 1997. *The Invention of Women: Making an African Sense of Western Gender Discourses*. Minneapolis: University of Minnesota Press.

Paap, Kris. 2006. *Working Construction: Why White Working-Class Men Put Themselves – and the Labor Movement – in Harm's Way*. Ithaca, NY: Cornell University Press.

Parsons, Talcott, and Robert F. Bales. 1956. *Family Socialization and Interaction Process*. London: Routledge & Kegan Paul.

Perkins, Roberta. 1983. *The 'Drag Queen' Scene: Transsexuals in Kings Cross*. Sydney: Allen & Unwin.

Peteet, Julie. 1994. 'Male gender and rituals of resistance in the Palestinian Intifada: A cultural politics of violence', *American Ethnologist* 21: 31–49.

Petersen, Jennifer, and Janet Hyde. 2011. 'Gender differences in sexual attitudes and behaviors: A review of meta-analytic results and large datasets', *Journal of Sex Research* 48 (2–3): 149–65.

Pfau-Effinger, Birgit. 1998. 'Gender cultures and the gender arrangement – A theoretical framework for cross-national research', *Innovation* 11: 147–66.

Pleck, Joseph H., and Jack Sawyer, eds. 1974. *Men and Masculinity*. Englewood Cliffs, NJ: Prentice-Hall.

Plumwood, Val. 1994. *Feminism and the Mastery of Nature*, London: Routledge.

Plumwood, Val. 2002. *Environmental Culture: The Ecological Crisis of Reason*. London: Routledge.

Poster, Winifred R. 2002. 'Racialism, sexuality, and masculinity: Gendering "global ethnography" of the workplace', *Social Politics* 9: 126–58.

Power, Marilyn. 2004. 'Social provisioning as a starting point for feminist economics', *Feminist Economics* 10 (3): 3–19.

Pringle, Rosemary. 1989. *Secretaries Talk: Sexuality, Power and Work*. Sydney: Allen & Unwin.

Pringle, Rosemary. 1992. 'Absolute sex? Unpacking the sexuality/gender relationship', in *Rethinking Sex: Social Theory and Sexuality Research*, edited by R.W. Connell and G.W. Dowsett. Melbourne: Melbourne University Press.

Prudham, Scott. 2009. 'Pimping climate change: Richard Branson, global warming, and the performance of green capitalism', *Environment and Planning A* 41 (7): 1594–613.

Radcliffe, Sarah A., Nina Laurie and Robert Andolina. 2004. 'The transnationalization of gender and reimagining Andean indigenous development', *Signs* 29: 387–416.

Rai, Shirin, and Vina Mazumdar. 2007. 'Emerging state feminism in India: A conversation with Vina Mazumdar, Member Secretary to the First Committee on the Status of Women in India', *International Feminist Journal of Politics* 9 (1): 104–11.

Ray, Raka. 1999. *Fields of Protest: Women's Movements in India*. Minneapolis, MN: University of Minnesota Press.

Razavi, Shahra, Camila Arza, Elissa Braunstein, Sarah Cook and Kristine Goulding. 2012. *Gendered Impacts of Globalization: Employment and Social Protection*. Geneva: United Nations Research Institute for Social Development.

Reid, Kirsty. 2007. *Gender, Crime and Empire: Convicts, Settlers and the State in Early Colonial Australia*. Manchester: Manchester University Press.

Reed, Evelyn. 1975. *Women and Evolution: From Matriarchal Clan to Patriarchal Family*. New York: Pathfinder.

Reynolds, Robert. 2002. *From Camp to Queer: Re-making the Australian Homosexual*. Melbourne: Melbourne University Press.

Rich, Adrienne. 1976. *Of Woman Born: Motherhood as Experience and Institution*. London: Virago (1991 edition).

Rigi, Jakob. 2003. 'The conditions of post-Soviet dispossessed youth and work in Almaty, Kazakhstan', *Critique of Anthropology* 23: 35–49.

Risman, Barbara J. 1986. 'Can men "mother"? Life as a single father', *Family Relations* 35: 95–102.

Risman, Barbara J. 1998. *Gender Vertigo: American Families in Transition*. New Haven, CT: Yale University Press.

Roberts, Adrienne. 2008. 'Privatizing social reproduction: The primitive accumulation of water in an era of neoliberalism', *Antipode* 40 (4): 535–60.

Roberts, Celia. 2000. 'Biological behaviour? Hormones, psychology and sex', *NWSA Journal* 12: 1–20.

Robinson, Kathryn. 2009. *Gender, Islam, and Democracy in Indonesia*. Oxford: Routledge.

Rockström, Johan, Will Steffen, Kevin Noone, Åsa Persson, F. Stuart Chapin III et al. 2009. 'Planetary boundaries: Exploring the safe operating space for humanity', *Ecology and Society*, 14(2): 472–5.

Rogers, Lesley. 2000. *Sexing the Brain*. London: Phoenix.

Roper, Michael. 1994. *Masculinity and the British Organization Man since 1945*. Oxford: Oxford University Press.

Rosenberg, Rosalind. 1982. *Beyond Separate Spheres: Intellectual Roots of Modern Feminism*. New Haven, CT: Yale University Press.

Rowbotham, Sheila. 1969. *Women's Liberation and the New Politics*. Nottingham: Spokesman.

Rubin, Gayle. 1975. 'The traffic in women: Notes on the "political economy" of sex', in *Toward an Anthropology of Woman*, edited by Rayna R. Reiter. New York: Monthly Review.

Rubin, Henry. 2003. *Self-Made Men: Identity and Embodiment among Transsexual Men*. Nashville, TN: Vanderbilt University Press.

Saffioti, Heleieth. 1976. *A mulher na sociedade de classes: Mito e realidad*. Petrópolis: Vozes.

Sahlins, Marshall. 1977. *The Use and Abuse of Biology: An Anthropological Critique of Sociobiology*. London: Tavistock.

Salleh, Ariel. 1998. 'Nature, woman, labour, capital: Living the deepest contradiction', in *Natural Causes: Essays in Ecological Marxism*, edited by James O'Connor. New York: The Guilford Press.

Salleh, Ariel. 2000. 'The meta-industrial class and why we need it', *Democracy & Nature* 6 (1): 27–36.

Salleh, Ariel. 2010. 'From metabolic rift to "metabolic value": Reflections on environmental sociology and the alternative globalization movement', *Organization & Environment* 23 (2): 205–19.

Sartre, Jean-Paul. 1968. *Search for a Method*. New York: Vintage.

Sawyer, Jack. 1970. 'On male liberation', in *Men and Masculinity*, edited by Joseph H. Pleck and Jack Sawyer. Englewood Cliffs, NJ: Prentice-Hall (1974 edition)

Sax, Leonard. 2002. 'How common is Intersex? A response to Anne Fausto-Sterling', *Journal of Sex Research* 39 (3): 174–8.

Schilt, Kristen, and Matthew Wiswall. 2008. 'Before and after: Gender transitions, human capital, and workplace experiences', *The B.E. Journal of Economic Analysis & Policy* 8 (1): article 39.

Schneider, Beth, and Nancy Stoller. 1995. *Women Resisting AIDS: Feminist Strategies of Empowerment*. Philadelphia, PA: Temple University Press.

Schofield, T., R.W. Connell, L. Walker, J. Wood and D. Butland. 2000. 'Understanding men's health: A gender relations approach to masculinity, health and illness', *Journal of American College Health* 48: 247–56.

Schreiner, Olive. 1978 [1911]. *Woman and Labour*. London: Virago.

Scott, Joan W. 1986. 'Gender: A useful category of historical analysis', *American Historical Review* 91 (5): 1053–75.

Seager, Joni. 1993. *Earth Follies: Coming to Feminist Terms with the Global Environmental Crisis*. London: Earthscan.

Seager, Joni. 2003. 'Rachel Carson died of breast cancer: The coming of age of feminist environmentalism', *Signs* 28 (3): 945–72.

Segal, Lynne. 1994. *Straight Sex: The Politics of Pleasure*. London: Virago.

Seifert, Ruth. 1993. Individualisierungsprozesse, Geschlechterverhältnisse und die soziale Konstruktion des Soldaten. Munich: Sozialwissenschaftliches Institut der Bundeswehr.

Severiens, Sabine, and Geert ten Dam. 1998. 'Gender and learning: Comparing two theories', *Higher Education* 35 (3): 329–50.

Shen, Zhi. 1987. 'Development of women's studies – the Chinese way: Sidelights of the National Symposium on Theoretical Studies on Women', *Chinese Sociology and Anthropology* 20: 18–25.

Shiva, Vandana. 1989. *Staying Alive: Women, Ecology and Development*. London: Zed Books.

Sideris, Tina. 2005. '"You have to change and you don't know how!": Contesting what it means to be a man in rural area of South Africa', in *Men Behaving*

Differently, edited by Graeme Reid and Liz Walker. Cape Town: Double Storey Books.

Simon-Kumar, Rachel. 2004. 'Negotiating emancipation: The public sphere and gender critiques of neo-liberal development', *International Feminist Journal of Politics* 6: 485–506.

Sinclair-Webb, Emma. 2000. 'Our Bülent is now a commando: Military service and manhood in Turkey', in *Imagined Masculinities: Male Identity and Culture in the Modern Middle East*, edited by Mai Ghoussoub and Emma Sinclair-Webb. London: Saqi Books.

Sinha, Mrinalini. 1995. *Colonial Masculinity: The 'Manly Englishman' and the 'Effeminate Bengali' in the late Nineteenth Century*. Manchester: Manchester University Press.

Spivak, Gayatri Chakravorty. 1988. *In Other Worlds: Essays in Cultural Politics*. New York: Routledge.

Spivak, Gayatri Chakravorty. 1999. *A Critique of Postcolonial Reason: Toward a History of the Vanishing Present*. Cambridge, MA: Harvard University Press.

Stacey, Judith. 1983. *Patriarchy and Socialist Revolution in China*. Berkeley: University of California Press.

Steele, Valerie. 1996. *Fetish: Fashion, Sex and Power*. New York: Oxford University Press.

Stienstra, Deborah. 2000. 'Dancing resistance from Rio to Beijing: Transnational women's organizing and United Nations conferences, 1992–6', in *Gender and Global Restructuring*, edited by Marianne H. Marchand and Anne Sisson Runyan. London: Routledge.

Stockholm International Peace Research Institute. 2011. *SIPRI Yearbook 2011*. Oxford: Oxford University Press.

Stoller, Robert J. 1968. *Sex and Gender, vol. 1: On the Development of Masculinity and Femininity*. London: Hogarth Press.

Stone, Merlin. 1976. *When God was a Woman*. New York: Harcourt Brace.

Strathern, Marilyn. 1978. 'The achievement of sex: Paradoxes in Hagen gender-thinking', in *The Yearbook of Symbolic Anthropology*, edited by Erik Schwimmer. London: Hurst.

Stryker, Susan. 2008. *Transgender History*. Berkeley: Seal Press.

Stryker, Susan, and Stephen Whittle, eds. 2006. *The Transgender Studies Reader*. New York: Routledge.

Swerdlow, Amy. 1993. *Women Strike for Peace: Traditional Motherhood and Radical Politics in the 1960s*. Chicago: University of Chicago Press.

Taga, Futoshi. 2007. 'The trends of discourse on fatherhood and father's conflict in Japan'. Paper to fifteenth biennial conference of Japanese Studies Association of Australia, Canberra, July.

Tanaka, Kazuko. 1977. *A Short History of the Women's Movement in Modern Japan*, 3rd edition. Japan: Femintern Press.

Taymour, Aisha. 1892. *Mir'at Al-Ta'mmul fi Al-Umur [The Mirror of Contemplating Affairs]*. Mohandessin: Women and Memory Forum (2001 edition).

Temkina, Anna. 2008. *Sexual Life of Women: Between Subordination and Freedom*. St Petersburg: European University at St Petersburg.

Terry, Geraldine, ed. 2009. *Climate Change and Gender Justice*. Rugby: Practical Action Publishing/Oxfam.

Thayer, Millie. 2010. *Making Transnational Feminism: Rural Women, NGO Activists, and Northern Donors in Brazil*. London: Routledge.

Theberge, Nancy. 1991. 'Reflections on the body in the sociology of sport', *Quest* 43: 123–34.

Thorne, Barrie. 1993. *Gender Play: Girls and Boys in School*. New Brunswick, NJ: Rutgers University Press.

Tienari, Janne, Anne-Marie Søderberg, Charlotte Holgersson and Eero Vaara. 2005. 'Gender and national identity constructions in the cross-border merger context', *Gender, Work & Organization* 12: 217–41.

Timmerman, Greetje, and Cristien Bajema. 1999. 'Sexual harassment in northwest Europe: A cross-cultural comparison', *European Journal of Women's Studies* 6 (4): 419–39.

Tinsman, Heidi. 2000. 'Reviving feminist materialism: Gender and neoliberalism in Pinochet's Chile', *Signs* 26: 145–88.

Tohidi, Nayereh. 1991. 'Gender and Islamic fundamentalism: Feminist politics in Iran', in *Third World Women and the Politics of Feminism*, edited by Chandra Talpade Mohanty, Ann Russo and Lourdes Torres. Bloomington: Indiana University Press.

Tomsen, Stephen. 1998. '"He had to be a poofter or something": Violence, male honour and heterosexual panic', *Journal of Interdisciplinary Gender Studies* 3 (2): 44–57.

Troiden, Richard R. 1989. 'The formation of homosexual identities', *Journal of Homosexuality* 17: 43–73.

Tsing, Anna L. 1993. *In the Realm of the Diamond Queen: Marginality in an Out-of-the-Way Place*. Princeton, NJ: Princeton University Press.

Tsing, Anna L. 2005. *Friction: An Ethnography of Global Connection*. Princeton, NJ: Princeton University Press.

Twenge, Jean M. 1997. 'Changes in masculine and feminine traits over time: A meta-analysis', *Sex Roles* 36: 305–25.

UNDP. 2013. Human Development Report 2013: The Rise of the South: Human Progress in a Diverse World. New York: United Nations Development Programme.

Vaerting, Mathilde [writing as Mathilde and Mathias Vaerting]. 1921. *The Dominant Sex: A Study in the Sociology of Sex Differentiation*. Westport, CT: Hyperion (1981 edition).

Valdés, Teresa. 2001. El índice de Compromiso Cumplido – ICC: Una Estrategia Para el Control Ciudadano de la Equidad de Género. Santiago de Chile: FLACSO.

Valdés, Teresa, Ana María Muñoz and Alina Donoso. 2003. *Han Avanzado las Mujeres? Indice de Compromiso Cumplido Latino Americano*. Santiago de Chile: FLACSO.

Via, Sandra. 2010. 'Gender, militarism, and globalization: Soldiers for hire and hegemonic masculinity', in *Gender, War, and Militarism: Feminist Perspectives*, edited by L. Sjoberg and Sandra Via. Santa Barbara, CA: Greenwood.

Vickers, Jill. 1994. 'Notes toward a political theory of sex and power', in *Power/Gender*, edited by H. Lorraine Radtke and Henderikus J. Stam. London: Sage.

Waetjen, Thembisa. 2004. *Workers and Warriors: Masculinity and the Struggle for Nation in South Africa*. Urbana: University of Illinois Press.

Waetjen, Thembisa, and Gerhard Maré. 2001. '"Men amongst men": Masculinity and Zulu nationalism in the 1980s', in *Changing Men in Southern Africa*, edited by Robert Morrell. London: Zed Books.

Wajcman, Judy. 1999. *Managing like a Man: Women and Men in Corporate Management*. Cambridge: Polity; Sydney: Allen & Unwin.

Walby, Sylvia. 1990. *Theorizing Patriarchy*. Oxford: Basil Blackwell.

Walby, Sylvia. 1997. *Gender Transformations*. London: Routledge.

Wamukonya, Njeri, and Margaret Skutsch. 2002. 'Gender angle to the climate change negotiations', *Energy & Environment* 13 (1): 115–24.

Ward, Lester. 1883. *Dynamic Sociology or Applied Social Science*. New York: D. Appleton and Company.

Warren, Karen, ed. 1997. *Ecofeminism: Women, Culture, Nature*. Bloomington: Indiana University Press.

West, Candace, and Don H. Zimmerman. 1987. 'Doing gender', *Gender and Society* 1: 125–51.

White, Sara C. 2000. '"Did the Earth move?" The hazards of bringing men and masculinities into gender and development', *IDS Bulletin* 31 (2): 33–41.

Williams, Walter L. 1986. *The Spirit and the Flesh: Sexual Diversity in American Indian Culture*. Boston: Beacon Press.

Wollstonecraft, Mary. 1792. *Vindication of the Rights of Woman*. Harmondsworth: Penguin (1975 edition).

WRI. 1990. *World Resources 1990–91: A Guide to the Golobal Environment*. World Resources Institute, Oxford: Oxford University Press.

Xaba, Thokozani. 2001. 'Masculinity and its malcontents: The confrontation between "struggle masculinity" and "post-struggle masculinity" (1990–1997)', in *Changing Men in Southern Africa*, edited by Robert Morrell. Pietermaritzburg, University of Natal Press.

Zhen, He-Yin. 1907. 'On the question of Women's Liberation', in *The Birth of Chinese Feminism: Essential Texts in Transnational Theory*, edited by Lydia H. Liu, Rebecca E. Karl and Dorothy Ko. New York: Columbia University Press (2013 edition).

Zulehner, Paul M., and Rainer Volz. 1998. *Männer im Aufbruch: Wie Deutschlands Männer sich selbst und wie Frauen sie sehen*. Ostfildern: Schwabenverlag.

Author Index

Subject Index